Laurent Giles

and His Yacht Designs

Adrian Lee and Ruby Philpott

Foreword by Olin Stephens

International Marine Publishing Company
A Division of TAB BOOKS
P.O. Box 220, Camden, Maine 04843

First published in Great Britain by Nautical Books,
1990.

ISBN: 0–87742–285–0

Printed and bound in Great Britain.

International Marine Publishing Company offers
software for sale. For information and a catalog, please
contact TAB Software Department, Blue Ridge
Summit, PA 17924–0850.

Photocredits

C.K. Adair: p 103
Albion Studios: p 145
Beken of Cowes Ltd: pp 13,21,27,43,48,52,55,
    66,69,73,77,85,91,109,112,116,118,123,135
Foto Contini: p 82
Miles Cooper: p 79
Foto Cresta: p 107
T. Davis: p 161
F. Drew: p 27
East Coast Yacht Agency: p 61
E. Hiscock: p 33
H. Jenkins Ltd: p 136, 141
W. Payne: pp 175, 183, 185
Saro (Anglesey) Ltd: p 154

Foreword

I am happy that Jack Giles' work will be there for us all to see with the publication of this book. To be reminded of Jack as I have been by the invitation to write a preface to the book makes me wish, for many reasons, that I had known him better.

My first visit to England was with *Dorade* in 1931, sailing into Plymouth to finish the Trans-Atlantic race of that year. We were welcomed there and entertained with great courtesy and enthusiasm and then sailed up to Cowes where we were further entertained. We then sailed the Fastnet finishing again in Plymouth. That year *Dorade* was shipped home. Readers may excuse the fact that with the passage of nearly sixty years on top of the excitement of that time, one's recollection is somewhat blurred. I think I see Jack's tanned, sharp face and quizzical expression among the many new friends.

Over the years one read the yachting press and studied the design sections of the magazines, becoming familiar with the work of certain designers. It was always easy to recognize the exceptionally distinctive and stylish plans of J. Laurent Giles. Photographs of the new boats gave the same impression and also showed practical working yachts whether in the field of racing, cruising or power. Because they usually had large deck structures, which so well blended with the hulls, the power boats seemed especially attractive.

In the years between 1933 and 1937 Professor Kenneth Davidson of the Stevens Institute of Technology in Hoboken, New Jersey, a great innovator in the field of technical yacht design, had developed his method of testing small models of sailing yachts. I had closely followed his work. It had contributed to the success of a number of racing yachts, including, in 1937, the *America's* Cup defender, *Ranger*. I think it was soon after *Ranger*, though it may have been a year later, that I heard from Jack asking about the model tests, my opinion of their usefulness and something about time, cost and procedures. Not much later he appeared in New York with lines for a model that was to become *Flica II*.

In anything having to do with Twelve-Metre design we worked with complete independence but he must have considered that my initial advice had been helpful because much to my surprise, some time, a good deal later, he sent me some shares of a limited company that had been organized to set up a testing facility similar to Davidson's in England. I think the onset of the war upset the project. He said that my help deserved recognition, while I felt that Jack's thoughtfulness had gone far beyond the call of duty.

The war interrupted work on yacht designs. When sailing could begin Jack's passion for boats was seen on offshore racing yachts. Success came to Jack at once with *Myth* and others. By the early sixties you might say that we were in competition as our office had some success with boats under the RORC rule. This brought us together and I was intrigued by his attitude as it seemed to me so objective, even rather detached, and maybe a little fatalistically oriented after a boat came out.

I became much involved in rating rules. I don't think he had the hopes that I had that we could improve the sport through rules. Nor was he then as active in offshore racing as he had been earlier. His larger cruising yachts and especially his fast motor sailers were highly successful and took a lot of his time.

Jack's *Blue Leopard* was an impressive motor sailer, clearly new in the way she combined speed under power and under sail. She and her sister designs were marked by great success. I'm sure that Jack will be long remembered for the practicality, the performance and the appearance of all kinds of designs.

Olin Stephens 29 Jan. '90

Contents

Jack Giles outside the Quay Hill office

Chapter 1
The History of Laurent Giles

Introduction

The name of Laurent Giles first appeared in the world of yacht design in the 1920s when Jack Laurent Giles R.D.I., M.R.I.N.A. set up a partnership in Lymington, Hampshire, England, and began his immensely successful career. One of the great names of yachting design, his reputation was based mainly on a very successful series of cruising, racing and motor yachts which are known throughout the yachting fraternity. Although many yachting books and magazine articles have written innumerable accounts of his famous boats, nowhere is the complete range of his most exceptional designs compiled.

This long overdue book was written as a tribute to the late and great Jack Laurent Giles and condenses into one volume some of his greatest yacht designs. This was no mean task since Giles was responsible for creating over 400 different designs. Although Jack Laurent Giles died in 1969, the company of Laurent Giles Ltd is still designing yachts

in the original tradition and maintains Jack's reputation for design excellence.

The book incorporates information from the original company files, which date back to the late 1920s, as well as pre- and post-war yachting articles and reports. Some of Jack Giles' original letters to yachting magazines as well as speeches and lectures on particular designs have also been included in the description of specific boats. This is not the first attempt at compiling a book of Laurent Giles designs since Jack himself had started to write a history of the company prior to his death. Entitled *Chocolate Boats* the manuscript provided an amusing reference to an inheritance from his relations the Fry family, the well-known chocolate manufacturers. It was this money that enabled him to follow his heart designing yachts rather than entering the conventional business world. Sadly the manuscript for this book was lost some time after his death.

Structure of the Book

The book is divided into six chapters. The first chapter contains a biography of Jack Laurent Giles followed by a review of the company origin, its development and evolution through to the present-day. In this chapter important and exceptional Giles designs are discussed in context and include some very distinguished designs from the pre-war and post-war period. The formation of the present-day company, Laurent Giles Ltd, a direct descendant of the original company is also included within this section and provides an interesting insight into modern-day yacht design methods, particularly with the introduction of computer technology and computer aided design (C.A.D.) systems.

The second, third and fourth chapters contain, respectively, 10, 19 and 15 one-off Laurent Giles yacht designs produced during 1927 to 1982. Each design is outlined in a separate section which provides information about the owner, builder and date of construction, together with the physical parameters of the boat. Following this there is a general description of the design together with information about its specific achievements, notable voyages and racing successes. Diagrams showing the sail plan, hull lines and plan views of the boat's interior accommodation are also included and, where available, there are original black and white photographs of the vessel. The boats are listed in chronological order and are separated into three distinct periods of design, pre-war 1927–1939, and post-war 1946–1958 and 1959–1982.

With over 800 designs produced during this period the selection of a representative set of boats proved difficult. From a wide range of unique yachts and classic motor boats, 44 of the most significant and famous Laurent Giles designs were chosen from the company files. The criteria for selecting the boats is based on their innovative design, such as their hull form or the unusual material used in their construction, or because of their light displacement, particularly with the advent of new technology. Several yachts are included because their highly successful ocean racing careers made the Laurent Giles name famous throughout the world's racing fraternity. Others appear because of the exceptional voyages made by some famous owners, whilst a few are here just because of their attractive style.

In Chapter five the introduction of glass reinforced plastic (G.R.P.) as a new boat construction material together with the advent of mass production boats during the 1960s is discussed. Laurent Giles had entered this field in the very beginning and was responsible for a number of very popular production boat designs. Seven of the most influential production yachts are described in detail.

The last chapter contains some of the most interesting recent Laurent Giles designs from 1982 to the present day, and include: a lifeboat, a U.L.D.B. (ultra-light displacement boat), a 70 ft. training vessel, a 190 ft. private schooner, an 80 ft. motor yacht, and the 1987 *America*'s Cup contender, *Crusader II*.

An appendix is provided at the end of the book listing all the Laurent Giles designs from 1927 through to the end of the original company in 1982. It is in chronological order with reference to the Laurent Giles Boat Design Number, this being assigned to each new design. The list was compiled after much research and cross-referencing of the original design files and drawing registers. In a few cases some of the information has unfortunately been lost; however, the list comprises the most complete historical record available. A glance at this document makes one appreciate the huge number and wide variety of successful Laurent Giles designs drawn over seven decades.

Jack Laurent Giles

Jack Laurent Giles was born at Scarborough in Yorkshire in 1901, the son of a medical practitioner. Although christened John Laurent Giles, he was known to all as Jack. He was educated at Winchester College and it was during this period that he fell in love with sailing. During the First World War, with his parents away assisting with the war effort in France, he would spend the summer holidays sailing off the coast of Ireland. After completing his schooling he went up to Magdalene College, Cambridge where he read for an engineering degree. He later continued his studies at Durham University where he finally qualified as a Naval Architect. On leaving university he started an apprenticeship with Vickers Armstrong at Newcastle-upon-Tyne designing merchant ships. However, during his spare time he entered yacht design competitions and won first prize with a design for the Swedish Cruising Club. Because of his love of yachts and sailing he decided to join the famous Camper and Nicholson company in Southampton where he learnt his craft under the supervision of the great yacht designer Charles E. Nicholson.

In a dinner speech in 1964 Jack spoke of his initial interest in yacht designing in his usual humorous manner. 'I first got the silly idea of designing yachts when I was at school. Then I had three years of comparative sanity doing engineering at Cambridge. At the end of my time there the lunacy took on a slightly different guise, and I found myself signed on as an apprentice at Armstrong Whitworths Naval Yard. There the crack in the brain opened out again and I started playing with design competitions.' It was a small local boat show in 1924 at the agricultural hall in Islington, where the famous yacht designer Morgan Giles was showing his pretty little boat *Black Raven*, that was to be the turning point and make Jack decide on a career as a yacht designer.

In the 1920s yacht design was only just beginning to leave the plateau at which it had remained for the previous 200 years. Although the shape of racing yachts had been developing since before the turn of the century, the vessels produced were of very similar form with hulls which were standard on all fishing smacks and pilot cutters of the day.

Jack Giles appreciated the need for new thought in yacht design and in 1927 at the age of 26 he decided to set up his own yacht design company, Laurent Giles and Partners with the late George R. Gill. They were joined shortly afterwards by the famous ocean farer Humphrey D.E. Barton. Giles applied sound engineering principles to his designs and combined this with his artist's eye to create efficient yet beautiful yachts. To him yacht design was not merely a question of mathematics; it was also an art form.

In the beginning the company office comprised a single room in a shoemaker's shop in Captains Row in the small Hampshire town of Lymington on the south coast of England. In 1929 the company moved a short distance to 4 Quay Hill a delightful Queen Anne building, where it remained for the next 55 years. The telephone number was just No. 6 and telegrams could be sent to Lymington 6. The famous seafarer Eric Hiscock who owned two Giles-designed cruising yachts *Wanderer II* and *Wanderer III* described the office as he had seen it some years before the war: 'Strolling dejectedly up Quay Hill, a steep and narrow cobbled alley, my eyes were attracted to a charming yacht model hanging in an equally charming bow-window. A brass plate on the door proclaimed it to be the office of that well known firm of yacht architects, Laurent Giles and Partners. Only then did it occur to me that it might be as cheap to build the ship I wanted as to buy an old one that I didn't ... So in I walked and found the great man himself poring over a vast drawing board on which were the pencilled lines of a ship-to-be, surrounded by curves, rules, battens and all the other paraphernalia associated with the designing of ships. "Please," I said, "will you design me a yacht?" "We shall be delighted," he replied, and introduced me to his partner George Gill who was busy warming his stern before a roaring fire.'

The town of Lymington is situated on the Solent, which is the strip of water that lies between the mainland and the Isle of Wight and is a well-known sailing mecca. Jack's choice of locating his company in Lymington was very wise since it was and still is a major centre of sailing activity, the

Solent being one of the most famous stretches of water for sailing regattas, the most notable being held at Cowes on the Isle of Wight. The Solent is also famous for some of the most difficult waters to race in, having double tides because of the tight restriction of water through this confined channel way and for its steep chop when there is wind over tide.

Lymington is located at the edge of the New Forest, and is one of the prettiest towns on the south coast. The town and the surrounding area has had a boat building history dating back to the 16th century, and at Buckler's Hard, several miles to the east of Lymington town, King Henry VIII had many of his naval warships built using the wood from the nearby forest. There were many boat builders situated near Lymington in 1927 and many are still flourishing today in this active yachting centre.

Two years after starting the company Jack married Elizabeth Falconar whom he met during his time in Newcastle. Over the next few years he was to become a father to twin sons and a daughter. Although the scope of his work and his family life allowed little time for other activities, Jack took a keen interest in local affairs. He was a great supporter and active member of the Lymington Players' Amateur Dramatic Society, a keen Rotarian, a supporter of amateur artistic talent, and was above all an admirer of old Lymington and its traditions. He lived in Lymington for the rest of his life at Normandy Mead, Woodside.

Jack Giles was one of the early members of the Royal Ocean Racing Club (R.O.R.C.) which he joined in 1930, and was responsible for many of the fast cruiser racers of pre-war days of which *Maid of Malham* was a well known example. In 1931 he participated in the Fastnet race aboard *Jolly Breeze*, and during 1933 to 1953 was a member of the R.O.R.C. Technical Committee. In 1938 the firm was registered as a limited company and during this time the Laurent Giles reputation for elegant, seaworthy boats was born. The company was disbanded during the Second World War and Jack went to work in special projects associated with the Special Boat Squadron (S.B.S.), along with Blondie Hassler and Captain John Illingworth. Among their projects were *Sleeping Beauty*, a one-man aluminium submarine which could be dropped by parachute, and also an exact double of a French tuny fishing boat which had a false bottom to the hull and was used to hide agents during missions to France. He later moved to the Royal Corps of Naval Constructors (which he called the 'obstructors'), and there he designed the H.D.M.L., 45 ft. picket boat and the Admiralty M.F.V. Unfortunately Jack did not get on with his ministry bosses whose slow pace of action was a constant frustration to him. When he heard that the Atlantic convoys were in jeopardy because of a shortage of lifeboats he visited and commissioned several small yards he knew to build them without any authority from the Admiralty. He was subsequently transferred to Washington D.C., where he was to become involved with wooden aircraft construction.

The Laurent Giles company was restarted after the war in 1946 with the original partners. In 1951 he was appointed to the faculty of Royal Designers for Industry, an honour of which he was greatly proud. During his long and distinguished career he gave numerous lectures and wrote many articles about his yacht designs and design techniques.

In 1968 Jack became ill with lung cancer and underwent an operation at the end of that September. During the convalescence holiday in Tenerife he was taken ill and flown home; however, his condition was too serious to operate and he died at Southampton Chest Hospital on 20th February 1969, aged 69. Even at the very end he spoke enthusiastically about the 225 ft. schooner which was being designed for L. Ron Hubbard and how his life with yachts had been a passion. His death was a great shock to the yachting world and many tributes to him were made.

Throughout his career Giles was to be one of the foremost yacht designers in the world, a man of vision, unfettered by convention and always an innovater and trend setter. Jack Lowis, who joined the company in 1951, described Jack as 'ambitious, brilliant, determined, alert, witty, observant, understanding and possessed of a forceful, dominant personality which, in conjunction with his unfailing charm, enabled his associates and those whose business it was to give effect to his designs, to do so with enthusiasm and in full appreciation that they were helping to fulfil the inspiration of the Maestro.' Jack Giles was a quiet man with a delightful sense of humour whom clients described as 'looking more like an artist than an engineer.' A very humble person, he regarded his work as a partnership and was the first to insist that the firm's successes were greatly due to the harmony and skill of the team with which he worked. He appreciated the fickleness of his craft and one of his most famous quotes was 'Beware of him who claims knowledge of yacht design, for we know only about the rudiments, the rest is conjecture.' Jack considered the sea as the most important element of a design, and not the owner's whims. He used to call the sea 'the old enemy' or 'the enchantress'.

It was said of Jack, by one of his partners, that he was fortunate in that he had the following characteristics which are most important in a yacht designer; a love of hard work, an inventive flair, a very strong aesthetic sense and a thorough knowl-edge of the mathematics associated with the technicalities of yacht design. His most outstanding characteristic was that he was able to develop a very distinctive style early on in his career which he maintained and developed for over forty years.

Jack Giles will perhaps be best remembered for his pioneering work in the fields of light displacement yachts, ocean racers, and his achievements with motor sailing yachts which really did perform well under sail. These alone, however, scarcely do justice to the variety and scope of his designs and it is only looking at his work as a whole that one can fully appreciate his talents.

Laurent Giles and Partners Ltd (1927–1969)

Laurent Giles and Partners was founded in 1927, the initial partnership comprising himself, G.R. Gill and Humphrey Barton. Their very first design was the 56 ft. gaff yawl *Clymene* and over 400 yacht designs were to be produced by this company over the following 45 years. Laurent Giles was a team effort, the others keeping a rein on Jack's radical ideas. George Gill used to argue with him for hours over aspects of design, one of the few brave enough to do so. In fact Gill contributed a great deal to the fame of Laurent Giles, producing many of the characteristics associated with the Giles look.

During the period from 1927 to the outbreak of war in 1939, they designed a variety of famous one-design cruising and racing yachts, as well as five classes of yachts and several motor boats such as the well known *Tamahine*. The classes of yacht designed include; the Lymington 'L' class, the famous 5 ton Vertue class boats, of which *Andrillot* was the first, the Channel, Flying Gull and Brittany Class yachts. Of the one-design yachts of this period, *Wanderer II*, *Wapipi* and her sister *Whooper*, *Valfreya*, the famous *Dyarchy* and *Fairlight* are best known. From amongst the pre-war racers, *Maid of Malham* was perhaps the most successful having won the R.O.R.C Open Class Points Championship in 1938 while in the following year the International 12-metre racing yacht *Flica II* was built for Sir Hugh Goodson. This yacht took many years to show her true performance since she was severely handicapped in having no winches on board, as her all-Devon crew refused to use 'winksies'. The Giles stock designs demonstrated Jack's attention to detail and his striving for perfection. Almost invariably he would achieve the right hull lines at the outset but would then improve the details of succeeding boats, for example on the lovely Brittany Class. Not content with the completed result he would inevitably sail the boats he designed to find out how they could be further improved.

Early in his career Jack Giles was the first to use a doghouse, which appeared in the 1930s on his second design, the 12-ton cutter *Etain*. In those days a coachroof was a rather unattractive wooden box which was considered to reduce unnecessarily the amount of deck space, and which reduced the elegance of a yacht. Giles early designs, however, featured a better looking superstructure which blended with the hull and formed an integral part of the yacht. Windows were shaped to the angles of the coachroof, something which had never been attempted before, and it was Giles who pointed the way to this now commonplace feature on yachts.

By the outbreak of war Giles had become established as one of the world's foremost designers, although up until this time his work had been

Laurent Giles' very first design, the 26 ton gaff-rigged yawl *Clymene* in 1929

The simple but elegant 1930's motor cruiser *Daphne*

entirely with heavy displacement yachts. To help the war effort, the company was disbanded and Jack joined the Admiralty where amongst other vessels he designed the Motor Fishing Vessel (MFV) and a midget submarine.

When peace returned, the original partners got back together and reformed the company. Having worked with wooden aircraft, as well as on naval vessel design during the war years, Giles saw the potential use of lightweight construction in racing yachts, and in 1946 the triumphant racer, *Myth of Malham*, was conceived. She was to be the first of a long line of successful light displacement yachts, and the design concept was to be one of the most important advances in yacht design. *Myth of Malham* was one of the most celebrated racing yachts of her day, winning a hat-trick in her first three races and the Fastnet Race twice. By the standards of her day she was considered ugly by the yachting establishment, yet she was brilliantly conceived and ruthlessly efficient sweeping all before her and changing the face of modern ocean racing.

Another two light displacement racing yachts *Gulvain* and *Fandango* immediatcly followed *Myth of Malham* off the drawing board. These too were later followed by *Bacchante*, *Tilly Twin* and her sister *Water Music*, and *Lutine*, all boats regularly achieving high places in ocean races. *Gulvain* and *Fandango* were both unusual for their day since they had a sawn-off counter stern with a reverse sheer and reverse transom. Although this design provided a stronger, lighter structure creating more

The 12-Metre *Flica II* built for Sir Hugh Goodson

freeboard and headroom, contemporary opinion was not favourable. Giles was the first English designer to use such a hull form and today it is rare not to find a modern yacht without a reverse transom; this was to be yet another of Giles' innovations. *Gulvain* was also the first ocean racing yacht to be built of aluminium and Giles was always quick to see the advantages of any new constructional methods. Later he was to design *Morag Mhor*, the first yacht in welded aluminium.

Giles believed implicitly in light displacement and was advocating its advantages long before his contemporaries. Over a period of five years he produced a series of light displacement boats, all with low wetted areas, generous freeboard, deep keels and high ballast ratios. These include, with those mentioned: *Sopranino*, the first of the tiny yachts of the Barchetta Class under 20 ft. in length, which sailed the Atlantic; the famous Mediterranean racing yacht *Miranda IV*, which was the first yacht designed for racing offshore to have a fin and skeg underwater profile; and the 21 ft. *Trekka*, the first of the very successful Columbia Class, which sailed twice around the world.

During this time Giles was also making advances and significant weight reductions in spars, mast and deck fittings. Because of the war there had been rapid technological advances made in industrial materials and products and by the late 1940s a whole range of new materials, and particularly glues, became available. Birmabright, an aluminium alloy, was a most promising material and Giles saw the potential of this new metal and designed a wide variety of strong, lightweight mast fittings using this product which replaced the then conventional heavy wrought-iron ones. Design of deck gear also took advantage of this material and the first sheet track and car systems were developed for *Myth of Malham*, which were the forerunners of all modern sail sheeting equipment.

During the period from 1947 to 1955 Giles was regarded as the foremost designer of ocean racing yachts in the world. It was therefore no surprise that the Royal Naval Sailing Association approached him to design a class of yacht to compete offshore in Class III races. In 1949 *Pocahontas*, the first of the R.N.S.A. 24's was launched, which carried light aluminium alloy masts to Giles design. These were the first yachts to have successful metal masts reducing their weight aloft and improving efficiency

as well as their seaworthiness. Fifteen of these boats were built, three of which entered and did well in the 1950 Fastnet and Wolf Rock Races, although at the time Class III boats were considered to be too small for such courses. The three R.N.S.A. 24's, *Blue Disa*, *Samuel Pepys* and *Minx of Malham* entered the race, and during bad gales continued double-reefed while the larger boats had heaved to. The Fastnet had been won by Giles' *Myth of Malham* and the first three places went to Laurent Giles designs.

Giles' light displacement ocean racers, including *Myth of Malham* in the U.K., *Miranda IV* in the Mediterranean and *Samuel Pepys*, were to dominate the racing scene. *Myth* had previously won the Sydney to Hobart race in 1946 and the Fastnet race in 1947 and 1950, and *Samuel Pepys* had won the Trans-Atlantic race in 1952. *Southern Myth*, built in the early 1950s along the same lines as the British yachting queen *Myth of Malham*, won the Australian 680-mile Sydney to Hobart race in 1955. By the mid 1950s the name of Laurent Giles and the company's formidable reputation was known worldwide. In Italy a succession of beautiful Laurent Giles yachts were built for racing and cruising. In 1951 *Miranda IV* proved to be an almost unbeatable racing boat in the Mediterranean, winning the Giraglia Cup, considered to be the Mediterranean equivalent of the Fastnet, and started a tradition which culminated in the three consecutive victories of *Susanna II* in the Giraglia race in the 1960s. From the early 1950s to 60s the following notable racing and cruising yachts were built: *Nina V*, *Nephele*, *Star Sapphire*, *Santa Anna II*, *Susanna*, *Alcor*, *Giga*, *Magadisen*, *Seconda Santa Lucia*, *Ilaria*, *Enteara*, *Airin*, *Cadama*.

During the late 1940s and 50s Giles yachts became known internationally for other reasons than just their racing abilities. *Wanderer III*, *Beyond* and *Trekka* circumnavigated the world and notable trans-ocean voyages were made by *Vertue XXXV*, *Sopranino*, *Speedwell of Hong Kong*, *Coimbra* and others. During these years Laurent Giles designs were being built not only in Europe but also in Australia, New Zealand, Tasmania, Africa, U.S.A., Canada, Hong Kong, Alaska, Singapore, India and Argentina.

Disenchanted with the fickleness of the rating rule changes and the changing atmosphere that was beginning to prevail in ocean racing, Giles turned

Jack Giles during his lecture on *Audacity*

his attention more and more to developing a sailing hull with a powerful auxiliary engine in an attempt to produce the ideal cruising boat. This was to be far removed from what was known then as a 'motor sailer'. Using information gained from his successful racing designs he was able to conceive higher performance cruisers and motor sailers. His aim was to produce a 100/100 motor sailer which would bring motor sailers into a new era, where they could compete in performance with sailing boats of the same size and under power respond as well as a motor boat.

Nina V racing in the Mediterranean

One of his earliest examples of this type of motor sailer is *Beyond*, which proved her capabilities by sailing around the world. She had only moderate displacement and was quite different in concept from any of his previous yachts which had circumnavigated the globe. Developed from the *Taylor Trusty*, built in 1949, she was a much advanced version of this 50/50 motor sailer. Similar and more improved designs quickly followed. Previous motor sailers tended to be motor boats to which sails were added almost as an afterthought. Giles, however, produced them with efficient rigs so that their sails could be sheeted flat enough to stand within three points of the wind, and this had the effect of reducing the leeway-making component to which the shallow draft of the motor sailer type was susceptible. Roughly the same size and type of design as *Beyond* was the ill-fated *Coimbra*. During a circumnavigation voyage, she was wrecked on Tristan da Cunha Island in the Atlantic Ocean. Following *Beyond* and *Coimbra* were a series of famous motor sailer designs, including the aluminium-hulled *Pinna II*, *Great Days* and *Donella*. The later design was so successful that a further fifteen, Donella Class, sister ships were built. In 1956 Giles designed the 73 ft. light displacement motor sailer *Star Sapphire* which carried over 2000 square feet of sail and in 1961 the Dhorus Mhor class was produced, of which seven yachts were built, the peak of development culminating with the famous *Blue Leopard* in 1962. *Blue Leopard* was the ultimate success in motor sailers which broke through the old barrier of (Speed $= 1.5\sqrt{\text{Length of Waterline}}$) both under power and under sail. She was large, graceful, powerful and luxuriously appointed, and although her underwater lines brought out all the advances that modern technology had instigated, above the water she was possessed of typical Giles fine looks. Both *Blue Leopard* and her smaller sister *Lamadine*, are considered the ultimate in motor sailers even today.

Jack Giles appreciated the need for tank testing hulls and this was undertaken on some of his pre-war boats, but was more commonly performed on post-war designs. Such tests were carried out on *Blue Leopard* and *Diadem of Dewlish*. It was by careful testing that the bow and stern overhangs of *Blue Leopard*'s hull were optimised and produced the most efficient hull form and her incredibly fast speeds. She clearly demonstrated the use of tank-testing techniques in providing the best possible performance of a hull. Giles also spent considerable time in experimental tank-test work on bilge keels and optimising their parameters for such boats as *Blue Bird of Thorn*.

In the post-war era, Laurent Giles designed some very impressive motor yachts and in particular the elegant *Woodpecker of Poole* in 1947. Much admired, she generated further work in this field and motor yachts of all types were produced steadily through the fifties. *Ravahine*, a fast fishing launch, was built in 1955, a replacement for the owner's previous pre-war motor boat *Tamahine*. In 1962 the majestic 96 ft. *Diadem of Dewlish* was designed and built as a tender for the *America*'s Cup 12-Metre yacht *Sovereign*. She was followed closely by the 105 ft. motor boat *Aetea* built in 1963.

The Giles name was not generally associated with commercial craft, but with the ever-increasing need for all types of working boats at home and worldwide, numerous designs were produced. The most notable were designs for a 90 ft. Pilot vessel for the Port Talbot Pilots, *Margham Abbey*, which was built in steel in 1959 by Richards Iron Works, and a 44 ft. wooden Pilot boat for the Dublin Pilots, built by John Tyrell of Arklow.

By the early fifties Jack Giles had gathered a skilled and loyal design team. Although Humphrey Barton had left the company and George Gill retired from the firm in 1959, Roger Heron and later Jack Lowis and Arthur Bayzand joined the company. They were shortly followed by Peter Anstey in 1960 and Vernon Sainsbury, the well known former Commodore of the Royal Ocean Racing Club and the owner of several Giles offshore racing yachts. During the 1960s the partnership began to dwindle, and on Jack's death in 1969 the firm was reformed. Control passed to the company's four senior members, who became the new company directors and included; Arthur Bayzand, Peter Anstey, Dick Stower and Bill Matthew, while Jack Lowis and Vernon Sainsbury remained with the firm as consultants.

The last years of Jack Giles' life were times of change. The new age of the production yacht in G.R.P. was dawning and the era of the one-off yacht was drawing to a close, so whilst producing some particularly beautiful boats like *Riwaru*, *Sails of Dawn* and *Tumbelina*, he was also involved with the Audacity class, a descendant of the tiny *Sopranino*,

The wreck of *Coimbra* on Tristan da Cunha

which had been sponsored by the *News Chronicle*. Other G.R.P. production boats include the Scimitar and Salar, but, alas, Giles never lived to see his most successful design, the Westerly Centaur of which 2500 were built. Giles never judged success in terms of financial reward, nevertheless this last project once again shows his versatility and readiness to adapt.

Sailing was beginning to appeal to a much wider public who had different requirements. Because of the increase in demand, boat builders were employing new methods of mass production in reinforced plastics as the only realistic way forward. These new yachtsmen were, more often than not, family men interested in a boat which was affordable, easy to sail and that could sleep the maximum number of people. Giles applied himself to these requirements and produced the Centaur, a light displacement,

bilge keeled boat with the identifiable Giles look. Once again he produced a boat which was just that bit better than its contemporaries and the Centaur was an instant success. Before many had been launched, Jack Giles was dead and the Centaur was left as a legacy to his surviving partners.

Just before Jack Giles's serious operation at the end of September 1968, he had drawn the lines of perhaps his most important commission, a 225 ft. L.O.A. four-masted schooner for L. Ron Hubbard. Although this vessel was never built, it was a fitting apotheosis to his distinguished career in the design of sailing yachts.

Many tributes were paid to Jack Giles on his death and a quote from *The Proper Yacht* says of Jack: 'The late Laurent Giles was perhaps the most skilled and innovative English yacht designer of his time. Boats for cruising and for racing, large boats and small, heavy boats and light, all came off his drawing board with equal facility. Probably he will be remembered as a pioneer of weight-saving methods of construction.' Colin Mudie, a well known ocean farer and designer, who spent five years in the Laurent Giles drawing office, regarded him as 'the first man to apply engineering principles to yacht design and take his work right through every facet of construction.' He had been a pioneer in yacht design in almost every type of design from pure sailing boats to motor sailers and motor boats. Many of his designs had been unique for their day and went against the conservative nature of the yachting fraternity, since he designed boats that were meant for their purpose. His yachts live on as a tribute to a truly great designer.

Laurent Giles and Partners Ltd (1969–1982)

The firm of Laurent Giles and Partners Ltd continued from 1969 to 1982 although during this period there were a number of changes within the partnership. A welcome addition to the firm was Michael Pocock who joined as a director, for a short time, in 1977. Prior to joining Laurent Giles and Partners Ltd, Michael Pocock had designed a yacht which was to become the production boat *Starlight* for Blue Water Yachts in Jersey. Mike provided the company with knowledge and experience of the I.O.R. rule, and was responsible for the design of the prototype half-tonner GK29 as well as other I.O.R. racers.

The production of standard yachts in glass reinforced plastic was developing rapidly, and Laurent Giles and Partners produced many designs for prominent building firms such as Westerly Marine, A.H. Moody and Son and a number of other well known yards. These designs ranged from 18 to over 66 feet in length and 33 tons displacement. For Westerly Marine, one of the most successful firms in the field, they designed a range of yachts, including Centaur, Pageant, Jouster, Longbow, Fastnet 27, Conway, Renown, GK 24, Westerly 33, Konsort, GK 29. It seems likely that the first of these boats, the Centaur, built in 1967, will become part of yachting history since more than 2500 have been built. The performance of this and subsequent designs for Westerly did much to counter the prejudice against twin bilge keeled yachts.

In addition to their work for Westerly, the firm designed a range of larger and more luxurious yachts in GRP for A.H. Moody and Sons Ltd. These include the Carbineer, Moody 44, Carbineer 46, Moody 66, Moody 48, Grenadier, Moody 50, Moody 183 and Moody 63. The earliest design, the Carbineer, dates from 1969 and is a classic Giles yacht, but the Moody 44 of 1971, one of the first production boats featuring a centre cockpit with a passage under the seats, began the series of modern hulls as used for the Moody 52 and 63 range and led on to the Grenadier range of 1978. A number of other designs such as the Buccaneer range, in 1973, for Eastwood Marine (Essex) and the Seamaster range for Seamaster Yachts, together with a large number of other production designs were also produced within this period. The success of the production boats was followed in the early eighties by the imposing 154-ft. schooner *White Gull*. Built in 1982 she was the largest motor sailer designed by the company and one of the largest private yachts launched in post-war times.

The company also chose this time to move their brokerage business from the top floor of 4 Quay Hill to a more suitable office at Yacht Haven marina. The brokerage was run by James Crawford and David Guthrie, keen yachtsmen and owners of two Laurent Giles designs, *Tom Thumb* a wooden Vertue and *Widgee* a Wanderer Class yacht.

In the last few years of the 1970s, the company saw the retirement of two of the partners, Arthur Bayzand and Bill Matthew, leaving Dick Stower and Peter Anstey to soldier on. By the early 1980s, both Dick and Peter were reaching retirement age and were looking for a way to retire from the day-to-day workload of the company. The solution lay with Alan Roy, a designer employed by the partners, who together with Peter Anstey decided to begin a new company. After negotiation, the firm of Laurent Giles Ltd was set up in April 1982. The new company moved from Quay Hill to Station Street, Lymington, taking with them by agreement all the data and designs held by Laurent Giles and Partners Ltd, allowing the traditions and reputation of the Laurent Giles name to continue. Many of the designs were then sent to the National Maritime Museum at Greenwich where they are now kept in their archives. Because of the recession in the yacht industry in the early 1980s, combined with the need for keeping in touch with new trends and ideas, it was considered necessary to inject new blood into the firm. The addition of younger directors, Stephen Wallis and Barry van Geffen, in 1983 fulfilled the company's requirements and completed the new design team. Barry had originally served his apprenticeship and worked at Laurent Giles during 1971 to 1980.

Laurent Giles Ltd (1982-Present)

During this period the company's workload began to increase and it became necessary to move to larger premises. The Laurent Giles design studio is presently situated in a suite of offices within the Old Lymington Town railway station building. This beautiful Victorian station, built in 1857, still operates as part of the Lymington/Brockenhurst branch line. The offices were extensively modernised to suit the company's particular needs and also afford views across the river and marinas of Lymington. Not only changes in the office location have occurred during this time. In 1986, director Peter Anstey retired after 34 years with the company and in 1987 Alan Roy left after nearly 20 years of service. At present there are four naval architects in the design team including the two directors. Student art illustrators and designers are also often found working at the offices during their period of industrial training.

The present Laurent Giles team has a broad based knowledge of design which encompasses cruising yachts, motor yachts, I.O.R. racers, 12-Metres, ultra light displacement boats, lifeboats and pilot-boats. They have experience with all types of structural materials such as wood, G.R.P., aluminium, steel, as well as modern and old fashioned working practices. Fully conversant with the various Classification Society Rules, including Det Norske Veritas, A.B.S. and Lloyds, many of their designs are required to comply with government safety rules. They have a close professional relationship with the Wolfson Marine Technology unit at Southampton University, British Maritime Technology and Liverpool University where new designs are thoroughly researched using their test tank, flume tank and wind tunnel facilities.

Over the past three years, the company has expanded its computing facilities and now has several IBM compatible computers and the latest Computer Aided Design and Drafting system (C.A.D.). This sophisticated facility achieves more accuracy and flexibility and allows the designer to manipulate and experiment with the hull form, in a way which previously would have been impossible. With such updated computer facilities, Laurent Giles Ltd now boasts one of the most modern design offices in the country. The company is expanding into new areas and after a break of almost 10 years has once again engaged in surveying and operates a brokerage.

Within the past six years the new company has designed a wide range of yachts and motor boats, including a design for the largest aluminium motor sailer ever built. It has also undertaken designs for a lifeboat, a 70 ft. training vessel and a 12-Metre challenger for the 1987 *America*'s Cup series. These and other interesting designs are included in the final chapter of this book.

Chapter 2

Pre-War Designs (1927–1939)

Introduction

The early years of Laurent Giles were not prolific in terms of the number of yachts designed, there being only 44 designs produced before the company was disbanded at the beginning of the war. This limited number is not surprising, since establishing a new name in the tight-knit yachting fraternity of the time was especially difficult and much of the company's work was initially involved with re-fit design work on yachts around the Solent.

From among those yachts designed during this period, a surprisingly high number were to become classic boats and well-established classes admired by many yachtsmen. These include of course, *Andrillot* and the Vertue Class, *Wanderer II* and *Dyarchy*. During the first years, there was also a wide range of motor boats, such as the lovely *Tamahine*, as well as yachts from the smallest dinghy to cruisers and ocean racers. *Wapipi* and her sister *Whooper* were both exceptional examples of centre board cruising yachts and were the first to have their mast stepped on the coachroof. *Maid of Malham* was the predecessor of perhaps one of the most famous racing yachts ever built, *Myth of Malham*. Even the very first of Jack Giles' yachts were to show revolutionary new ideas with many innovations in design already making them stand out from the crowd. The ten boats selected from this era best represent the range and skills of this historic designer.

The second Laurent Giles design, *Etain*

Etain

Owner	Miss Marjorie Goodson
Builder	Unknown
Date Built	1930
Design No.	2
L.O.A.	46 ft. 0 in. (14.03 m)
L.W.L.	31 ft. 0 in. (9.45 m)
Beam	9 ft. 0 in. (2.75 m)
Draft	6 ft. 6 in. (1.98 m)
Displacement	10.0 tons (10.16 tonnes)
Sail Area	814 sq. ft. (75.70 m²)
Rig	Cutter

Etain was Laurent Giles' second commission designed after the much admired 52 ft. gaff yawl *Clymene*. She was designed for a lady client, Miss Marjorie Goodson, who had very specific ideas for the type of yacht she wanted. *Etain* was to be based loosely on the International Yacht Racing Rule 8-Metre class, but she was to be a yacht for cruising rather than racing. Laurent Giles produced a sea-going 8-Metre yacht with good accommodation but which maintained the fast easy handling characteristics of the class. *Etain* proved to be well balanced and could sail herself, both features being essential for single-handed sailing, one of the main requirements of the commission since Miss Goodson often sailed alone or with few crew.

Etain's elegant interior looking forward

Etain was traditionally constructed; however, one important and unusual feature of this yacht was her deckworks. She had a skylight and doghouse which extended over a large area of the deck, a new and revolutionary idea for the time, and they were styled to blend in with the overall appearance of the yacht. The style of the windows also complemented the geometry of the doghouse and improved her looks, as well as increasing the amount of light internally. The whole arrangement was found to be most beneficial and provided additional headroom maximising the amount of usable space below decks. *Etain*'s accommodation was also unique in as far as she was designed to provide maximum comfort for one person, with room for only an occasional guest. The galley was placed in the fo'c'sle, an uncommon and today an unpopular position for the cooking area, and there was a single folding cot with the mast on the aft bulkhead. Behind this was the owner's full-width stateroom which contained a dressing table, bookcase, two wardrobes, wash basin and a W.C. hidden in a commode. In the saloon two settees provided seating with stowage lockers arranged below and behind them. There were also additional stowage lockers for oilskins in the doghouse, easily accessible in the main navigation area.

Etain's unique superstructure was to set the trend for small cruising yachts. The coachroof and doghouse were to appear in later Giles designs, where they evolved into a wide variety of styles enabling the designer to experiment with the arrangement of the interior and improve the overall accommodation. As a matter of interest one of the Laurent Giles partners, George Gill, married Marjorie Goodson shortly after the boat was completed.

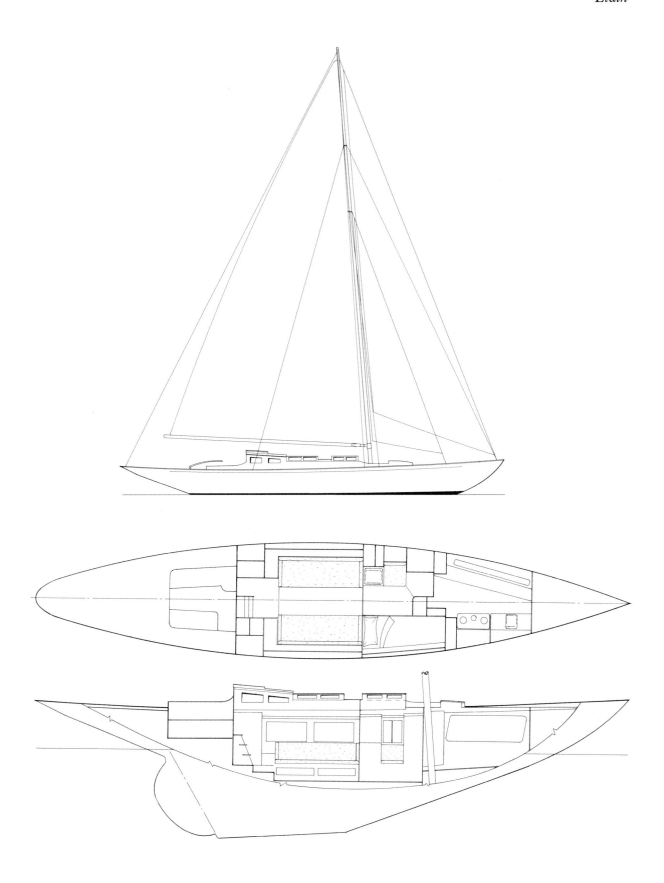

Lymington 'L' Class

Owner	Various
Builder	Elkin and Son, Christchurch
Date Designed	1931
Design No.	8
L.O.A	23 ft. 3 in. (7.09 m)
L.W.L.	19 ft. 6 in. (5.95 m)
Beam	6 ft. 10 in. (2.08 m)
Draft	3 ft. 8 in. (1.01 m)
Displacement	2.7 tons (2.74 tonnes)
Sail Area	275 sq. ft. (25.58 m²)
Rig	Sloop

The Lymington class was originally designed as a day sailer or weekend cruising yacht and one which was affordable to a large number of yachtsmen. To minimise building costs, the construction of the yacht was made as simple as possible and their straight-forward design allowed them to be built almost anywhere using locally established and traditional techniques. The materials used in the construction of these boats comprised English oak frames at 3-foot centres, American rock elm timbers at 9-inch centres, and oak floors on all grown frames. The hull was carvel planked using Oregon pine with a finished planking thickness of three-quarters of an inch. The keel was of English elm with 4-inch siding, and the transom and fittings were of mahogany. Owing to the simple sections, the planks were able to run from stem to sternpost along the garboards and round the turn of the bilge with almost parallel seams, thereby saving much waste in the cutting of timber.

The design for the class was based on sturdy little boats that had been sailing and racing in the West Solent for a number of years. The result was a seaworthy little yacht, with a large freeboard, that would sail happily to windward and keep the crew dry. Like most Giles designs they were light to handle and, as their owners would say, 'a pleasure to sail'. Their large volume provided plenty of room for accommodation, and if the owner chose there was room to fit an auxiliary engine and all the paraphernalia that a boat owner seems to require. There was also a choice of rigs which included a Bermudan sloop, lugsail sloop and gaff sloop, although most were built with the Bermudan sloop rig.

The first two boats were built for Brigadier General Lubbock and Colonel Bland-Strang. They commented that, 'both boats handled admirably and were conspicuously dry, well mannered and sailed suprisingly well in light winds.' Such performance from these little boats attracted much attention at the time and further orders were placed with the company. The local owners of these yachts proposed that they should be adopted as a class at Lymington and so their name was born. To be a member of the Lymington L Class fleet back in the 1930s, there were thirteen rules under which a competitor had to abide and these are listed here for historic interest:

1. Membership is restricted to members of any recognised Yacht or Sailing Club.
2. Races will be sailed under Y.R.A. rules
3. All hulls to be built of one design and must have a certificate from the official measurers (Messrs Laurent Giles and Partners) before racing in the Class.
4. The rig is optional but the area of the sails is restricted to 275 sq. ft. by Y.R.A. measurement.
5. Solid spars to be used.
6. One new mainsail is allowed every two years. Head sails may be renewed when required, but if the boat is rigged as a Bermudan sloop the sails must not exceed the measurements of the original design. The same applies to spinnakers.
7. Spinnakers may be used on the river.
8. The spinnaker boom when in use must be shipped in its socket on the mast and must not be tacked down to the stem head.
9. There is a penalty of 1 cwt. if no auxiliary engine is fitted.
10. Boats may only be slipped for scrubbing once a month, June, July and August.

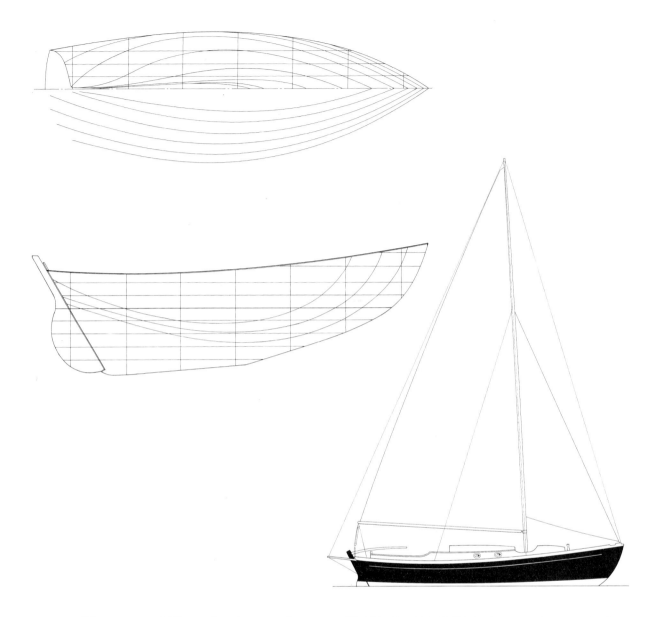

11. The sewer outfall boom is to be treated as a mark in the Course.
12. Sounding sticks are permitted.
13. All boats must be steered by an amateur helmsman.

Eighteen boats were built over the years and are listed in chronological order; *Isabella*, *Shuna*, *Wingsong*, *Penguine*, *Lotus*, *Wavecrest II*, *Grey Jane*, *Mayflower*, *Shaheen*, *Malista*, *Skipjack*, *Peri*, *Syvona*, *Mermerus*, *Saving Grace*, *Ariba*, *Iduna* and *Cavalier*.

The Lymington 'L' Class

Tamahine

Owner	H.W. Hall
Builder	Vosper and Co.
Date Built	1933
Design No.	10
L.O.A.	63 ft. 0 in. (19.22 m)
L.W.L.	60 ft. 3 in. (18.38 m)
Beam	13 ft. 1 in. (3.97 m)
Draft	4 ft. 3 in. (1.3 m)
Displacement	25.0 tons (25.4 tonnes)
Engines	2 × Gleniffer DC 6

One of the main requirements of *Tamahine* was to achieve as high a speed as possible on a 60-ft. waterline with the proviso that she had to be built using standard construction methods and materials. This meant that little weight could be saved in her construction and therefore any gain in speed would have to come from her hull shape. To attain the best possible form three models were tank tested and from this information the final hull shape was derived. The lines plan shows the fine lines and surprisingly well V'd aft body sections.

The construction was of transverse steel frames at 14.5-inch centres, planked with inch-and-a-quarter teak. Weight was saved by using an all-welded steel structure rather than the more common riveted construction of the day and the hull had 18 ft. bilge keels which were 6 inches deep to reduce rolling and improve her motion in a seaway. Her deck beams were also of steel and she sported a yellow pine deck and a mahogany deckhouse while the displacement was kept down to 25 tons, the displacement length ratio being 114, and powered by her two Gleniffer DC6 120 b.h.p. diesels she achieved a good maximum speed of 12 knots.

Her external styling, which no doubt was thought very modern for the day, gave the designer the opportunity of creating a full-width saloon, something that is now regaining popularity. With three large windows either side of the saloon allowing plenty of light and good visibility her internal decor was very modern with painted panelled bulkheads and ceilings, electric wall lights and light wood furniture with striking striped fabrics covering the settees. The combination of these elements set this boat firmly in the high fashion of the 1930s and even the sign writing of her name on the bows is in a style synonymous with the period.

Her accommodation comprised a double stateroom cabin at the stern with a single cabin forward of this with a washroom serving both cabins. The crew's quarters were placed in the fo'c'sle and consisted of four pipe cots, heads and the galley. Behind this was a spacious saloon with two large settees, from which there was access to the wheelhouse via a stairway. In the wheelhouse two doors, port and starboard, were positioned in the aft bulkhead, providing easy access to the wide side-decks. Between these doors and raised on a step was a plush settee with the same striped fabric as those in the saloon.

Tamahine was a very impressive sight, with her sleek hull and distinctive topsides, underway she proved comfortable with little noticeable vibration. Unfortunately little is known of her whereabouts today except that she has been sold and renamed *Meribru*.

Tamahine at full speed

Looking aft on *Tamahine*'s main deck

Tamahine's main saloon looking forward with
her classic 1930's style

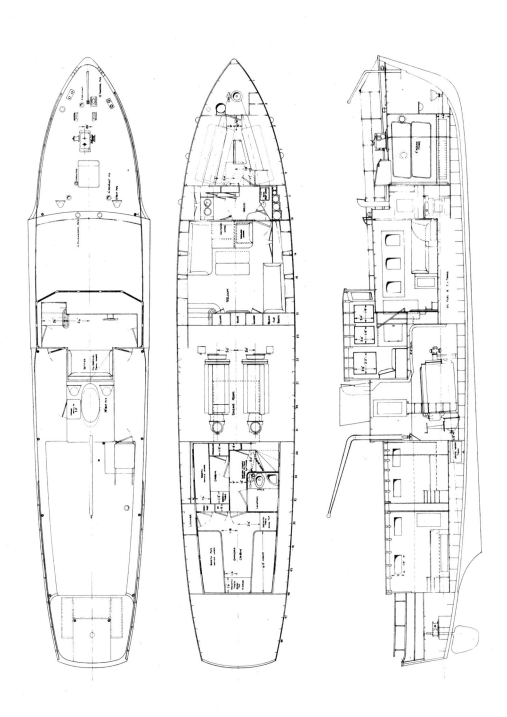

Andrillot

Owner	R.A. Kinnersley
Builder	A.H. Moody and Sons
Date Built	1936
Design No.	15
L.O.A.	25 ft. 0 in. (7.63 m)
L.W.L.	21 ft. 6 in. (6.56 m)
Beam	7 ft. 2 in. (2.21 m)
Draft	4 ft. 5 in. (1.37 m)
Displacement	4.28 tons (4.35 tonnes)
Sail Area	366 sq. ft. (34.04 m²)
Rig	Gaff Cutter

The little gaff cutter *Andrillot* was designed in 1936 for Dick Kinnersley, who had sailed with Roger Pinckney in his original yacht *Dyarchy* and had been impressed with this transom-sterned 24-ton Bristol Channel Pilot Cutter. Dick had also been brought up with the local fishing boats of his home in the Channel Islands and was keen to own a boat with similar characteristics. *Andrillot* was therefore designed as a modernised but miniature version of a pilot-cutter and was built and launched in Southampton in 1936.

Andrillot's hull maintained the general outward character of the pilot-fishing vessel, but was specifically designed as a cruising yacht. She had the benefit of a fresh mind and a clean piece of paper in her creation, and from the start was far superior to any working boat conversion. Although *Andrillot* had a transom-stern, similar to a pilot-cutter, with very little bow overhang and a gaff rig, she had very clean lines below the water and her sections showed that she was designed to give a great deal of room inside. An unusual feature for the day was the very short low coachroof with sitting headroom and only two berths below. In those days the look of a dog-house was not considered aesthetic on such a small boat.

The sail plan shows the highest development of the gaff cutter with a clean and efficient rig. The mast was situated well aft, and as the forestay went practically to the stem head, she had a large staysail. The jib stay ran parallel with this and made for an efficient combination of headsails. This type of rig required only a single spreader and had considerable advantages for short-handed cruising. *Andrillot* was an excellent example of simplicity throughout, this being obtained without loss of efficiency, as some of the cruises she undertook in record time have shown.

Andrillot soon became a celebrity, not only because of her good looks, but also for the long passages she made, some being quite exceptional for a small yacht by the standards of the day. One remarkable trip, which has been documented and reiterated many times over the years, was that undertaken by Humphrey Barton, one of the partners in the firm in 1937. He had borrowed *Andrillot* and cruised with his wife Jessie to the West Country, Scillies and Brittany. They covered 855 miles in 23 days and visited 22 places. 'She certainly did go' was Barton's enthusiastic comment on the yacht's abilities, and it was for this trip he won the Royal Cruising Club's Founders Cup.

She was the smallest cruising yacht designed by Laurent Giles yet set a style and character marked by her distinctive sheer, raised strake and moderate ends. Jack Giles described the design as: 'Shaped to maintain the general outward character of the pilot fishing boat, but having the benefit of the concentrated thought on the design of seagoing yachts that the activities of the Royal Ocean Racing Club had then fostered. The result was a straightforward little boat with a modest forward overhang, full displacement, outside ballast, moderate beam and a reasonably cut-away profile.' At this time they could not have guessed that *Andrillot* was to be the forerunner of a series of famous cruising yachts, the Vertues.

Andrillot has recently been discovered and painstakingly restored to her former glory by Tim Stevenson. She is currently rigged as a Bermudan sloop and can be seen today sailing on the Lymington river.

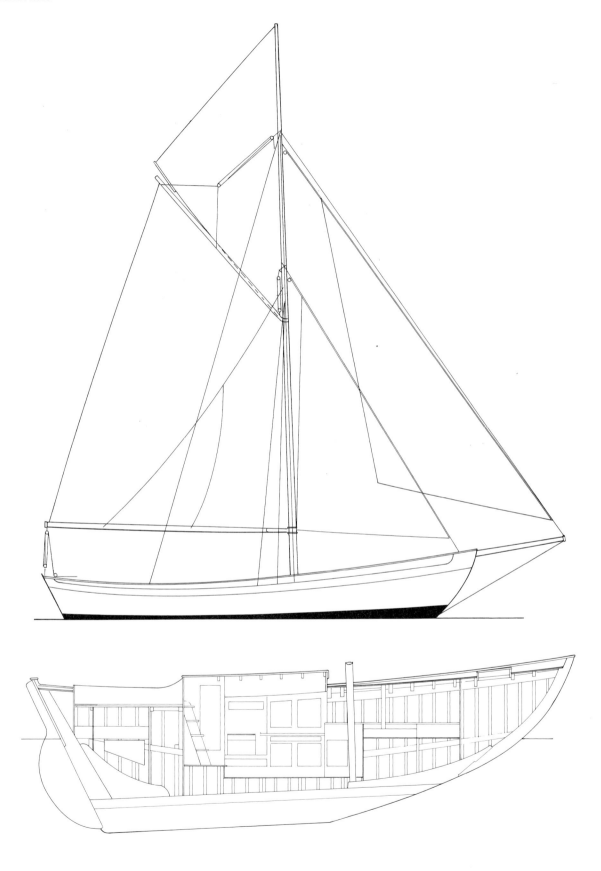

Andrillot, with her original gaff rig, in light airs

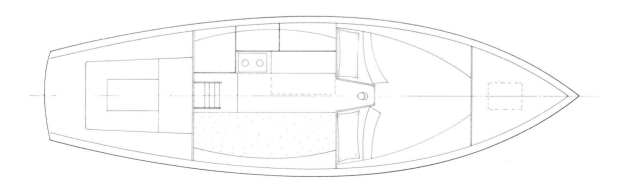

The Vertues

The class name was not adopted until 1945; however, a number of sisters of *Andrillot* were produced prior to the outbreak of war in 1939. The second boat *Sally II* was built by E.F Elkins of Christchurch in 1937, and in 1938 a third boat *Monie*, was built by Berthon Boatyard. *Sally II* carried a Bermudan rig and had a 4hp Stuart Turner petrol engine, while *Monie* was a similar design to *Andrillot* but had dispensed with the gaff and bowsprit rig, setting the trend with the 'Slutter' rig, a cross between a sloop and cutter. This rig is characterised by an inner forestay landed on the stem instead of nearer the middle of the foretriangle base. *Monie* differed from her sisters, having a lengthened coachroof although keeping the original trunk-like style. She was followed in the summer of 1938 by the fourth Vertue, *Charis*, and in December of the same year *Yachting World* reported a further six boats were being built, including two by Topham and Rooker.

It was the fifth boat *Epeneta*, built by Woodnutt & Co for Colonel Lawrence Biddle, that was to give the class its name. A member of the Little Ship Club, Biddle entered her into the 1939 Poole-Cherbourg race as her maiden passage with himself and Humphrey Barton as crew. After the race the two men sailed the engine-less boat to the Bay of Biscay and on their return were rewarded by the presentation of the Little Ship Club's Vertue Cup. As a tribute to *Epeneta*'s achievement, Laurent Giles decided, at the close of the war in 1945, to name their 5-ton class the Vertue.

In 1939 there were ten Vertue boats afloat, and in order of the Laurent Giles boat design numbers, these were: *Andrillot, Sally II, Monie, Charis, Epeneta, Francolin, Kawan, Caupona, Candy* and *Almena*. Naturally there were some variations between the boats, depending on the owners' requirements, but these were minor and mainly associated with accommodation or sail plan. All except *Andrillot* have had lead keels.

The principal achievements and notable cruises of some of the Vertues

Of the pre-war Vertues, Humphrey Barton made an interesting delivery trip with *Monie* to North Wales in 1938, going the hard way and sailing west through the Caledonian Canal. For the first leg of her cruise she covered 104 miles between Ryde and Dover in fifteen and a half hours, indicating a remarkable average speed of six and three-quarter knots. Within four days of leaving Ryde, she had reached Scotland. On her return passage to Wales, she covered a distance of 1,056 miles in 25 days, and the weather she had faced included a total of four gales. In the same year *Epeneta* cruised to Spain and back, and twelve years later in 1950 *Monie* made several notable voyages to Gibraltar via the Bay of Biscay. Such voyages at the time were thought to be quite considerable for such small yachts.

The most famous passage in a Vertue was made by Humphrey Barton and Kevin O'Riordan in 1950 with their epic trans-Atlantic crossing in *Vertue XXXV*. The boat was bought from stock from the builders Elkins of Christchurch, with only slight modifications being undertaken for the voyage. The crossing was made, using the intermediate route from the Lizard to Sandy Hook off New York, taking 47 days 11 hrs at an average of 3.38 knots, the equivalent of 77.26 miles a day. During the voyage they faced 23 days of head winds and were under bare poles on three occasions. Humphrey Barton commented after his voyage: 'I honestly believe that she is the best designed, built and equipped small ocean-going cruising yacht that has yet been produced. Her ability to stand up to bad weather, her remarkably high performance under sail and the comfort of her accommodation are outstanding.' They had encountered a hurricane 200 miles northwest of Bermuda and only the deckworks were damaged by a freak sea. *Vertue XXXV* was the

Humphrey Barton's Vertue 35 heavily reefed prior to her trans-Atlantic crossing

smallest yacht to have sailed over that route and the first to have crossed the Atlantic with her mast stepped on deck. Her voyage was considered to be an outstanding achievement.

The next major voyage was by *Icebird*, an especially designed ocean-cruising Vertue, cutter rigged, with extra planking in her topsides to assist with carrying the extra weight of the additional provisions needed on long voyages. Her reinforced coachroof was made with a low profile to increase the chances of survival in a knockdown. In 1952, skippered by Dr Joe Cunningham, *Icebird* sailed from England to the West Indies, then to Newfoundland arriving in 1953. After working for several years in Newfoundland, Cunningham made the return journey back to Ireland in 1957.

Speedwell of Hong Kong, built in Hong Kong for A.G. Hamilton, was sailed by the owner with one companion to England in 1953. His route took him from Singapore to England via the Cape of Good Hope. Door to door the voyage took six months ending in a gale at Portsmouth. He had undertaken the journey in 140 sailing days and covered a distance of 14,000 miles. Later in *Salmo*, a sister ship, he made an Atlantic crossing by the northern route from Scotland to Quebec, then to Panama and Tahiti via the Pitcairn Islands, ending his journey in California. Prior to this voyage, he had sold *Speedwell* to John Goodwin who sailed her first to the West Indies via Gibralter, and then to South Africa.

Easy Vertue, Ex. *Jonica*, was sailed by Dan Robinson from Christchurch, England via the Azores to the Bahamas. Robertson headed southwest from the Azores and ran for ten days under his running sails without touching the helm, doing 80 to 100 miles a day. He encountered a hurricane and winds of 60–70 knots but working to windward neither the boat nor owner suffered any damage.

In 1959 Brian Bleasdale built *Mea* in Hong Kong to the ocean cruising design and the standard rig. Over a three year period he sailed her leisurely home to England. In the first year he sailed to Borneo, in the next to Ceylon and South Africa, finally returning at the end of the third year to Falmouth, England. On Bleasdale's death in 1967, ownership passed into Swedish hands and *Mea* was refitted in anticipation of a voyage to New Zealand.

David Lewis in *Cardinal Vertue* made two notable trips in 1959 and 1960. The first was a singlehanded cruise to Norway and back from Burnham-on-Crouch, and the other was the inaugural Singlehanded Trans-Atlantic Race in which he finished third. *Cardinal Vertue* was sold to an Australian, Bill Nance, who in 1963 left Brixham on the first leg of his circumnavigation and reached San Fernando in Argentina in 61 days. His next leg was to Cape Town and then on to Melbourne. During the Cape Town to Melbourne voyage he lost his mast off St Paul's Island. He managed to reach Fremantle using a temporary rig and carried out repairs there before continuing to Auckland, where *Cardinal Vertue* was refitted for the last leg of her circumnavigation to Buenos Aires via Cape Horn. It was on this leg that Bill Nance held the singlehanded speed record for a long passage: 122.5 miles per day for 53 days. It was later taken from him by Sir Francis Chichester in the much larger *Gypsey Moth IV*. At that time *Cardinal Vertue* was also the smallest yacht to have rounded Cape Horn and she was one of four Vertues to complete circumnavigations.

Other reported trips include two trans-Atlantic crossings and a three-year circumnavigation by *Kantread*, which was considerably faster than Ed Bowden's 14-year circumnavigation during 1962–76 in *Kittiwake*. This later cruise, however, took in the French Canals, the Mediterranean Sea, the Atlantic Ocean, the West Indies, the Galapagos Islands, South Sea Islands, New Guinea, Singapore, South America and back to the West Indies. In 1969, *Bonaventure De Lys*, skippered by her Canadian owner John Struchinsky, completed his round-the-world trip in six years. Other recorded trans-Atlantic crossings by Vertues have been made in *Pavan* by Olaf Nissen, *Aotea* skippered by R.H. Montgomery, *Stelda* by Peter Woolass, *Blue Jenny* by Dan Bowen and *Charis* by Peter Pike.

In 1965 L.E.L. Sills accompanied by R. Mayhew and R. Craig, logged 2,242 miles on a round trip from Scotland to Iceland in the Vertue, *Fialar*. Leaving Fraserburgh on 30th May, they made Reykjavik, just under 600 miles in 8 days. They completed their all round trip in a month, sailing direct to Iceland on their outward leg, circumnavigating the island which took them into the Arctic Circle, returning via the Faroes and Hebrides Isles back to Scotland.

More recently a notable Vertue cruising trip was made by David Hays in a G.R.P. Vertue II. Between July 1984 and May 1985 he and his son

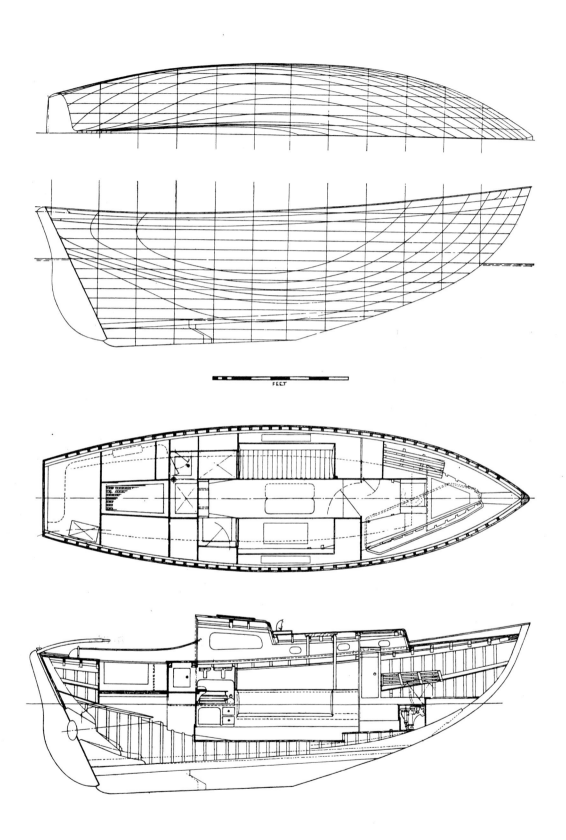

FEET

sailed *Sparrow* from Connecticut through the Panama Canal to Easter Island, around Cape Horn and back up the Atlantic to Connecticut. The boat had no engine and no radar and the trip took five months, forty-two days of which were sailed singlehanded by his 25 year-old son Daniel after his father was called home unexpectedly. *Sparrow* began life as a bought fibre-glass hull and was fitted out by father and son over a period of two years. It is believed that no boat that small has rounded Cape Horn for over twenty years, the last one in 1965 also being a Vertue.

Notable cruises in the southern hemisphere include that of *Kotimu*, which had an original gaff cutter rig, and was sailed from New Zealand to Australia and finally to New Guinea by Neils and Billie Powell. *Austral Vertue* was sailed from Melbourne via Sydney to New Zealand then to the Gilbert Islands via Fiji by Mike McKeon. Many ocean voyages and successful cruises have been logged by Vertues, but so commonplace have these voyages become that fewer reports are made concerning the exploits of these remarkable vessels.

The solid construction and strength of the Vertue can be summed up by the story of the pre-war *Kawan*. She was over 30 years old when she was accidentally driven into a coral reef off Tahiti, then pounded by the surf over the reef and into the quiet waters of the lagoon beyond. In this incident she suffered only superficial damage. Unfortunately, only a few days away from completing her round the world trip, which had begun in England with Don Nealey and had been taken over by Francis Gildas Le Guen in Papeete, *Kawan* was shipwrecked in the Red Sea.

Vertues have been built around the world by amateurs and professionals in wood, steel and glassfibre, and the 200th Vertue was built some two years before the class half-centenary. Approximately 80 of these have been built either by E.F Elkins and Sons of Christchurch, or R.A. Newman and Sons of Poole, in England, and many have also been built by the Cheoy Lee Shipyard in Hong Kong. These and other Vertues have criss-crossed the Atlantic and sailed around the world, and many of these voyages have been made singlehanded. Perhaps a most fitting story which enforces the sailability of the Vertue was from a *Yachting and Boating Weekly* report: 'One of my most vivid memories of a Vertue is of trying to catch a halyard that had come adrift

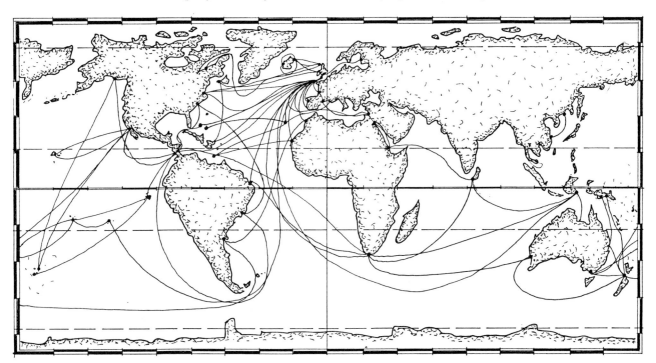

Ever since Humphrey Barton crossed the Atlantic in Vertue XXXV in 1950, "Vertues" have been sailing all round the world

and was just out of reach . . . "here, use this" said the helmsman, who handed me the tiller as the boat sailed on.'

During the post-war years, small adjustments were made to these boats in the topsides and deckworks. The basic *Andrillot* hull, however, remained the same. The important changes which were made in the design during the first decade of the war are as follows. In 1945, at last daring to offer this feature to the general public, an optional doghouse was added and the coachroof was extended forward of the mast. Although this meant less deck space, comfort below improved considerably. Up until 1946, boats had been built on all grown frames, but the more modern approach of using bent timbers was now adopted for construction. At about the same time the centreline shaft and aperture were introduced, allowing for the installation of high power auxiliary engines. Self-draining cockpits had also become standard on these boats. In the same year the first Vertue mast was stepped on deck, which automatically gave more space below. There was great concern at the time with this arrangement, but Humphrey Barton demonstrated its security when he used it in *Vertue XXXV* for his trans-Atlantic crossing.

In 1949 Jack Giles made a major change and altered the sheerline by raising the freeboard in line with current yachting design trends. The sheerline was flattened, giving more sitting headroom below and masking the height of the doghouse. This gave the Vertues the benefit of a roomier drier hull and a new look which transformed the pilot-fishing yacht of 1936 into the smart yacht of the fifties. No further changes occurred until 1954 when it was considered more practicable to extend the doghouse further. This provided much better proportions in the structure and also increased the amount of light and space below.

Changes in the sail plan began immediately after *Andrillot*, from a gaff to a Bermudan rig with the building of *Sally II*. The bowsprit was removed and the length of the mainboom was reduced by about 18 inches. It was not until the third boat *Monie* that the slutter rig, a modified sloop and cutter, was developed. Other Vertues were given a fractional rig, fitted with jumper struts and a cut-down mainsail. This included the loss of the bumpkin, to balance the reduction of the forward sail area, and a taller mast was fitted to some Vertues to compensate for this. The most popular rig of all was the masthead, simplified in design in 1961.

Vertue II

Although over the years there have been various alterations made to the deck and rigging of Vertues, the basic hull form of the original, *Andrillot*, has changed very little. This attests to the fact that the hull design had, in a first attempt, reached the pinnacle of its development. Originally Vertues were built of wood, but in the mid-seventies the G.R.P. Vertue II class was launched. The new yacht was very closely based on the original Vertue design but took advantage of modern G.R.P. construction. At deck level the beam was increased by four inches, without changing the underwater shape, providing extra interior space. This together with the addition of an attractive coachroof and doghouse gives Vertue II somewhat better accommodation. The G.R.P. construction produces a lighter yacht with an increased ballast ratio, thus improving the seaworthiness and performance. Vertue II is in every

way a 'Virtue'. Initially built by Rossiter yachts and then for a short period by Westerly Marine Construction, Vertue II is now built by Bossom Boatyard at Oxford and very much keeps alive the Vertue tradition. So far more than twenty Vertue II's have been built, five of which have been delivered overseas and include *Faire Vertue* to Australia, *Josphine* to Scandinavia, *Sparrow* to America, *Nimrod of Larne* to Northern Ireland and *Sallie* to San Francisco.

It is perhaps a little ironic that the Vertue, such a small and unassuming boat, should become the hallmark of Laurent Giles, since their main designs have been for large luxury yachts and ocean racers. This must surely then give tribute to Jack Giles who focused all of his creative energies into a project which at the time must have seemed relatively minor.

Wanderer II

Owner	Eric C. Hiscock
Builder	T. Napier and Co
Date Built	1936
Design No.	18
L.O.A.	24 ft. 0 in. (7.32 m)
L.W.L.	21 ft. 0 in. (6.41 m)
Beam	7 ft. 1 in. (2.14 m)
Draft	4 ft. 11 in. (1.52 m)
Displacement	4.5 tons (4.57 tonnes)
Sail Area	395 sq. ft. (36.74 m²)
Rig	Gaff Cutter

Wanderer II was built as a replacement for the owner's old 1898 sloop of the same name. Eric Hiscock, who was to become a legendary ocean farer together with his wife Susan, was impressed with Laurent Giles's designs and so approached Jack with his general ideas and requirements for a practical cruising yacht. Hiscock considered the most important aspects of the boat were that it should be comfortable, seaworthy, easy to handle, with a gaff rig and a displacement of about 4 to 5 tons. He left the dimensions of the boat entirely to Giles, the result of which Eric later commented on saying: 'He produced a lovely set of lines with plenty of sheer and fair waterlines.' The plans and specifications were put out to tender and a local boat yard in Poole built the boat in the summer of 1936 for £350. She was constructed from sawn frames with intermediate steam bent frames of elm, this being at the time a more favoured and cheaper method of building than using all grown frames.

The boat's hull-shape was not considered modern for her day since she did not have long overhangs or the preferred Bermudan rig. She did, however, have a reasonable amount of draft, a beamy hull with a transom stern and bowsprit which were built for serious cruising. Laurent Giles simplified the gaff rig with a combined main and topmast, in a similar fashion to *Dyarchy* and *Andrillot*. This had the benefit of setting a topsail without a yard and improved the rather stubby look of a conventional gaff mast. This meant that the final mast was considerably taller, and the total height was a remarkable 37 feet.

The accommodation layout was very practical although there was only sitting headroom due to the low coachroof. This arrangement was practicable since it allowed for a 7-foot dinghy to be carried on deck. One of the most interesting features below decks was the stove which was sunk flush into the bulkhead, with a locker close by which could store a half-hundredweight of coal. The thoughtful position of the stove allowed for sails and clothing placed in the forepeak to be dried easily and out of the way of the saloon.

Wanderer II is a classical example of the approach that owners and designers took as the norm for a boat designed and built in the 1930s. Today the idea of serious cruising, with all that it entails, in a boat with only sitting headroom would not be considered reasonable; few people today would want to prepare a full meal at sea in gale conditions, as the Hiscocks regularly did. Nor are boats today designed with solid fuel stoves and the space to carry the large supplies of coal necessary for heating.

In August 1936 *Wanderer II* made her maiden cruise to the Channel Islands. After this trip twin spinnakers were carried on all following voyages. A number of notable journeys were made by *Wanderer II* including trips to the West Country, Ireland, Skye and Brittany. In May 1950 a remarkable voyage was made to Spain and the Azores and is recorded in detail in one of Eric Hiscock's books, *Wandering Under Sail*.

In 1951 *Wanderer II* was sold to an Australian, Bill Howard who, with Frank McNully, sailed her to Tahiti. After this trip Bill sailed her singlehanded to Seattle where she was sold again. Since then she has changed hands a number of times and is now thought to be sailing in Hawaii.

Eric Hiscock's *Wanderer II* with his wife Susan at the helm

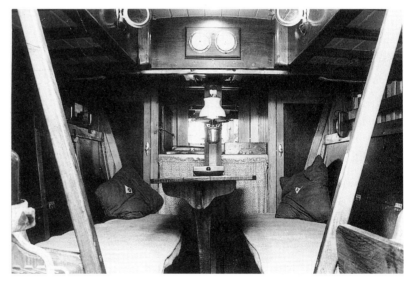

Wanderer II's tiny but classic interior

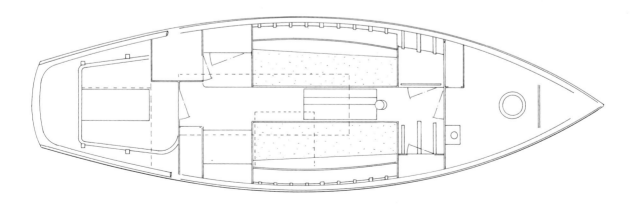

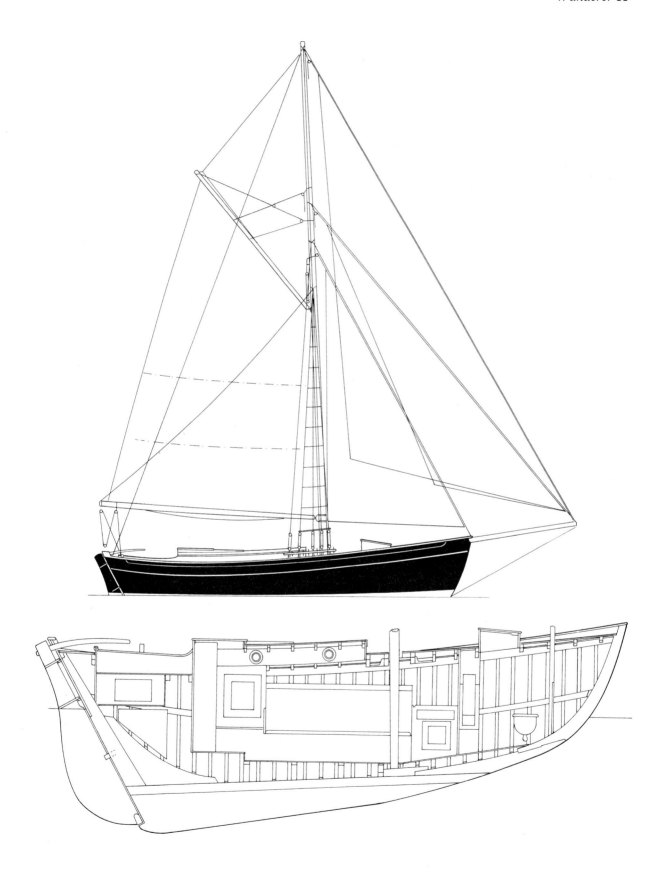

Verity A and the Channel Class

Owner	Unknown
Builder	Unknown
Date Built	1939
Design No.	19
L.O.A.	38 ft. 5 in. (11.77 m)
L.W.L.	26 ft. 0 in. (7.93 m)
Beam	8 ft. 10 in. (2.67 m)
Draft	5 ft. 6 in. (1.68 m)
Displacement	6.9 tons (7.01 tonnes)
Sail Area	624 sq. ft. (58.03 m²)
Rig	Bermudan Cutter

Verity A was one of the most attractive little yachts of her day and was designed for the smaller R.O.R.C. Class. The design was standardised by Laurent Giles and *Verity A* was to become the first of the popular Channel Class. This class, which had a close relationship with Giles's successful ocean-racer *Maid of Malham*, proved to be a most practical design and was equally suitable as a fast cruiser or as a handicap racer. Because of this, only minor modifications were made to later Channel Class yachts such as *English Lass* and *Triune of Troy*.

The Channel Class yacht *Triune of Troy* was also a very pretty ship with graceful lines and sheer, and was originally built for Lord Russell. Onboard she appeared much larger than she actually was and gave an air of confidence in her seagoing abilities. The mast and boom fittings, together with everything on deck, were planned in great detail as though she were a large ocean racer. Her sailing abilities are quoted here from the *Yachtsman's Annual Who's Who 1938–39*, 'She was stiff, extremely handy and light on the helm under all conditions, close hauled, reaching and running.' The sail plan showed the then modern all inboard rig with the mast stepped well into the centre of the yacht, and a wealth of headsails.

Seven Channel Class yachts were built between 1935 and 1946 though curiously little was seen of them in ocean racing. The probable reason for this was put down to their bold sheer and fairly long ends, giving them a disadvantage in the R.O.R.C.

rule which called for a profile with short overhangs. In 1939 the first of the Brittanys was launched, and these small and cheaper to build yachts began to eclipse the success of their elder sisters.

A feature of the Channel Class, of some historic interest, is that these yachts were the first to set the 'doghouse' fashion. The now universal doghouse had not previously been seen on small yachts until one was introduced on the second Laurent Giles design, *Etain*, in 1930. It had originally been introduced as a means of getting really habitable accommodation without unsightly deckworks on 8-Metre dimensions. However, the doghouse in this design and in the contemporary *Argo*, was used with restraint but became very successful. This was because it not only improved accommodation but also gave a balance to the design. The interest shown in *Verity A* was so great that the designers let themselves go and the doghouse on small yachts was rapidly established as an accepted convention.

Little is known of the present whereabouts of *Verity A*, but one of her sisters, *Triune of Troy*, was restored in 1988 and should be seen sailing again soon on the south coast of England.

The second of the Channel Class, *English Lass*

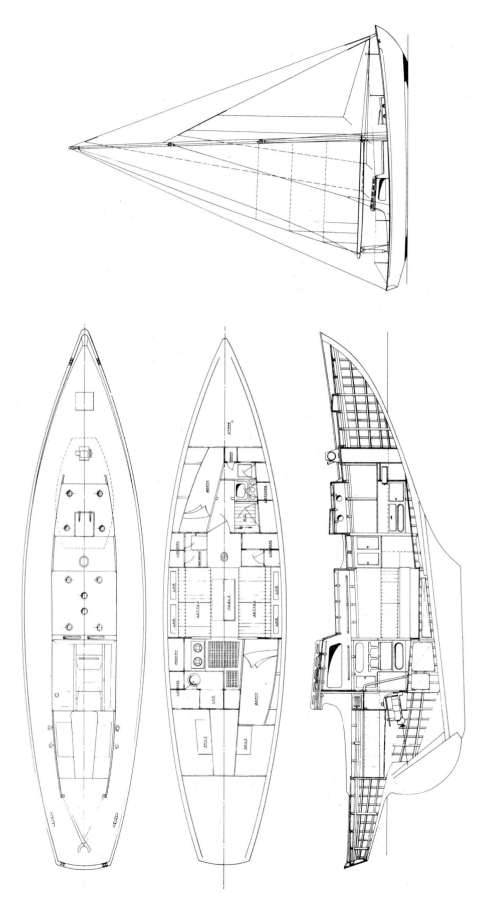

Maid of Malham

Owner	John Illingworth
Builder	King and Son
Date Built	1936
Design No.	23
L.O.A.	48 ft. 6 in. (14.79 m)
L.W.L.	35 ft. 0 in. (10.68 m)
Beam	10 ft. 8 in. (3.28 m)
Draft	7 ft. 6 in. (2.29 m)
Displacement	13.5 tons (13.72 tonnes)
Sail Area	955 sq. ft. (88.82 m^1)
Rig	Bermudan Cutter

Maid of Malham was designed as a serious racing yacht. Both John Illingworth and Jack Giles were members of the Royal Ocean Racing Club (R.O.R.C.) committee whose racing rules, like todays I.O.R., had many loopholes. Much thought was put into creating a yacht with a very low rating and there was also much attention to detail in her rig and general design.

A hull model of *Maid of Malham* was tank tested at the Stevens Institute of Technology in New Jersey to investigate her upright resistance and her close hauled performance. To obtain the Velocity Made Good (V.M.G.) figures a wind tunnel model of *Maid* and her rig were tested in association with Fairey Aviation. This information, along with observations made on board *Flica*, regarding her sails, trim, heel and V.M.G., was used to create vector diagrams of *Maid*'s predicted sailing performance with various combinations of rig and sails.

Her construction was fairly conventional for the day, being of carvel planking with wood frames and steel floors and straps. The deck was laid in a rather unusual manner, with the planking forward of the midships running parallel to her centre line and aft of the midships running parallel to her covering board. The transom on *Maid of Malham* was cut short to reduce her weight and rating, and at the time this sawn-off appearance was considered radical and, to some, not aesthetically pleasing.

Her rig, optimised from the model predictions, was basically a cutter, with a large foretriangle and

consequently proportionately smaller mainsail. The ability to set her twin inner forestays in two different positions fore and aft, or to stow them against the mast by the simple means of quick release levers, gave her an enormous variety of headsails from a large Genoa to small working jibs, and the ability to set twin spinnakers. These quick release levers like many other deck fittings, for example the sail handling winches, were designed exclusively by Laurent Giles for *Maid of Malham*. Another unusual feature of this yacht, for the time, was her backstay which could be adjusted whilst racing by a calibrated register which could measure the amount of tension in her rig. This allowed the crew to quickly optimise the mast-bend during a race, so that the sails could be set to maximise speed for a wide variety of wind conditions.

An auxiliary engine was installed for her role as a cruising yacht, which would normally necessitate dragging a propeller around the racing course. *Maid of Malham*, however, had a folding propeller positioned out through the quarter which could be removed for important races. If the propeller had not been removed prior to a race, a member of the crew would dive down and place thick rubber bands around the blades to make sure they remained closed while sailing.

The arrangement of the interior accommodation was designed for eight members of crew, but could be extended to sleep nine by using a pipe cot slung over one of the saloon settees. The saloon was placed in the centre of the boat and was large enough to seat the whole crew for meals. Forward of the saloon was a double cabin to starboard with the head to port, and forward of this was a large fo'c'sle with a built-in berth. Aft of the saloon to port was the navigation room, and to starboard there was an oilskin locker with a recess bunk. In the stern there was a double cockpit, the smaller was for the helmsman and the larger for the crew, a very useful arrangement which keeps the helmsman free of the crew's distraction and activity.

Maid of Malham was an exceptionally well designed racing yacht, as her racing history shows. In her very first season, in 1937, she entered the Coronation Race and won easily against fifty other

notable entries. This was no mean feat since the
course, for this her maiden race, was from Brixham
to the Eddystone lighthouse, across the Channel to
Cherbourg, and then returning to Southsea leaving
the Isle of Wight to port. This was to be the first of a
long line of victories through her racing career until
1973, when she was lost at sea in the middle of the
Pacific Ocean.

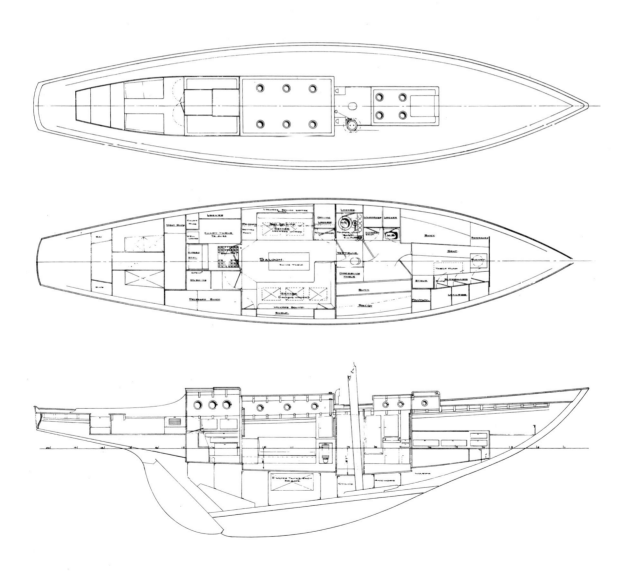

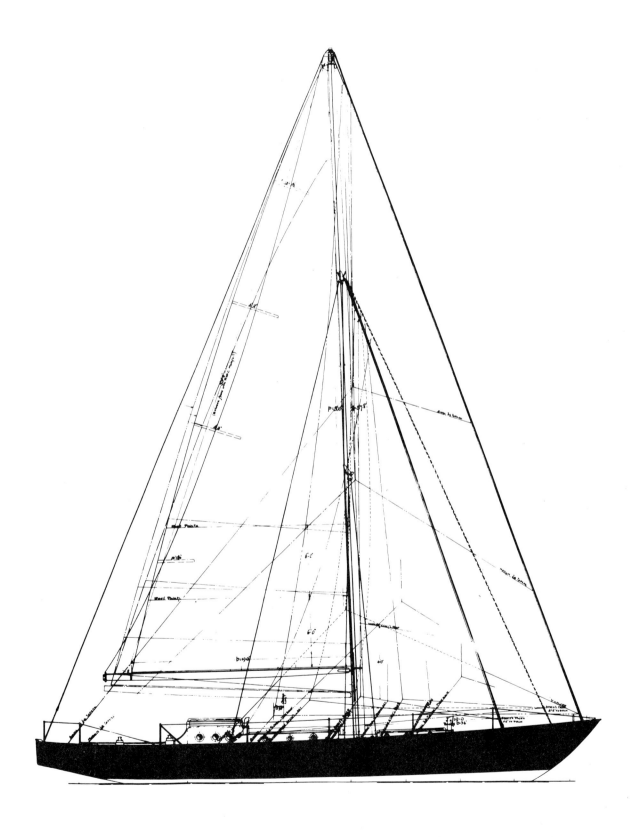

Captain John Illingworth's *Maid of Malham*

Wapipi and Whooper

Owner	Commander Pirie
Builder	Morgan Giles Ltd, Teignmouth
Date Built	1937
Design No.	31
L.O.A.	38 ft. 10 in. (11.82 m)
L.W.L.	28 ft. 0 in. (8.54 m)
Beam	9 ft. 6 in. (2.90 m)
Draft	3 ft. 6 in. (1.07 m)
Displacement	5.4 tons (5.49 tonnes)
Sail Area	490 sq. ft. (45.6 m²)
Rig	Bermudan Cutter

This famous design is described by Jack Giles in a letter to *Yachting World* in March 1949, the contents of which are as follows:

'Yacht designing is often said to be an art. In fact it is a combination of calculations and controlled guessing with art. Calculations are fine. The more precisely a solution can be calculated, the smaller is the margin for error. In the course of time and designing, an imposing mass of data is collected and a considerable technique for finding one's way around it is developed. But there has always to be a beginning and at best the limits of calculations are never more than just around the corner. Sooner or later the designer has to summon his courage and guess. *Wapipi* was a case in point.

When Commander Pirie commissioned the design we had very little to work from. We had ideas, half-formed ideas, possibly half-baked ideas of what a shoal draft boat of such size might be. The owner advanced a German design as a "take-off". It was ahead of any known contemporary English practice, typically German, thorough and complete in detail. But somehow it seemed to us that it should be possible to produce a shoal draft cruiser with better looks and more promise of fun under sail.

British, American and European designs were studied but the final conception was, I think generally, and in detail, unascribable to any direct outside inspiration. But it was all rather long ago to remember surrounding detail. The broad outline of the argument remains, however, pretty clear. Ballast, with no depth of keel, did not offer much profit, so for stability there must be beam. With ballast at a discount, light displacement was indicated. At that time the 30-Square Metre boats were in the eye and the argument would develop from them along the lines: first how much displacement must be put up to compensate (1) for engine (2) for accommodation weights, (3) for a rather more robust construction; secondly, what increase of beam was necessary to compensate for lack of draft and lever. Here the French 8.50s, attractive boats in their way, were not forgotten, and the final answer, as the photograph alone is sufficient to show, was a break away from the precedent with a general style more in keeping with post-war than pre-war notions. Beyond the photograph lies the fact of an overall satisfactory performance, charming manners, speed at moderate heel and some ability to windward. *Wapipi* showed the way to nearly, if not all the ocean racing fleet on a light weather beat from Dinard to Brehart in 1938 and considerable speed down wind. Otherwise she will beat a Solent tide on the wind without her plate; has weathered a severe gale in West Bay; has proved far less unsatisfactory at sea than we ever hoped; had a ramming match with the Warden Ledge buoy

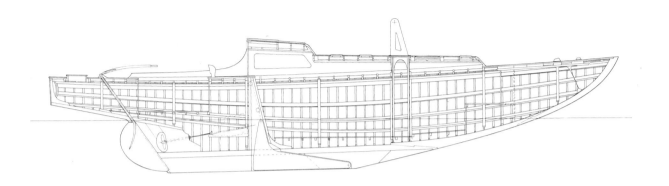

running up the Needles Channel at over 8 knots on a spring flood and, though a little shaken, needed no attention until the end of the season; and could, in general, be said to have not only met requirements, but to have exceeded expectations. For much of her success we and she are beholden to the lovely job which Morgan Giles did.

Some details of the basic argument may be of interest.

The displacement/length ratio (246) which we finally chose was a little over 240. This was low in those days. Our previous "dare" had been *Maid of Malham* at 315 and we did not quite make it for she floated a little deep. Some figures from the calculated weights will, however, illustrate the argument. Allowances of 540 lbs. for engine room weights, 100 lbs. for electrical fittings, 1036 lbs. for joinery, 100 lbs. for plumbing, 100 lbs. for water and 460 lbs. for normal cruising equipment, something very like 1500 lbs. over what one may describe as "racing practice", and with 600 lbs. in the sail plan left a balance of 4900 lbs. for struc-

tural weights to hit the target, with 4250 lbs. in hand for ballast keel. The complete build-up totalled 11,980 lbs., with a ballast ratio of 35.4%.

The beam was finalized at 9 feet 6 inches. There may have been solid argumentation behind this figure but I imagine that we were satisfied to reply with Sir Andrew, "I have no exquisite reason, but I have reason good enough." The best possible reason I can offer is the boat.

About this time the owner decided to step the mast on deck. "In for a penny, in for a pound", we suggested that it might as well go on the coachroof. Then and there I clearly remember partners and others having fits and advancing a number of very good reasons against balancing the thing on the roof, but onto the roof it went and on the roof it has remained up and down the coast and to and fro across the North Sea. As usual, Morgan Giles made a lovely job of the steel work and much of the credit is his; also, I suspect, much of the cost. But the contraption was a success and

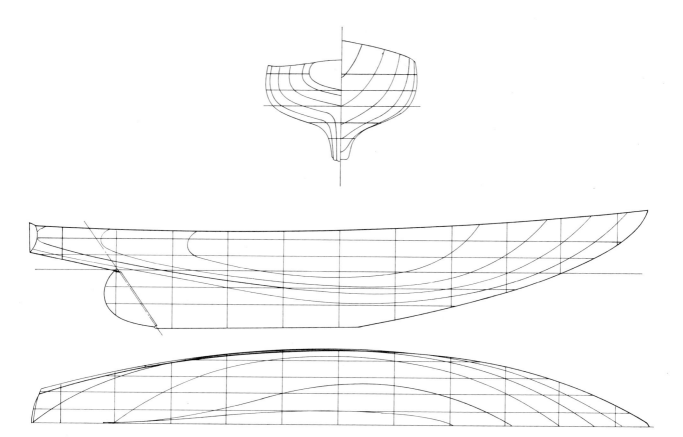

that's that. Now we are beginning to get used to it and I suppose an ever increasing number of boats will put to sea with masts balanced on their hats. Heigh-ho for the good old days when masts landed on the step, and garboards opened up on the wind like a concertina and all hands queued up at the pump.

Looking inside it can be said that the accommodation was generally successful and quite unexpectedly spacious. The position of the galley was argued on the basis of the proportion of meals expected to be served underway. If the proportion is as high as a third then almost certainly the galley is better aft, for cooking forward at sea is too much to ask of the stomach.

Despite the hope inspired by the bridge deck and the natural foundations of the centre board case an enclosed engine compartment was not possible, and in the common manner of the small yacht it is in the accommodation. In the interest of general openness the WC was denied the seclusion of a separate compartment, an arrangement which is far more acceptable in practice than in contemplation.

In conclusion, the proof of the pudding is in the eating. For once in a way we found ourselves delighted both with the appearance and the performance of this yacht, and if designers have any doubt of the value of the type I can only advise them to consider the history of *Wapipi* and her sister *Whooper* in the sale ring. Each time these boats have come onto the market they have commanded freak prices. Buyers have queued up and it has been a matter of selling to the highest bidder rather than accepting best offers.

As a parting shot, attention may be called to the doghouse, a commonplace today but at that time very exceptional. This device, first turned to effective use in *Etain* and *Argo* in 1930, started the revolution in the accommodation of small yachts, now being continued with this elevated mast business.'

Today *Wapipi* can still be seen sailing in southern Ireland.

Wapipi's sister *Whooper* sailing in perfect conditions

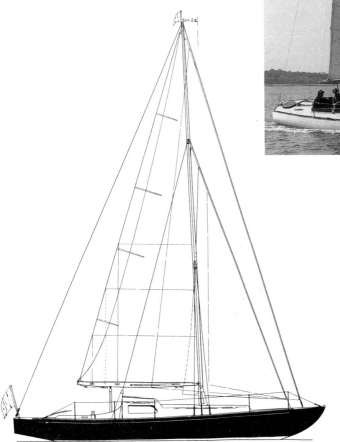

Dyarchy

Owner	Roger Pinkney
Builder	Sture Truedesson, Karlsknona, Sweden
Date Built	1938
Design No.	37
L.O.A.	45 ft. 10 in. (13.95 m)
L.W.L.	38 ft. 0 in. (11.59 m)
Beam	12 ft. 3 in. (3.74 m)
Draft	7 ft. 6 in. (2.29 m)
Displacement	24.2 tons (24.58 tonnes)
Sail Area	1,410 sq. ft. (131.13 m²)
Rig	Gaff Cutter

Dyarchy is an unforgettable name for a boat which has been envied and admired throughout the world. Although her cruising record was far from modest, she never boasted any outstanding feats or broke any records. Her reputation was gained purely as a beautifully conceived cruising boat both in function and appearance.

The new *Dyarchy* was to be a replacement for an old Bristol Channel pilot cutter of the same name. Because of the attachment of the owner, Roger Pinkney, to the original boat and his requirements for a similar type and style, the new *Dyarchy* was modelled on the old. Pilot cutters were developed to withstand heavy seas and winds and therefore were strong in both hull and rig. Roger specifically wanted a boat purely for cruising, and his instructions to Jack Giles were 'Design me a transom sterned gaff cutter 38ft. on the water line with, if you think this is enough, not more than 7ft 6in. draft, and above all let her be a cruiser that can sail and not a racer that can cruise.' Jack Giles knew that Roger was impressed with his lines for *Andrillot*, the forerunner of his famous Vertue class, and therefore *Dyarchy* emerged as a direct descendant, although much larger.

Dyarchy was built in Sweden at the yard of Sture Truedesson at Karlsknona in 1938 just prior to the beginning of the Second World War. She was built in the Scandinavian tradition using very heavy one-and-a-half-inch Swedish oak planking, close seamed with no caulking on alternative grown and steamed oak frames. She was launched successfully in Sweden, but, with the outbreak of war Roger was unable to sail her home to England and so she was kept in a berth ashore in Sweden until the end of hostilities in 1945. On re-launching *Dyarchy* it was appreciated that there would be inevitable leaks due to the original method of construction and the fact that she had been in dry dock for over five years. However, those responsible forgot to treat the seams with soft soap before putting her back into the water, and did not pump the yacht out, with the result that she sank. Fortunately this happened in shallow water and did little damage to the boat except for drowning the engine. The boat was made ready to sail in July 1945 and *Dyarchy* was taken home to England, but without an engine. That year Roger was commissioned to sail *Dyarchy* to the West Country and Guernsey and was accompanied on that trip by Eric and Susan Hiscock, the story of which is told in their book *Wandering Under Sail*. In 1947 she made a notable round trip of 1900 miles to the Baltic, and in 1950 took an adventurous trip to Spain which was reported in the November edition of *Yachting Monthly*.

Dyarchy was a beautiful, classically designed boat, with fair lines, a flush deck and deep bulwarks and her line was hardly encumbered by the small protrusion of her doghouse. She was specifically designed above decks for short-handed sailing and a large topsail was added, an obvious necessity in a gaff cutter. The size of the topsail posed a big problem for efficient short-handed sailing, so assisted by Bill Martineau, Roger Pinkney devised a very

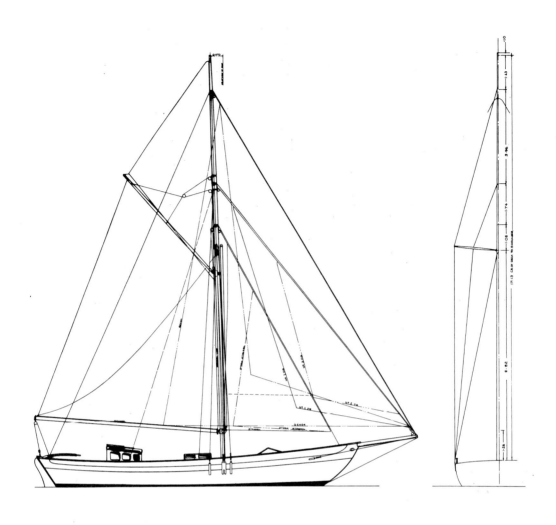

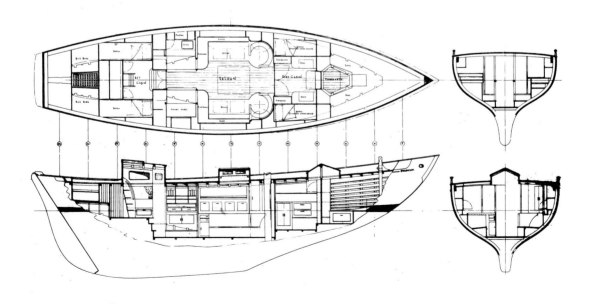

The classic *Dyarchy* with all sails flying

Dyarchy

effective and novel system for easily hoisting and lowering it. This utilised a luff rope groove in the aft face of the mast above the gaff. Permanently mounted inside the groove was a small bronze traveller, through which the wire topsail halyard ran freely. The halyard was attached to the sail by a screw-on fitting so that it was a continuation of the luff rope. The metal traveller remained at the bottom of the groove, thus keeping the halyard in the right place, until the head of the sail entered the bottom of the groove. The head of the sail then pushed the traveller up as it was hoisted; once the sail had entered the groove it could not jam or escape, and it was consequently under control when either setting or lowering the sail. Provided the wind was forward of the beam the sail would always enter the groove. Another special feature of *Dyarchy* was the position of the mast, which was far aft for a gaff rig boat but achieved a more manageable size of mainsail whilst increasing the size of the foresails.

Below decks *Dyarchy* was particularly interesting and was designed by the owner. His requirements were for a much more open-planned layout which could sleep four people comfortably, although a maximum of six could be accommodated if necessary. Of special interest was the saloon, 9ft. long with settee berths on both sides and with one built-in semi-circular armchair on either side. The table was an ingenious invention built by Harrison Butler, which folded and collapsed into a special compartment below the sole.

Roger Pinkney was very pleased with *Dyarchy*,

finding her dry and comfortable in a seaway. He commented that 'she was light to steer on all points although not very good at sailing herself close hauled'. He also noted that in confined waters or rough sea 'she was very certain and manoeuvrable.' The light weight and simplicity of her equipment made it very easy for one or two people to sail. There were originally no sheet winches fitted and runners and back stays were designed to be operated by the same levers. Originally she carried no radio, echo sounder nor ship-to-shore radio since the owner believed these to be redundant to the cruiser. The comfort, safety and ease of handling of *Dyarchy* can best be summed up by the fact that Roger often sailed her crewed only by his octogenarian mother, who made her last Channel crossing in *Dyarchy* at the age of 91. As part of the design fee for *Dyarchy* Roger Pinkney, who was an architect, designed Jack Giles a house which was to become his family home for the rest of his life.

Roger owned *Dyarchy* for 22 years before selling her to Bill Batten. Since 1961 Bill and his family have sailed her to Scotland, Ireland, Holland, Denmark, Norway, Sweden; her first ocean passage was to the West Indies, returning via the Balearic Islands. She was sold in 1982 to an Austrian, Peter Weisner, who now keeps her in Trieste in Italy where she is well cared for and is still sailing, the centre of attraction. Even today there are enthusiasts building sister ships and there are several replicas of *Dyarchy*, including *Acorn* which can be seen sailing on England's East Coast.

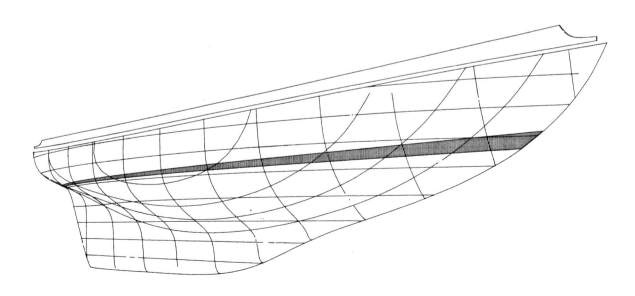

Bettine and the Brittany Class

Owner	Unknown
Builder	R.A. Newman and Sons of Poole
Date Built	1939
Design No.	48
L.O.A.	33 ft. 6 in. (10.22 m)
L.W.L.	25 ft. 3 in. (7.70 m)
Beam	8 ft. 3 in. (2.52 m)
Draft	5 ft. 3 in. (1.6 m)
Displacement	6.4 tons (6.50 tonnes)
Sail Area	502 sq. ft. (46.69 m²)
Rig	Bermudan Cutter

Bettine, the first of the Brittany Class, is usually thought of as a post-war Laurent Giles design but was in fact instigated in the 1930s. Although she was originally designed to meet the requirements of the owner, the design was to become very popular with a further 20 sister yachts being constructed. *Bettine* was built and launched just prior to the war in 1939. Her sister *Daula*, the second boat of the class, which was also being built at the same yard, was not finished before hostilities began and sustained war damage. Luckily the damage was not major and she was repaired and launched at the end of the war in 1946.

One of the marked characteristics of the Brittany Class was its large, useful doghouse which had big windows allowing plenty of light and standing headroom below. High teak coamings around the sheer had the effect of lowering the apparent height of the coachroof as well as keeping her deck drier. The first six boats had their masts keel-stepped, but on successive Brittanys, following the success of Laurent Giles' earlier design, *Wapipi*, the masts were stepped on the cabin top. This allowed for more space in the accommodation below decks and reduced the number of potential leaks. The deck fittings such as the runner levers, inner forestay release lever, halyard and sheet winches, the track and slides on the mast and boom were all specially designed by Laurent Giles.

Jack Giles commented that 'these yachts balance perfectly under almost any combination of sails, and are remarkably well mannered and responsive on all points of sailing.'

The design was of a fairly heavy displacement, but in their appearance and performance they proved to be notable boats both in cruising and racing. The fourth Brittany to be built, *Droleen II*, won the R.O.R.C. Channel Cup and also the Hamble to Poole race in her first year afloat in 1948. Of the Brittany Class still sailing, *Asali*, the ninth Brittany to be built, was recently bought by Dave Molesworth from a yard in Portsmouth. Although she was in poor condition he has now restored her to her former glory, and she can now be seen with her new owner sailing in the Western Approaches of the English Channel.

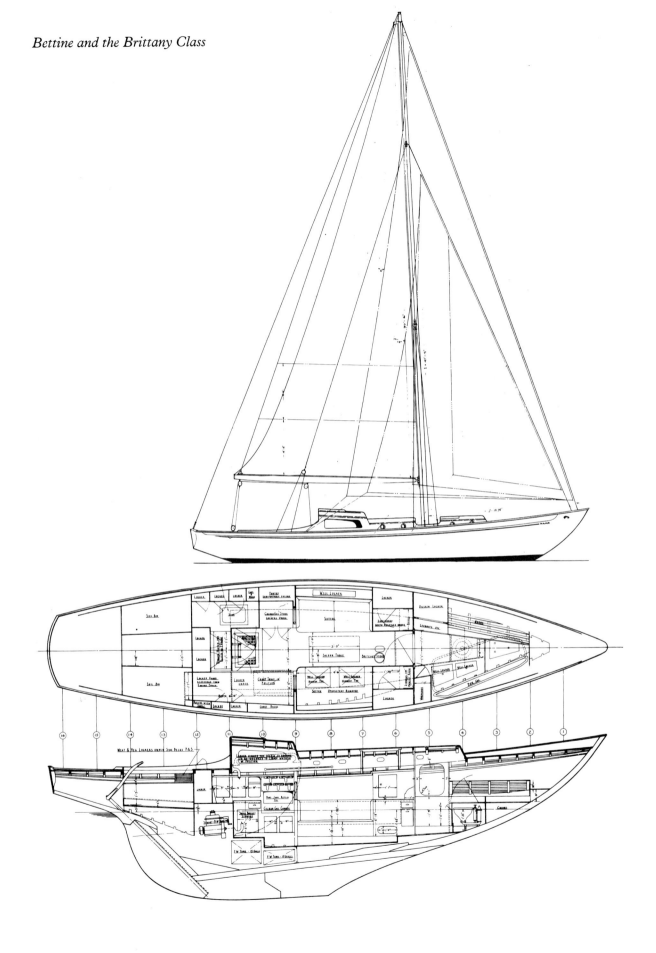

Daula, the second of the popular Brittany Class

Chapter 3
Post-War Designs (1946–1958)

Introduction

After the war the Laurent Giles partners returned to the company's office in Quay Hill to continue their design work. The war had caused many changes and there were new ideas, as well as new materials which had become available. Jack Giles was quick to use these and to adapt to the changing social structure of society which would see a wider range of people becoming interested in sailing. It was during this period that two of Jack's true quests were to be initiated: firstly the reduction in the displacement ratio of all forms of boat, and secondly, the perfection of the motor sailer. The nineteen designs chosen chart both of these endeavours, as well as illustrating how these different construction materials and techniques were used on the wide variety of craft that the company was designing.

It was also during this period that the company's reputation began to grow and the output of designs became truly prolific. Several of the yachts designed, *Trekka*, *Sopranino* and *Wanderer III* were to become household names for their trans-Atlantic crossings and circumnavigations of the world. Whilst on the British racing circuit *Myth of Malham* was to become one of the most successful and talked-about racing yachts. In the Mediterranean the far more graceful *Miranda IV* was to be as successful as *Myth* and was the forerunner of a whole series of fine Laurent Giles racing yachts.

A Peter Duck Class yacht showing the typical Laurent Giles knightshead, raised strake and caveta

Peter Duck and the Peter Duck Class

Owner	Arthur Ransome
Builder	Harry King and Son, Pin Mill, Suffolk
Date Built	1946
Design No.	54
L.O.A.	28 ft. 0 in. (8.54 m)
L.W.L.	25 ft. 0 in. (7.63 m)
Beam	9 ft. 0 in. (2.75 m)
Draft	3 ft. 6 in. (1.08 m)
Displacement	5.61 tons (5.7 tonnes)
Sail Area	293 sq. ft. (27.25 m²)
Rig	Bermudan Ketch

Peter Duck was designed for the well known author of *Swallows and Amazons*, who wanted Laurent Giles to design a boat with 'the maximum of liveability with the absolute minimum of work.' The yacht was to be based upon a style and character evident in previous Giles designs such as *Argo*, *Wanderer II* and *Kalliste* and the bow had similarities with his motor cruisers of the Samaki type. Since *Peter Duck* was to be used mainly for shoal water sailing the draft was kept to a minimum, and the beam was therefore increased to compensate for the loss of stability.

Prior to the war Arthur Ransome had owned several large yachts, but due to ill health his requirements changed and he wanted a smaller yacht in which he could sail the waters around Pin Mill in Suffolk. The result was *Peter Duck*, which was named after a character in one of his books and which he referred to as 'a marine bath-chair for my old age'. Unfortunately he was only able to sail her for a few seasons before leaving the East Coast and returning to the Lake District. *Peter Duck* was later to be sold to the well known artist George Jones who used her for 27 years as a mobile studio on the Suffolk rivers. So admired was this little yacht, Laurent Giles produced the Peter Duck Class, which comprised a slightly modified hull and superstructure. The overall length was increased by

three inches and the same amount was added to the draft. The coachroof was also lengthened so that it extended forward of the mast, these alterations being undertaken to further improve her sailing performance and accommodation. This class of yacht was incorporated into the company's stock plans in 1947 and proved popular with yachtsmen keen to sail in the creeks and estuaries of the English East Coast. True to her owner's original wishes for his *Peter Duck*, the Peter Duck Class was described by many yachtsmen as 'an easy to handle shoal water cruising yacht giving maximum liveability with the minimum of upkeep.' At sea they are quoted as being 'a duck by name and a duck by nature, dry, buoyant, with a very easy motion.' The firm turn to the bilge and good beam meant they sailed well with a small angle of heel with seldom any need to reef.

The boats were easy to handle with few crew and if necessary they could be managed by a single person. Their popularity lay in the fact that not only were they strongly built, safe and reliable in the open sea, they were also able to sail creeks because of their remarkably shallow draft. This provided other advantages including being able to reach anchorages and moorings denied to deeper keeled yachts. These factors, together with the comfortable full-sized headroom below decks, made the Peter Duck Class a most suitable choice for a young family. The boat was well mannered, it could sail as nearly upright as possible and had wide side-decks as well as ample room below. The accommodation was arranged so that there were two sleeping cabins, a separate W.C., chart table and a proper galley, the latter being a tall order in a 28 ft. yacht of the period.

The Peter Duck Class proved very popular indeed with over 45 boats being built, the majority by Porter and Haylett. Eighteen years after the first design a Mark II version of the Peter Duck Class was produced with a more modernised profile, and which offered the owner a choice of internal accommodation. In 1964, one of these new Peter Duck yachts would have cost only £4600.

The original *Peter Duck* is alive and well and living in Woodbridge, Suffolk, and can be seen sailing on the River Deben.

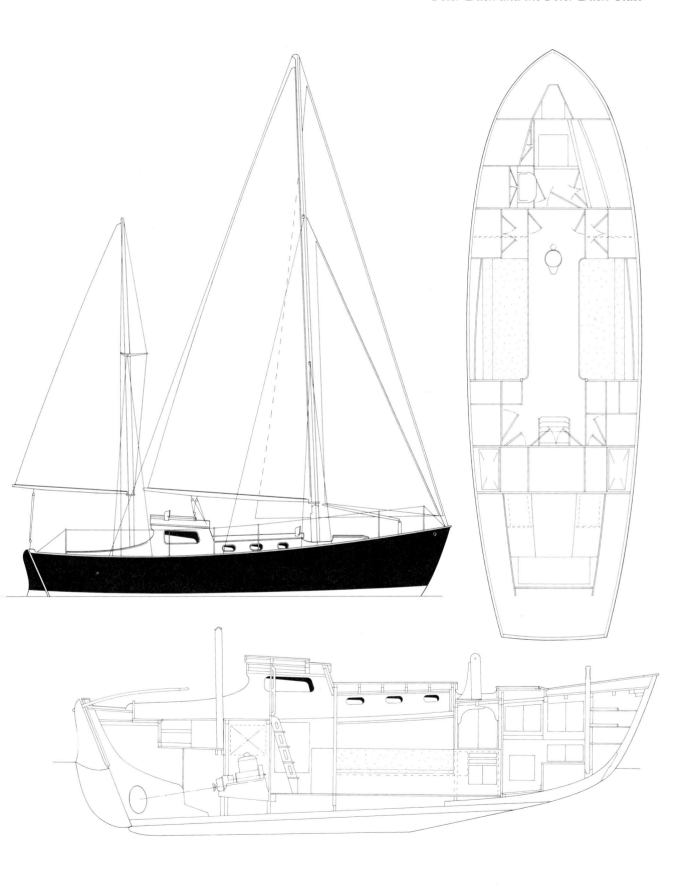

Woodpecker

Owner	A.A. Hall
Builder	R.A. Newman and Sons, Poole
Date Built	1948
Design No.	62
L.O.A.	70 ft. 0 in. (21.35 m)
L.W.L.	65 ft. 0 in. (19.82 m)
Beam	14 ft. 1 in. (4.3 m)
Draft	4 ft. 0 in. (1.22 m)
Displacement	24.75 tons (25.15 tonnes)
Engines	Twin Dorman 8-cyl. Diesels

Had Laurent Giles never designed an ocean racer he would still have become famous for his beautiful motor yacht designs. In 1948 he created the lovely *Woodpecker*, a 70-ft. light displacement motor yacht, which had a displacement length ratio of 90. She had a bold stem, with a good deal of flare in the bow sections and a wide sloping-transom stern. She had a fine, narrow, easily driven hull form with the longitudinal centre of buoyancy (L.C.B) well aft with straight buttock lines and straight run aft. 'Her hull is a delight to the eye, for her freeboard is not excessive and she has a lovely sheer,' was a quote from a report in *Yachting World* dated May 1948. *Woodpecker* bears little similarity to the Motor Fishing Vessels (M.F.V.) Giles had designed during the war, yet she retained the elegant workmanlike simplicity that her naval sisters had.

An interesting feature above deck was the small deckhouse immediately forward of the wheelhouse, where passengers could sit in comfort with a good, unobstructed forward view. Below decks the accommodation was simple and consisted of a forward double cabin with WC compartment and dressing room, which all opened into a vestibule giving access to the main saloon. The deckhouse could be reached via a corridor past the galley. Aft of the engine room was the owner's bathroom and stateroom, and a most interesting feature was the placement of the crew's quarters in an unusual position being at the aft end of the boat. This area, over the propellers, is more often than not a noisy part of the boat where so often the stateroom is placed. Another benefit of having the crew's cabin aft, was

to produce an uncluttered foredeck without a crew's access hatch. The position of these foredeck hatches could be a nuisance and were often unusable in bad weather.

Woodpecker was fitted with two 8-cylinder high-speed Dorman Diesel engines, which could produce 100 b.h.p. each at 2,300 r.p.m. These were some of the most powerful engines of the day and were installed, along with a generating set and work bench, beneath the wheelhouse. *Woodpecker* is a seaworthy motor yacht with light displacement and is an example of a design well ahead of her time. At just under 25 tons she weighs 35% less than contemporary fishing boat styled yachts with 40 or 50 tons displacement.

Several sister ships have been built and the original *Woodpecker* was recently for sale in the Isle of Wight. She is undergoing a major refit and we look forward to seeing this beautiful motor yacht again in the near future.

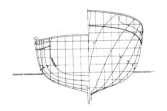

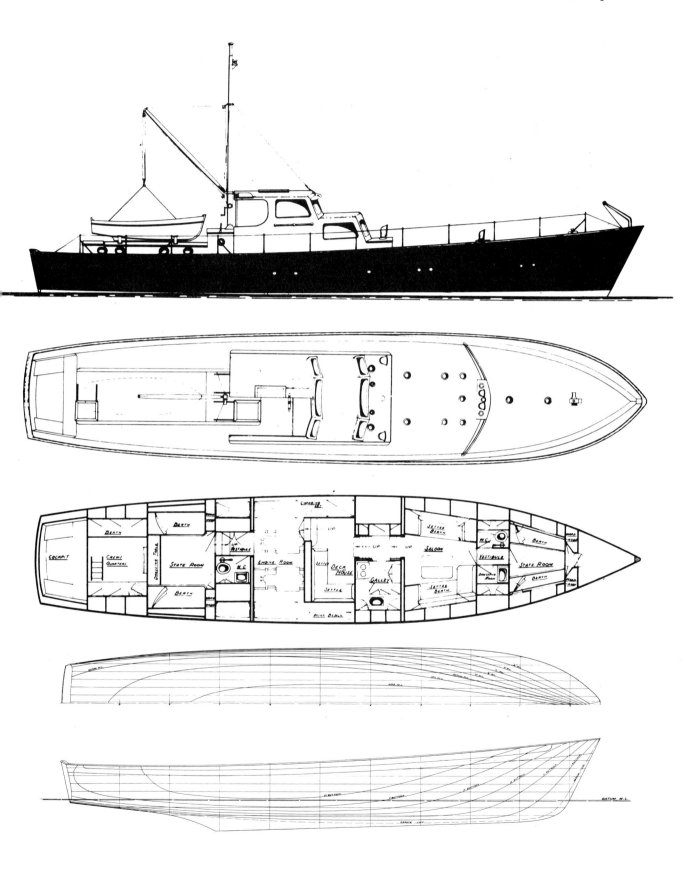

The impressive *Woodpecker* cleaving gracefully through the water

Myth of Malham

Owner	Capt. John H. Illingworth, R.N.
Builder	Hugh McLean & Sons, Gourock
Date Built	1947
Designer No.	64
L.O.A.	37 ft. 6 in. (11.44 m)
L.W.L.	33 ft. 6 in. (10.22 m)
Beam	9 ft. 3 in. (2.82 m)
Draft	7 ft. 3 in. (2.21 m)
Displacement	7.6 tons (7.72 tonnes)
Sail Area	626 sq. ft. (58.22 m²)
R.O.R.C Rating	27.5 ft.
Rig	Bermudan Cutter

Myth of Malham was designed with the intention that she should be the fastest possible sailing yacht under all conditions and within the limits of the Royal Ocean Racing Club (R.O.R.C.) rule. She was specifically built for John Illingworth who had previously owned *Maid of Malham*, a 1936 pre-war Laurent Giles design.

She was constructed in an unconventional, although not unusual way which incorporated the use of steam bent timbers with fore and aft stringers, running inboard of these frames. In high load areas a second steam bent timber was laid over the stringers, forming a very light and strong girder. This was then sheathed with a 3/8th inch diagonal inner skin with a 1/2 inch fore and aft outer skin. She was of light displacement and had only 4 ft. of overhangs. Her bow had a separate stem section which was fastened to the fore transom. It was not in any way readily detachable, although the original idea at the design stage was to build on a different bow if required.

She was fitted with twin companionway hatches which were new in conception at the time and proved to be most practicable. The design was originally developed from *Maid of Malham* and her cockpit arrangement was not unlike her earlier sister, except that it was deeper. The original design was for the helmsman to have a small cockpit to himself right aft with the wheel arranged in a similar position to that in a car though this was never fitted.

Innovations in her deck gear included a main sheet track on the bridge deck as opposed to the old style 'horse'. This allowed the mainsail to be sheeted into any position and to control the flow of the sail. Likewise, jib sheet tracks were fitted along both sides of the boat, from the mast to the transom, to cope with her large wardrobe of sails. With this arrangement, the sheet leads slide and were locked in their desired position by spring plungers. These tracks were constructed out of an early form of aluminium alloy which was a high technology material of the day. All of the deck gear was specially designed for her by Laurent Giles with much care taken in saving weight. Many of the ideas we now take for granted were first tried out on *Myth* and were the forerunners of most of today's deck hardware.

The sailplan shows a mainsail of 3:1 aspect ratio which comprised a little less than half the total rated sail area. This placed the mast almost halfway along her waterline. There was a wide variety of headsail combinations which could be set to suit every possible condition. The twin backstays set up to the quarters were an unusual feature in a Bermudan rigged yacht in her day. Giles also designed and fitted an extra large sheet winch for handling the wire sheets on her powerful Genoa and Yankee.

The accommodation was arranged to sleep six people and was simple and workmanlike. It was practically open from bow to stern without doors or other unnecessary weighty items. In her first season of racing she won the first four ocean races she

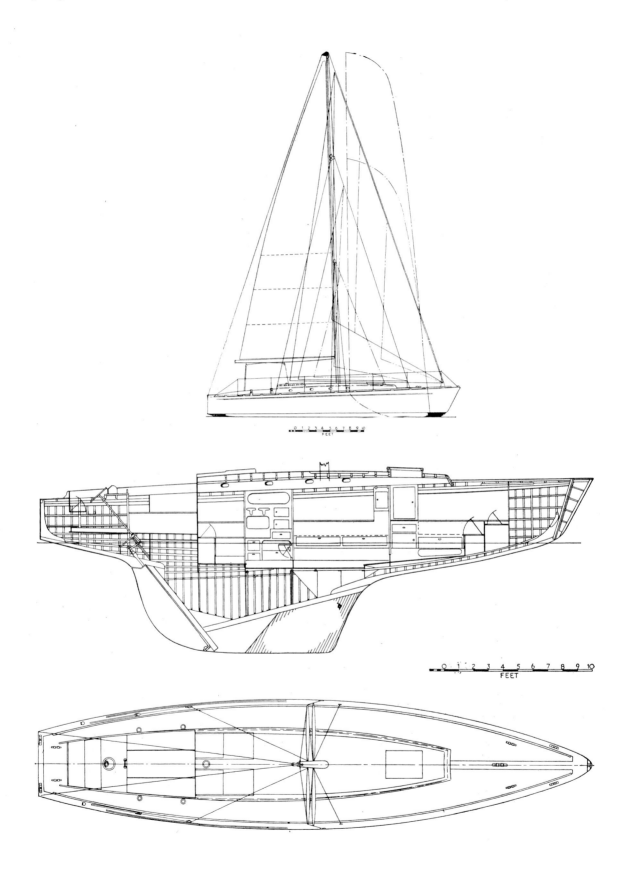

The highly sucessful racer *Myth of Malham* commissioned by Captain John Illingworth

entered, which were the Clyde to Portsmouth, the Channel, the Fastnet and the La Rochelle races.

Laurent Giles broke with the traditions of the day and Jack was aware from the start that she would be a revolutionary yacht. *Myth of Malham* was radical for that time, and although she was not considered by many to be an attractive yacht, she was extremely successful in her intended purpose. Her excellence can be summed up by a statement from *Yachting World* in 1948, 'For her displacement we do not suppose that any boat has previously combined, to the same extent, speed with good accommodation and seaworthiness as *Myth of Malham*.'

Myth of Malham was the forerunner of light displacement ocean-going yachts and was one of the first boats where one could see the evolution of the fin keel with its aerodynamic shaping. Perhaps the most important contribution to the art of design lay in her demonstration of the effectiveness of short ends and light weight. Although described here as a light displacement yacht, it must be appreciated that this is a term used relative to the displacement of current boats in the 1940s and her displacement length ratio of 202 would not be considered quite so light today. Modern light displacement boats have ratios of around 100. However, it is interesting to note that the ratio of today's modern Admiral's Cup yachts are of about 200 to 220. Numerous yachts have followed *Myth*'s example since 1947 and today we see the evolution of the ultimate ultra-light displacement boat (U.L.D.B.).

John Illingworth had many successful races in *Myth of Malham*, which included her winning her first three races, the Fastnet race twice in 1947 and 1949, as well as the Australian Sydney to Hobart race in 1955, which he was responsible for initiating. In 1956 he started his own design company with Angus Primrose although he continued a close association with Laurent Giles. *Myth of Malham* completed three transatlantic voyages including two OSTARs but was unfortunately lost at sea off the Brittany coast in 1972.

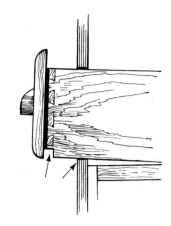

Typical Laurent Giles draw detail

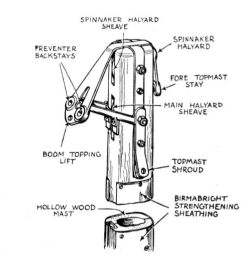

Light-weight mast-head fittings

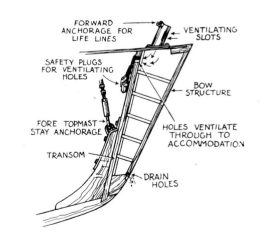

Myth's detachable bow structure

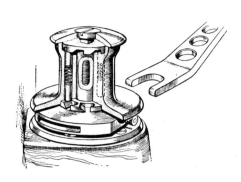

Laurent Giles designed bottom action winch

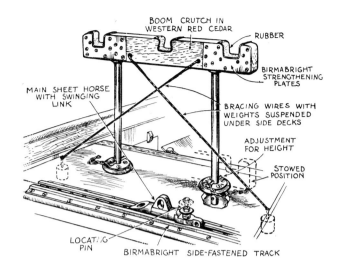

Myth's controllable mainsheet track with a retractable boom crutch

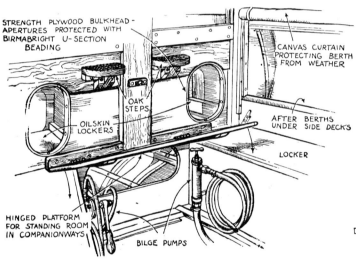

Details of *Myth*'s saloon at the companion way entrance

Myth's double sliding companion way hatches

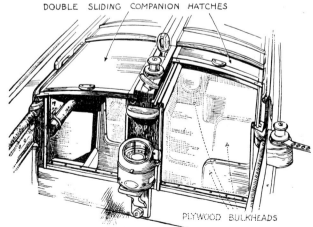

R.N.S.A. 24 Class

Owner	Various
Builder	Various
Date Designed	1947
Design No.	81
L.O.A.	31 ft. 0 in. (9.46 m)
L.W.L.	24 ft. 0 in. (7.32 m)
Beam	7 ft. 6 in. (2.29 m)
Draft	5 ft. 10 in. (1.75 ml)
R.O.R.C. Rating	22 ft. 6 in.
R.O.R.C. Sail	465 sq. ft. (43.25 m²)
Displacement	4.3 tons (4.37 tonnes)
Rig	Bermudan Sloop

In 1947 the Royal Naval Sailing Association considered the idea of a one-design fast cruiser suitable for ocean racing and for short distance and handicap events. These boats were to form a local class at the main centres of the Association and to race offshore in Class III events. The R.N.S.A. approached Laurent Giles for this design and the result was a stable 24 ft. on the waterline, fast cruiser to the R.O.R.C. specifications. The yachts were designed to carry a large sail area and they had a fractional rig which was ideal for simplified sail handling. The masts were constructed from aluminium and the R.N.S.A.s were the first boats ever to have metal rather than wooden masts, another Giles first, which considerably reduced the weight of the rig and improved stability. The hull form was also unusual for the day, with short ends, light displacement and a short straight keel following the general ideas of *Myth of Malham*. Costs were to be kept to a minimum and so a transom stern was used together with a lightweight but strong construction method. This consisted of longitudinal stringers supported by the transverse bulkheads in the interior accommodation of the boat. The bulkheads were also employed as moulds for building the hull, and since they were cut as templates this also ensured that variation in the shape of the hull was kept to a minimum. The final design of the R.N.S.A. 24 became a restricted class and their keels, bulkheads and other moulds were batch produced for cheapness.

There was a great deal of space in the interior which was designed to sleep a maximum of four people. A large cockpit was incorporated to allow extra room when racing, and the shallow coachroof allowed for plenty of deck space. Within the limits of the class rules, the internal fitout, the rig and deck plan could be customised by each owner.

Boats of this class were not only built for racing in the U.K. but also built abroad in Hong Kong and Australia. Fifteen of these Class III yachts were built and did remarkably well in offshore races, including courses for which they were considered, at that time, to be far too small. Three of the R.N.S.A.s, *Blue Disa*, *Samuel Pepys* and *Minx of Malham* took part in the 1949 Fastnet and Wolfrock Races and did very well against some of the larger boats. During the Fastnet Race gales were blowing for much of the course, and while the larger boats had heaved to, these three continued under double reefed mainsails completing the course with high placings. A further indication of the abilities of these little yachts was shown in 1952 when *Samuel Pepys*, the fifth R.N.S.A. to be built, won the prestigious Trans-Atlantic race.

The RNSA 24, *Minx of Malham*, during the 1949 Cowes to Dinard Race

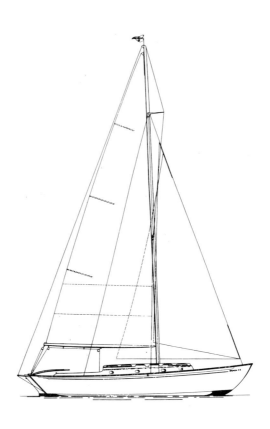

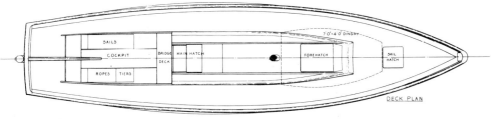

DECK PLAN

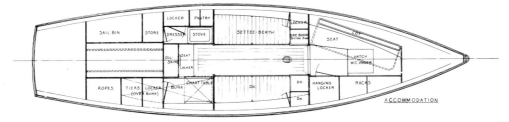

ACCOMMODATION

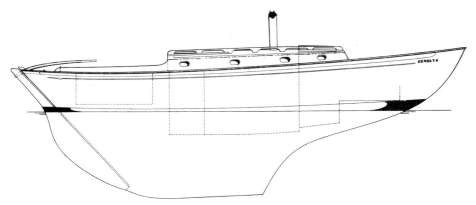

Gulvain

Owner	Jack Rawlings
Builder	Sussex Shipbuilding Co., Shoreham
Date Built	1949
Design No.	104
L.O.A.	55 ft. 0 in. (16.76 m)
L.W.L.	43 ft. 0 in. (13.12 m)
Beam	11 ft. 7 in. (3.5 m)
Draft	8 ft. 9 in. (2.67 m)
Displacement	16.5 tons (16.76 tonnes)
Sail Area	1160 sq. ft. (107.89 m²)
R.O.R.C. Rating	44 ft. 5 in.
Rig	Bermudan Cutter

Gulvain was the first ocean racing yacht to be built totally of the aluminium alloy Birmabright, and was the result of a fruitful collaboration of the owner, designers and builders. She showed in every detail that no expense was spared in producing this first-class ocean racer. The choice of aluminium was aimed at strength rather than weight reduction, although this allowed the designers to limit the displacement to a maximum of 16.5 tons. The ballast/displacement weight ratio was therefore high, roughly 45%, through having 8 tons of iron in the ballast keel. Her hull form was a direct descendant of the *Myth of Malham* but with a fully developed reverse sheer, which allowed for greater mid-ships freeboard and more room below decks. The overhangs were moderate and she had a better proportioned bow.

Among the numerous innovations on this yacht was the mast, which like the hull and deck was made of lightweight aluminium alloy. This made *Gulvain*, like the R.N.S.A.s, one of the first yachts to carry a metal mast and this particular design was registered by the company that built her. It is interesting to note that rod rigging and internally run halyards, possibly another Laurent Giles design first, were used to reduce windage. Yet another unusual feature was that the halyard sheaves were made of Tufnol. Other deck fittings such as the rigging screws, forestay slip hook, mast fittings and some of the winches were also designed by Laurent Giles and made of stainless steel. The forestay was detachable and led through a pipe in the foredeck to the fo'c'sle where it was set up with a specially designed lever.

A notable feature of *Gulvain* was her superstructure amidships which provided a navigation doghouse, with a big chart table forward where the navigator could work without interruption and where he had a clear view in every direction. The forward end of the casing provided what was really a large watertight ventilator, which at the same time allowed plenty of light through the big skylight. The casing also provided useful stowage space for warps and halyards and the whole arrangement was considered ingenious and very practical. Steering was by a wheel in a small steering cockpit aft. This was semi-circular in section allowing the helmsman to sit or stand with comparative ease when the yacht was at any normal angle of heel. Forward of this was the main cockpit, from which all the sheets and sheet winches were worked, and from the cockpit a hatch led from the doghouse down a semi-spiral enclosed stairway into the saloon.

The accommodation below decks was very roomy and was far greater than on any other contemporary yacht of comparable size. There was a great deal of height below decks which partly explained the reason for the unconventional profile of her reverse sheer. *Gulvain* not only provided the owner with a good ocean racer, but also provided a cruising boat on which it was possible to live for long periods and in considerable comfort.

Gulvain was one of the most advanced experiments in design of hull shape, structure and deck gear for her day. She was built in an incredibly short time, five months, and was launched on June 27th, 1949 just in time for the Dinard Race. She won this, her maiden race, easily and went on to win many other races, proving herself to be one of the fastest ocean racers of that era. *Gulvain* is currently in America competing and winning club races.

DECKHOUSE

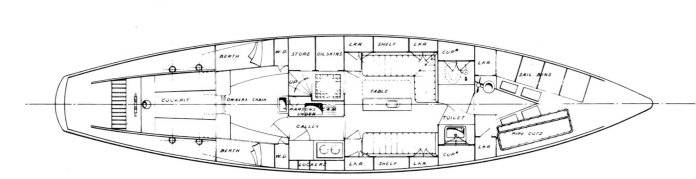

Gulvain, the first Aluminium ocean racing yacht

Sopranino and the Barchetta Class

Owner	Patrick Ellam
Builder	Messrs. Wottens, Cookham Dene.
Date Built	1950
Design No.	130
L.O.A.	19 ft. 8 in. (6.03 m)
L.W.L.	17 ft. 6 in. (5.34 m)
Beam	5 ft. 3 in. (1.60 m)
Draft	3 ft. 8 in. (1.14 m)
Displacement	0.35 tons (0.356 tonnes)
Sail Area	208 sq. ft. (19.34 m²)
Rig	Bermudan Cutter

Sopranino was designed for Patrick Ellam who wanted a very small, fast yacht for racing and cruising. Her size was specifically chosen so that two men, with provisions, could undertake a hundred mile or more leg of a race or cruise in relative comfort, but was still to be of a size that could be trailed behind a car. This latter requirement in the 1950s, placed considerable restrictions on the size and weight of the yacht. She was designed to plane and so her displacement was kept as light as possible, and by counting the crew as ballast a high ballast ratio of 50% was achieved. This meant that she had to be sat out in a breeze and *Sopranino*, in fact, carried a single trapeze, a very unusual feature on a boat of this size, which was rigged from the lower spreaders so that it could be used on either side of the boat. Her beam appeared to be narrow for a boat intended to plane, but this was necessary to maintain momentum in the typical choppy sea of the English Channel. Many of her design features were unique and some ideas were borrowed from model yacht design; for example, the fin and bulb keel, now a commonplace solution for the small trailer/sailer, and the separate rudder being hung on a skeg. She also carried a model yacht type Braine steering gear so that she could sail for short periods without anyone at the helm when off the wind. Within her small hull two full-sized bunks, a proper chart table, galley, toilet and equipment had to be fitted. An interesting feature of her design was that the aftpeak served as a buoyancy compartment which could be used to store fenders, while the forepeak was purely

a buoyancy chamber. The interior was divided into a wet and a dry compartment separated by a waterproof curtain, the dry compartment containing the two bunks and lockers to store clothes. *Sopranino* was designed and built for low budget sailing, and consequently a clinker construction was chosen as a strong and cheap method which could be easily repaired by the average boat builder.

One week after *Sopranino*'s launch she sailed in the R.O.R.C. Santander race in which much bigger yachts sail from Plymouth across the Channel, around Ushant and across the Bay of Biscay to Spain. *Sopranino* was too small to officially enter the race but accompanied Captain John Illingworth, who was sailing in *Myth of Malham*. Prior to the race Jack Giles went sailing in *Sopranino*, as he did many of his yachts, in particular to see how the theory of such a small and unusual design had turned into reality.

Sopranino has, during her lifetime, undertaken a number of adventurous journeys which include a cruise from Falmouth to New York via Coruna in Spain, stopping at Lisbon, Morocco, Casablanca, Las Palmas in the Canary Islands, Barbados, several other Caribbean Islands, and finally New York. This was a remarkable achievement when you consider that she was under 20 feet in length. Colin Mudie sailed with Patrick Ellam on this trip, and a quote from a letter written from Colin to Jack whilst in Las Palmas in January 1952 says, 'The little boat is magnificent in a sea and cannot do anything wrong. She is vastly overloaded and we carry stores

Patrick Ellam's *Sopranino* clearly showing her diminutive size prior to her trans-Atlantic crossing

to excess ... we bobble along happily with seventy or a hundred miles tucked away on good days. Once as Patrick was coming on watch we surfed furiously for twelve seconds. Shortly after that we lowered the main and did a fine hundred miles under Genoa staysail alone.' On many of their legs they covered over 100 miles a day. Colin Mudie's book *Sopranino* provides a diary and fascinating insight into living and sailing on such a small yacht and is very amusing to read.

Sopranino was built as a midget off-shore racer, named after a small wind instrument. She was to become the forerunner of a successful class of yachts called Barchetta which were eligible to race in the Junior Offshore Group (J.O.G.). The Barchetta Class, although similar to *Sopranino*, had a modified hull which was beamier, and the design

proved to be very popular with over 40 of them having been built over the years. Jack himself had an open version of this class called *Minion*, the only boat he ever owned.

In 1988, whilst visiting the Newport Museum of Yachting in Massachusetts, USA, the authors were suprised to find *Theta*, the 15 sq. metre centre-board sharpie, which had inspired Patrick Ellam to conceive his ideas for *Sopranino*. They were further delighted to find that the Museum had rescued *Sopranino* from a lingering death on Long Island, New York, and now have her stored in an old ammunition bunker at Fort Adams, Newport, Massachusetts. She was found to be in remarkably good condition, though not seaworthy, and the Museum is trying to decide whether to restore her or to display her in her present condition.

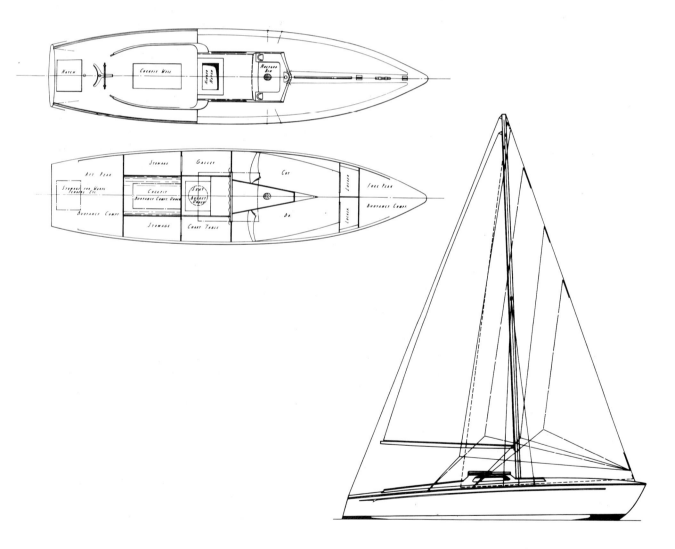

Miranda IV

Owner	Carlo Ciampi
Builder	Cantieri Baglietto
Date Built	1951
Design No.	146
L.O.A.	52 ft. 6 in. (16 m)
L.W.L.	39 ft. 0 in. (11.9 m)
Beam	11 ft. 4 in. (3.45 m)
Draft	7 ft. 6 in. (2.29 m)
Displacement	13 tons (13.21 tonnes)
Sail Area	1060 sq. ft. (98.58 m²)
Rig	Bermudan Sloop

Miranda IV with her complete sweep of victories in Mediterranean offshore racing started something of a fashion in yacht design for that part of the world. Many requests were made of Laurent Giles to develop and advance this design, and such famous yachts as *Cypsella* and *Nina* were evolved. The demand at the time was 'to beat *Miranda IV*.'

The following description of *Miranda IV* and design review is taken from an original company article written shortly after her successful first season in 1951.

'*Miranda IV* was built in Italy as the Italian entry for the Bermuda Race. She took to the water without a hitch, handled like a top and, designed without thought of racing or racing rules, outsailed all opposition in the Mediterranean passage races organised by the U.S.V.I. First to finish and first in her class in the race from St Tropez to Barcelona; first to finish Barcelona to Palma di Majorca; and first to finish, first in her class and in all classes in the race from Majorca to Ibiza, *Miranda IV* attracted more attention than any yacht of British design for many years. Imitation is the sincerest form of flattery, and soon there were six yachts of similar type under construction in Italy, Spain and Switzerland.

The occasions are rare when the designer finds himself with a free hand and after years of austerity we found the design of *Miranda IV* to be a holiday. The only requirements given

were for a yacht to sail out of Genoa, to be approximately 12 metres on the water line and to be sweet on the eye and fun to sail. There were no rule requirements, no power requirements and no accommodation problems, no whims and no prejudices. *Miranda IV* was a designer's benefit. At first sight our choice of light displacement – indeed very light displacement – may seem wayward, for light winds prevail on the Riviera coast and in light winds light displacement is not seen to advantage. It is only with a good deal of weight in the wind that the higher potential speed of the light displacement hull becomes effective, and in light airs the small sail area and proportionately large wetted surface can result in a sluggish boat. The fact of the matter is that given proportionate sail area and ballast, two 35-footers will sail side by side, mile after mile, heavy, light or moderate displacement, in other than extreme conditions one way or another.

But that is by no manner of means all the story. If we have learned anything in recent years, it is that the value of sail area is just what you make of it. If you want light weather performance you must have sail, but you must not go on piling up sail, even on moderate displacement, or you will end up with lanky rigs. It seemed reasonable to give *Miranda IV* substantially greater beam than the *Myth of Malham*/*Fandango* family. With no end penalties to consider and plenty of length and beam, *Miranda IV* at a light displacement would have a platform on which any amount of sail could be set in a taut and simple inboard rig. The rig was, in fact, reduced at a later stage to keep rating within bounds, but fortunately by then construction was too far advanced for racing and rating considerations to have any other effect on the design.

Below water *Miranda IV* offered a full-scale opportunity to try out a fin and skeg rudder. At the close of the 19th century, lack of balance gave the fin keel boats a bad reputation. Not all were ill balanced but a great number were, and without exception designers were content to revert to a conservative profile if only as a sort of insurance policy. In the intervening years a vast amount of experience had been gained by the model sailers with whom both the well known Major Heckstall-Smith and Admiral Turner have co-operated. But though the fin keel boat has been tamed, the solution of one problem has the habit of creating another, and it has become evident that a short fin in the middle of the boat is not a happy position to hang the rudder. The obvious development was to follow the lead of model designers, but conservatism had so far held back this development in full scale yachts, and apart from Uffa Fox, designers have had little

opportunity to develop in this direction. The success of a yacht of *Miranda IV*'s size was therefore of some importance.

Below decks there is little on which to comment, for construction follows the lines made familiar by *Myth of Malham*. The deck saloon is an interesting feature; it is now twenty years since the designers introduced the now universal after doghouse and this development is becoming an increasingly common feature of their designs. The arrangement plan is curious in these days as the saloon is furnished only for day sailing, but the provision of ships' side berths presents no difficulties and would complete an excellent plan for racing or normal cruising.'

Miranda IV ghosting along in the Mediterranean

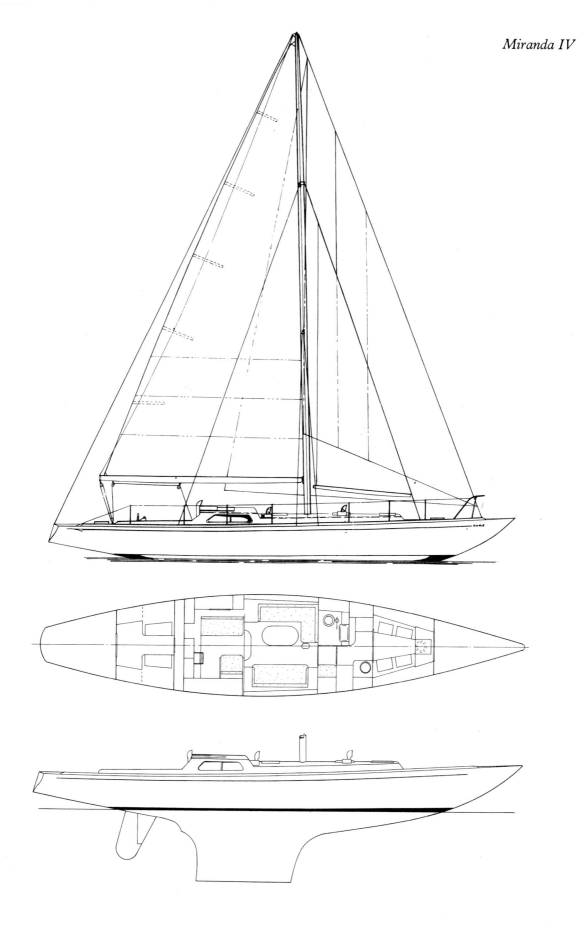

Lutine

Owner	Lloyds Yacht Club
Builder	Camper and Nicholson Ltd., Gosport
Date Built	1953
Design No.	163
L.O.A.	58 ft. 6 in. (17.84 m)
L.W.L.	41 ft. 6 in. (12.66 m)
Beam	13 ft. 2 in. (4.01 m)
Draft	8 ft. 6 in. (2.59 m)
Displacement	26.5 tons (26.92 tonnes)
Sail Area	(R.O.R.C.) 1400 sq. ft. (130.2 m^2)
Sail Area	(C.C.A.) 1730 sq. ft. (160.89 m^2)
Rig	Yawl

The prime consideration for designing this yacht was to produce a vessel strictly within the type envisaged in the general concept of the Cruising Club of America. Jack Giles studied the workings and implications of the C.C.A. rule at very great length and considered the dimensions affecting the rating such as beam, displacement and sail area. These were to be very carefully combined to produce the optimum balance between speed and rating. The result was a fine vessel with nice overhangs, wide clear decks and plenty of beam. A yawl rig was chosen because the Bermuda Race for which she was built entailed a good deal of reaching, and a yawl has the ability to set more canvas off the wind but still retain power in the main mast rig for efficient work to windward.

Although *Lutine* was built to the American rule she still has the Giles characteristics such as the bow overhang, a feature first development in *Maid of Malham*, and the doghouse labelled her unmistakably as a Giles design. Her accommodation was arranged first and foremost as a club ship intended primarily for ocean racing. With this in mind the whole of the middle portion of the hull was open plan, with sleeping accommodation for six in quarter berths and behind the settees. There was a two-berth stateroom at the bow intended for use as a comfortable cabin when the boat was out on charter. Most importantly for racing, the chart table was placed at the after end near the cockpit.

Lutine's original engine, a Parson Ford, was of comparatively low power by her American standards and was installed on the centre line beneath the galley and drove a Newall Petticrow folding propeller. An important feature of *Lutine* was her deck winches, which did not require the coffee grinder system usually considered essential on board the larger American yachts for handling the big headsails permitted by the C.C.A.

Lutine barely had time to undergo trials after launching before being shipped to the USA. Once in America she had little time for 'working up' before the Bermuda Race and it was not surprising that in this race she did not perform to the best of her abilities. *Lutine*'s racing days are now over and today she is being used as a charter boat.

Lutine going to windward

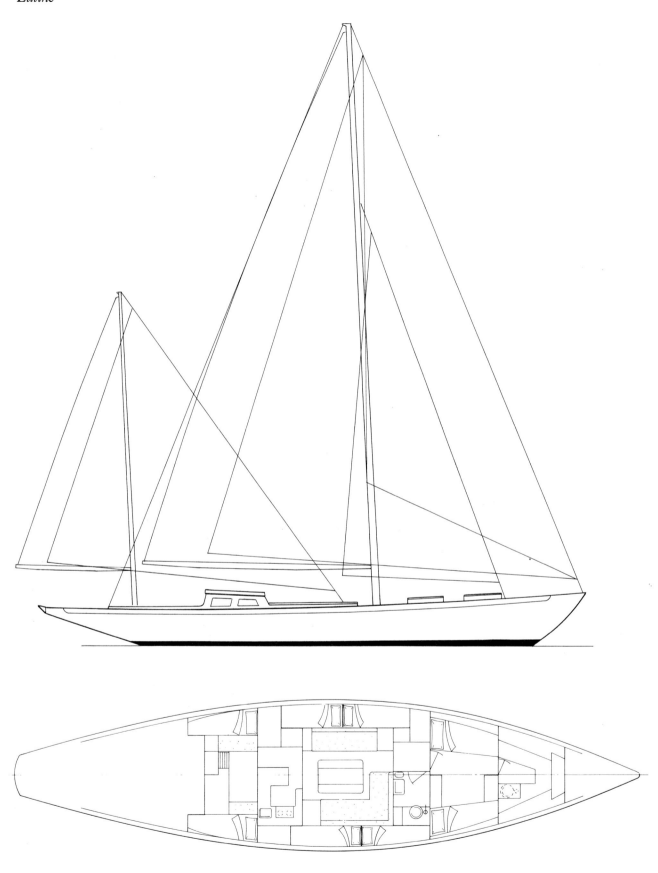

Wanderer III

Owner	Eric Hiscock
Builder	William King, Burnham on Crouch
Date Built	1951
Design No.	164
L.O.A.	30 ft. 3 in. (9.23 m)
L.W.L.	26 ft. 5 in. (8.06 m)
Beam	8 ft. 5 in. (2.58 m)
Draft	5 ft. 0 in. (1.53 m)
Displacement	8 Thames Tons
Sail Area	423 sq. ft. (39.34m²)
Rig	Bermudan Cutter

After many happy years with his pre-war yacht *Wanderer II*, Eric Hiscock naturally turned to Laurent Giles for his new larger yacht *Wanderer III*. Having undertaken a number of long voyages with his wife in *Wanderer II*, notably to the Channel Islands, Spain and the Azores, he found the boat too small to undertake more extensive cruising and to live onboard for long periods. He found that she was incapable of carrying the sheer weight of stores and equipment needed on their long voyages and so decided that they required a larger vessel.

One of his main design specifications to Laurent Giles was that *Wanderer III* must have as much volume as possible for a given cost. This therefore dictated a moderate forward overhang with a transom stern, and had the advantage of being able to fit a trim tab vane steering gear which would be necessary for short-handed ocean passages. Laurent Giles based the lines of the hull on an existing yacht *Kalliste* a 7-tonner built in 1938. The gaff rig of Hiscock's previous yacht was exchanged for a Bermudan sloop rig, as this could be handled more easily with only two people. A great deal of thought was put into its design, especially the running rigging, since she would be used for more extensive sailing.

Wanderer III was built under the standard construction practices of the time, with iroko planks on steam bent oak timbers and a lead ballast keel; and she was afforded the luxury of a copper sheathed hull. The accommodation was unusual and designed to Eric Hiscock's own unique requirements, since she would be used for living and working on board whilst cruising around the world. He was a professional photographer, so the forepeak had to double as a dark room for processing photographs and a light-tight door was installed. Another interesting feature was that the main purpose of the auxiliary engine was to generate electricity for the dark room and navigation lamps, rather than for propulsion. Additional stowage had to be provided for some 450 Admiralty charts and 200 books along with the owner's photographic and journalistic equipment. As there were only two people onboard, the cockpit was kept small. This had the advantage of reducing the danger of being swamped in heavy seas and no doghouse was fitted, providing space for a dinghy to be carried on the coachroof.

Wanderer III was owned by the Hiscocks for 17 years, during which they circumnavigated the world twice and covered over 110,000 miles. On most of her long passages she averaged 100 miles a day, and on one occasion in the Indian Ocean she logged a day's run of 169 nautical miles. Eric Hiscock said of her, 'she proved to be an able, good mannered, seaworthy little ship.' Eric Hiscock replaced *Wanderer III* with *Wanderer IV* in the late 1960s and her next owner Giselher Ahlers continued to sail her extensively.

Eric Hiscock went on to have two further yachts designed, *Wanderer IV* and *Wanderer V*, in which he sailed frequently in the waters of his home in New Zealand. Both he and his wife Susan, who were both notable ocean farers, wrote innumerable accounts of their voyages and were sailing well into their seventies. Sadly Eric died in 1986.

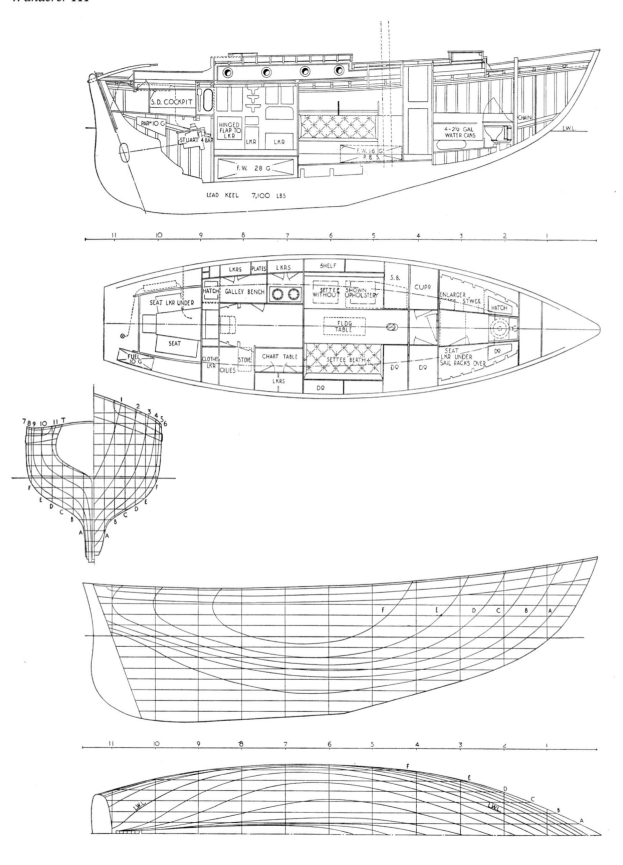

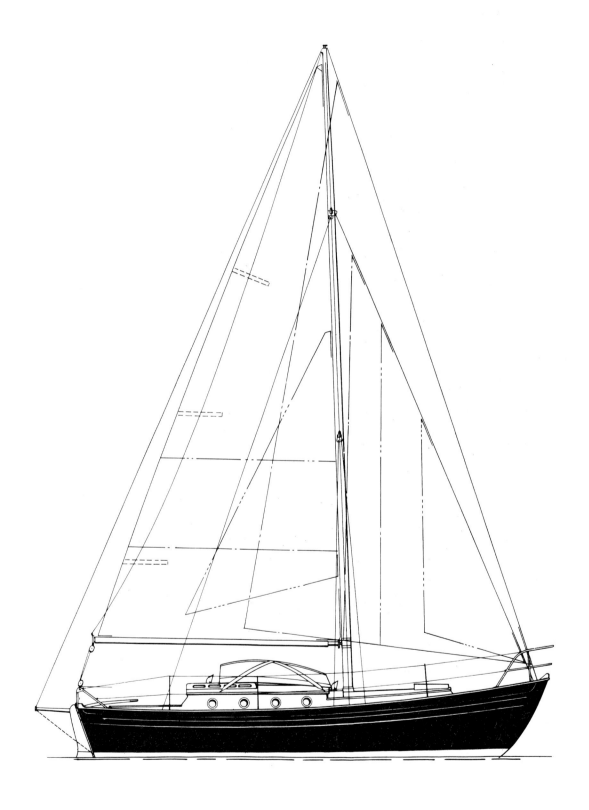

Rose of York and the New Channel Class

Owner	Colonel Norman S. Birch
Builder	John Tyrrell and Sons Ltd, Arklow.
Date Built	1951
Design No.	183
L.O.A.	38 ft. 4 in. (11.68 m)
L.W.L.	27 ft. 0 in. (8.24 m)
Beam	9 ft. 1 in. (2.76 m)
Draft	6 ft. 0 in. (1.83 m)
Displacement	12.9 tons (13.11 tonnes)
Sail Area	627 sq. ft. (58.31 m²)
Rig	Bermudan Cutter

During the 1940s there had been a decline in interest in the Channel Class yachts but interest continued in the more popular pre-war Brittany Class. Jack Giles had always retained his respect for the Channel yachts, in particular their really excellent performance as well as their ample deck space which allowed plenty of room necessary for their cutter rig. They were also beautifully balanced, and so with these beneficial characteristics in mind he decided to update and modify the Channel design. One of the main problems of the original design had been their high handicap in the R.O.R.C. rule which favoured small overhangs and low freeboard. When the Channel Class had first been produced the company had gambled that sooner or later the R.O.R.C. rule would change, allowing these lovely boats to come into their own. This, however, never happened, and it was therefore decided to increase the Channel hull to a 27 ft. waterline length as a definite step up from the Brittany's 25 ft. 3 in. For this alteration the 27 ft. W.L. *Tilly Whim* one-off design boat was adopted as the basic design for a New Channel Class.

The first of the new modified Channel Class design, *Rose of York*, was built for Colonel Birch as replacement for his previous Laurent Giles Brittany Class yacht *Maid of York*. The result of Giles' modifications was a yacht which was well balanced, docile and easy to handle with plenty of deck space and sufficient accommodation for five people. Compared to the original Channel Class, her sheer was flatter, her bow overhang was shorter, as was her counter which had a more vertical transom. On deck her coachroof had been brought up to date and there was more deck space due to an increase in the beam. Her construction was straightforward and sound, consisting of English oak in the centre lines and frames with galvanized mild steel floors. Larch was used for the stringers, shelves and some deck beams with English oak for the remainder. The deck trim and coamings were iroko with a canvas covered red pine deck, and planking was of sapele or larch.

Company records indicate that at least nine of these yachts were built between 1951 and 1955.

Rose of York at Cowes in 1952

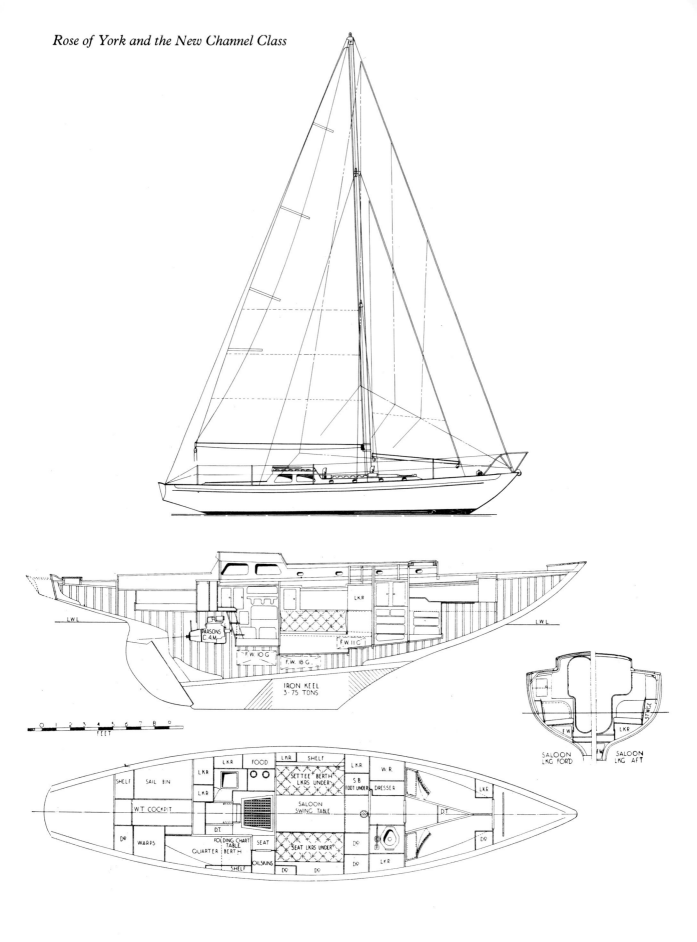

Taylor Trusty

Owner	Commissioned by James Taylor Ltd
Builder	James Taylor Ltd
Date Built	1949
Design No.	184
L.O.A.	36 ft. 3 in. (11.06 m)
L.W.L.	31 ft. 0 in. (9.46 m)
Beam	10 ft. 0 in. (3.05 m)
Draft	5 ft. 0 in. (1.53 m)
Displacement	8.6 tons (8.74 tonnes)
Sail Area	380 sq. ft. (35.34 m²)
Rig	Bermudan Sloop

After the war, more and more people were becoming interested in sailing as a hobby and there was a growing demand for motor sailers. These were considered, by the weekend sailer, to be safer and had the added ability of being able to make for a mooring under adverse wind conditions, so ensuring a return to work on a Monday morning. With these points in mind, and having been impressed with their strikingly handsome motor yacht *Woodpecker*, James Taylor Ltd commissioned Laurent Giles in 1949 to produce a motor sailer design that would appeal to the family yachtsman.

The motor sailer has never been an easy vessel to design, mainly because they have to be built more heavily and strongly than a motor boat. They must be able to take the strains imposed by the rigging and sails, and because of their larger and heavier keels, compared to a motor yacht of comparable size, they have greater wetted surface areas and a larger displacement. They are also at a disadvantage under sail because of the extra weight of the engine, and the flow of water past the hull is disturbed by the presence of a large propeller. *Taylor Trusty* was designed to achieve a good standard of performance under both sail and power, which required a well designed hull. With all these problems in mind, Giles managed to produce an exceptional boat. A quote from *Yachting World* in November 1949 stated that 'She has well-balanced proportions, those qualities required in a motor sailer and her hull is very neat and looks thoroughly seaworthy.'

Trusty was built with light scantlings and the planking is of two skins of mahogany, the diagonal inner skin being 3/8 in. thick and the outer 7/16 in. thick, running fore and aft. The mast was stepped on the coachroof to allow clear passage through the galley; this being unusual for the time, although this design idea would be tried and tested by *Vertue XXXV* in her trans-Atlantic voyage in 1950.

The rigging was made as simple as possible and incorporated a Bermudan mainsail and a staysail on a set boom, the total area being 380 sq. ft. Below decks there was full headroom in the saloon, something which was considered unnecessary in pre-war boats. An interesting feature of the layout is the after cabin, which was designed with the younger family in mind so that the children were not disturbed once put to bed.

The standard engines fitted were either the 30/40 h.p. Perkins P4M diesel or a 20/40 h.p. Morris Commodore petrol engine. During sailing trials, the 40 h.p engine produced a remarkable speed of 8 to 9 knots. It is amusing to think that the size of these engines today would be considered only suitable as an auxiliary for a sailing yacht.

Trusty was exhibited at the 1950 London Boat Show where it attracted much attention. This design was to show that Laurent Giles, although famous for his ocean racing and luxury yachts, could design boats which were attractive and affordable to the average yachtsman.

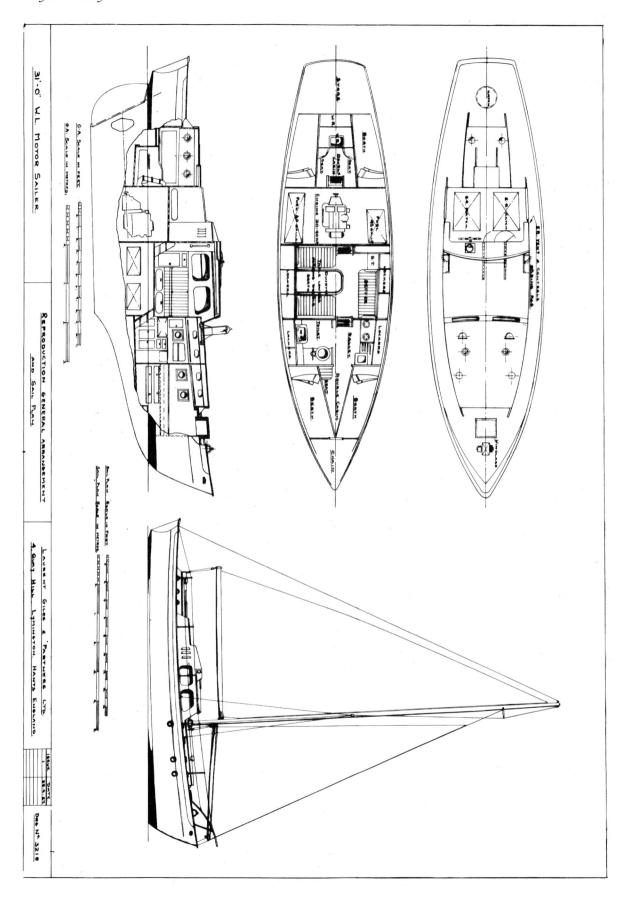

Morag Mhor

Designed for British Aluminium Co.

Date Built	1953
Design No.	195
L.O.A.	72 ft. 3 in. (22.04m)
L.W.L	60 ft. 4 in. (18.39 m)
Beam	16 ft. o in. (4.88 m)
Draft	7 ft. o in. (2.14 m)
Displacement	45.0 tons (45.72 tonnes)
Sail area	1408 sq. ft. (130.94 m²)
Rig	Ketch

Morag Mhor was a 72-ft. motor sailer which was designed in conjunction with the design staff of Saunders Roe, Anglesey Ltd. She was commissioned for the British Aluminium company to illustrate the application and further the development of the welding of aluminium alloys for use in ship construction. This ocean-going yacht was constructed at the Beaumaris Yard of Saunders Roe, and she was at the time the largest all-welded aluminium alloy hull ever constructed in any country except America. She was designed and built under Lloyds survey to class 100 A1.

The advantages of using aluminium alloys in yacht building include the fact that the hull is watertight at all times, unlike timber, and the maintenance costs are low when designed and engineered properly. There is no water absorption, unlike G.R.P. or timber, and advantage can be taken of using integral tanks so saving space and weight, since they constitute part of the hull structure. In comparison with steel, aluminium has a better strength-to-weight ratio and has a greater resistance to denting.

The hull was framed on the longitudinal system, transverse strength being provided by nine bulkheads and a system of frames spaced generally at 3-foot centers. The shell plating was welded directly to the longitudinal sections and bulkhead boundary bars, but there was no connection of the hull to the transverse frames, these being attached to the inboard flanges of the longitudinals. The ballast was encapsulated in the lower half of the keel, the upper half being used for double-bottomed tanks.

The superstructure was a riveted construction with double skins, the outer skin being of 16 s.w.g. and the inner skin of 18 s.w.g. Both main and mizzen masts were fabricated from aluminium plate rolled in two halves and then joined together with longitudinal butt welds. Sections of mast ten feet long were then welded together to produce the final structure. The two 70 b.h.p. diesel engines were coupled to three-bladed variable pitch propellers, and engine cooling was provided by a closed recirculating system, the water being cooled as it passed through specially constructed surface cooling tanks built onto the shell plating adjacent to the engines.

The deck equipment included two aluminium alloy boats, also of welded construction, one being a 12-foot motor launch fitted with a 4 h.p. Stuart Turner engine and the other a 10-foot sailing dinghy.

Morag Mhor is still sailing today, providing a fine example of how aluminium can be a very effective material for building boats when used correctly. Great care was taken to avoid electrolytic corrosion due to bimetallic joints and improper paints, sealants and poor electrical systems, since this would have caused the aluminium to deteriorate.

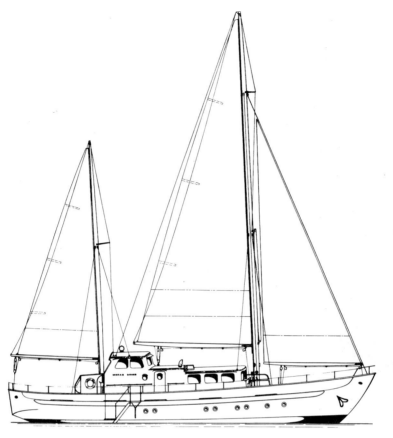

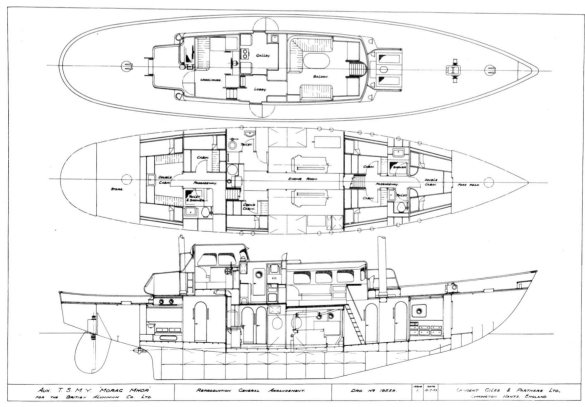

AUX. T.S.M.Y. 'MORAG MHOR' FOR THE BRITISH ALUMINIUM CO. LTD. | REPRODUCTION GENERAL ARRANGEMENT. | DRG. Nº 18558. | LAURENT GILES & PARTNERS LTD. LYMINGTON. HANTS. ENGLAND.

Shyraga

Owner	Sen. Rizzi
Builder	Abeking and Rasmussen
Design No.	227
Date Built	1955
L.O.A.	95 ft. 0 in. (28.98 m)
L.W.L.	88 ft. 0 in. (26.84 m)
Beam	19 ft. 6 in. (5.95 m)
Draft	7 ft. 0 in. (2.14 m)
Displacement	100 tons (101.6 tonnes)
Engines	Twin Foden F.D. 12

In 1954 Laurent Giles were approached by an Italian client who wanted a 95-foot twin-screw motor yacht of displacement form for use in the Mediterranean. The result was *Shyraga*, a purposeful looking canoe sterned motor yacht with some features that indicated *Tamahine*, the company's famous pre-war motor boat, to be a distant relative. The rounded stern was very much in style and produced a certain balance to the look of the hull. *Shyraga* was built in welded steel by the well known German yard of Abeking and Rasmussen, who employed a modular construction technique to build her. After the modules had been assembled the whole boat was zinc sprayed inside and out, a process which although initially increasing construction costs, paid handsome dividends in reducing the maintenance over the following years. An interesting feature in the construction was the boat deck, which had the transverse beams mounted on top of the steel saloon roof and cantilevered over the side decks. The teak boat deck was then fastened onto the steel beams, leaving an air gap between the saloon roof and the deck which helped to keep the interior cool.

The main machinery was a pair of Foden F.D. 12's, 12-cylinder twin crankshaft diesel engines each producing an intermittent output of 240 b.h.p. at 200 r.p.m. and a continuous output of 210 b.h.p. at 180 r.p.m. These gave the yacht a maximum speed of 12 knots and a cruising range of 1500 miles. Due to the short overall length of the engines, Giles was able to utilise this extra space and to design a fuel tank which ran the full width of the boat and the full depth of the hull from the keel to the deck. This then separated the engine compartment from the owner's cabin and acted as a useful heat and sound baffle. The interior of the yacht was also lined with glass wool insulation to further reduce the transmission of noise and heat.

The accommodation was designed for a crew of six, including captain, engineer, steward, and two hands. The crew occupied the forward part of the vessel and aft of their area was the galley, store room and steward's pantry. The only part of the guest accommodation forward of the engine room was a smoking room/study. Aft of the engine room was the owner's suite, two single cabins and a double cabin with ensuite bathroom. At deck level there was a large wheel-house and an open-plan lounge and dining room.

Shyraga was to establish Laurent Giles as designers of large motor yachts, and many other commissions were to follow over the next decade.

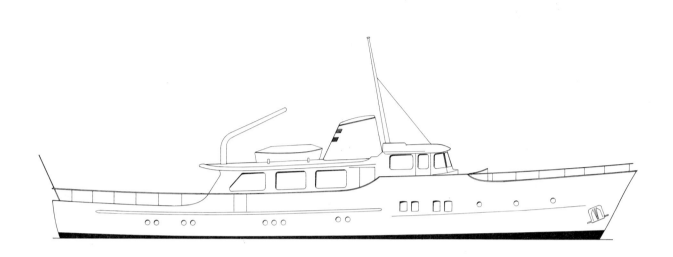

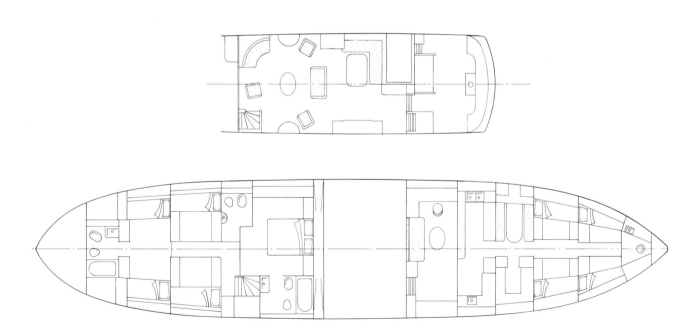

Trekka and the Columbia Class

Owner	J. Guzzwell
Builder	J. Guzzwell
Date Built	1954
Design No.	231
L.O.A.	21 ft. 2 in. (6.47 m)
L.W.L	18 ft. 6 in. (5.64 m)
Beam	6 ft. 6 in. (1.98 m)
Draft	4 ft. 6 in. (1.37 m)
Displacement	1.4 tons (1.42 tonnes)
Sail Area	197 sq. ft. (18.32 m²)
Rig	Yawl

The exploits of *Sopranino* fired the imagination of numerous yachtsmen throughout the world, among them John Guzzwell, an experienced English shipwright reared in a sea-faring family. John wanted to build and sail a 20 to 21-foot yawl in the same manner as *Sopranino* and accordingly approached Laurent Giles for the design. Among his requirements for this larger and more comfortable version, which later became the first of the successful Columbia Class, was sufficient length of straight keel to facilitate slipping, a self draining cockpit, watertight compartments fore and aft and additional headroom. The hull was also required to be robust enough to cope with the common hazards likely to be encountered in British Columbia waters, such as collision with water saturated logs, known as 'dead heads', which float down from the rivers and into the more open waters of the British Columbian coast.

To fulfil all of these requirements, it was necessary for Laurent Giles to use considerably more displacement in this design than they had used in *Sopranino*, and the construction shows the same understanding of light, small-boat building that was evident in her. *Trekka* was carvel built of edge-glued western red cedar planking on steam bent timbers. In the hull there was not one single piece of timber, apart from locker lids, that did not contribute to the structure of the hull, and even the shelves provided stiffening. The fin keel was of steel plate with an iron ballast bulb to make the most

efficient use of the ballast weight and a yawl rig was chosen to help self-steer the boat.

In September 1955 *Trekka* was launched at Victoria, British Columbia, and John sailed her to San Francisco, 800 miles away, as a preliminary trial. He encountered all kinds of weather in this 16 day voyage, and having arrived unscathed was well pleased with her handling and performance. Keeping his intentions to himself he continued to cruise *Trekka* around the world. His cruise took him from San Francisco to New Zealand via Honolulu, Samoa and Tonga, several legs of the journey being completed in surprisingly short time. In one particular gale he achieved 120 miles in 24 hours under staysail alone. During a refit in New Zealand, steam bent knees in the way of the mast partners were replaced with laminated mahogany and the whole of the hull was fibre glassed. He then sailed on, still singlehanded, to Australia, passing the Great Barrier reef, going on to Mauritius and South Africa. From Cape Town past the Cape of Good Hope his voyage continued to Ascension Island, Barbados and then through the Panama Canal to complete his circumnavigation and return to Honolulu. Finally he returned to his home port in British Columbia in September 1959. *Trekka* is now housed in a museum in British Columbia. The epic circumnavigation voyage is recounted in John Guzzwell's book *Trekka Round the World*.

The Columbia Class was a direct descendant of *Trekka* and was named after her home port. This design was to prove very popular, partly because of John Guzwell's adventures but also because their size made them affordable to many keen yachtsmen. Because of these factors, together with their ease of construction, over 75 Columbia yachts have been built throughout the world, mostly by amateur builders. Even today there are Columbia yachts still being built.

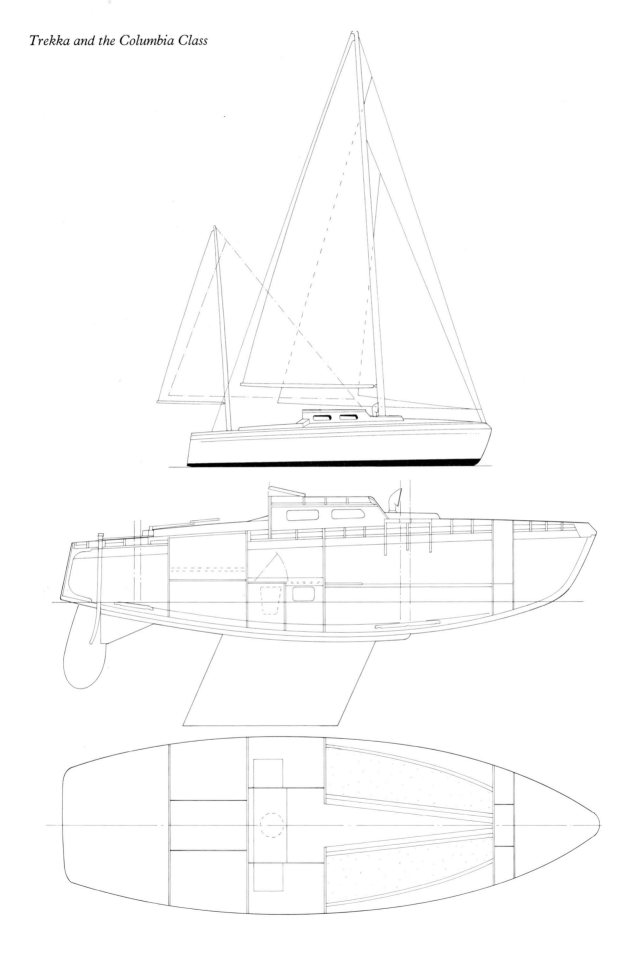

Ravahine

Owner	Major H. Hall
Builder	Port Hamble Ltd.
Date Built	1955
Design No.	244
L.O.A.	48 ft. 0 in. (14.64 m)
L.W.L	44 ft. 6 in. (13.57 m)
Beam	12 ft. 0 in. (3.66 m)
Draft	3 ft. 6 in. (1.07 m)
Displacement	10.5 tons (10.67 tonnes)
Engines	2 × 240 hp Foden F. D. 12

Major Hall had previously owned the famous motor boat *Tamahine* which had been designed for him by Laurent Giles in 1934. In 1955 he wanted a new fast fishing launch and asked Laurent Giles to design him a powerful, seagoing launch of robust construction which could achieve a speed of 20 knots. The hull, which was tank tested at the National Physics Laboratory at Teddington, was of a hard chine bow fading into a round bilge stern, showing Giles's pre-occupation with seakeeping qualities.

The hull was of triple skin construction with two inner skins of mahogany and the outer of teak, with stem and keel assembly of teak and English oak. Spruce longitudinal stringers were used with structural bulkheads of mahogany plywood. Decks and covering boards were of teak with a superstructure of mahogany. The engine beds and girders were made of aluminium alloy to conserve weight, and the engines were mounted on flexible feet with special attention being given to exhaust silencing. The boat proved to be remarkably free of vibration and cruised at 17 knots, reaching a maximum of 20.5 knots in sea trials. The owner was extremely pleased with the design and performance of *Ravahine*, particularly in varying weather conditions since she proved to be very manoeuvrable.

In 1963, eight years after *Ravahine* had been built, the owner considered replacing the original engines with identical but updated and more powerful ones. Laurent Giles took this opportunity to research the hull form thoroughly to ensure that she would attain maximum possible speeds. A model of *Ravahine* was again tank tested at Saunders Roe division of Westland Aircraft to evaluate her performance with these uprated engines and modifications to the hull. The new engines were to produce a total of 800 b.h.p., and the alterations to the hull entailed varying transom wedges and applying additional chine strips to the hull. It is now an accepted fact that the addition of transom wedges can improve a boat's performance by changing the trim angle. The tank test results showed that with the new engines, but with no changes to the hull, *Ravahine*'s maximum speed could be increased to 28.8 knots. However, by fitting an optimised transom wedge she would be able to achieve 30.7 knots. This project provides an excellent example of how Jack Giles was always keen to improve and optimise his designs.

Ravahine was built as a day boat and therefore had limited accommodation, but her manners and performance at sea were so pleasing that preliminary plans for a similar hull were drawn as a motor cruiser with good accommodation for four to six people. The well known yacht designer Peter Thornycroft, who is renowned for his design of semi-displacement motor boats, said that *Ravahine* influenced him more than any other boat.

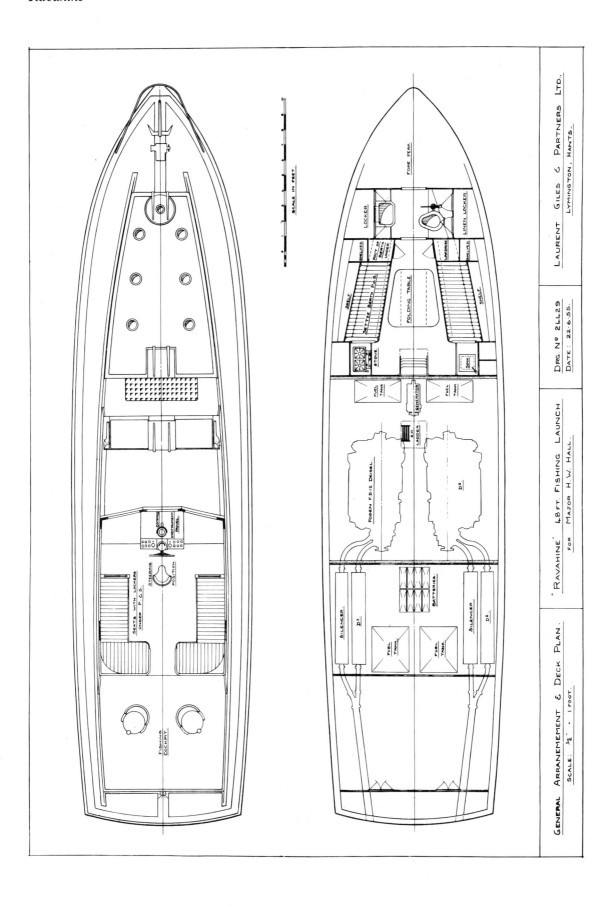

GENERAL ARRANGEMENT & DECK PLAN.   'RAVAHINE' 48 FT. FISHING LAUNCH   DRG. Nº 2LL29   LAURENT GILES & PARTNERS LTD.

SCALE: ½" = 1 FOOT.   FOR MAJOR H. W. HALL.   DATE: 22·6·55.   LYMINGTON, HANTS.

SCALE IN FEET.

FORE PEAK

LOCKER   LINEN LOCKER

SHELVES   FOOT OF BERTH UNDER   WARDROBE   SHELVES

SHELF   SETTEE BERTH P&S   FOLDING TABLE   SHELF

STOVE   SINK

FUEL TANK   GENERATOR   FUEL TANK

FODEN F.D.I2 DIESEL   LADDER   Dº

BATTERIES

SILENCER   Dº   SILENCER   Dº

FUEL TANK   FUEL TANK

SEATS WITH LOCKERS UNDER P. & S.   STEERING POSITION

COMPASS   INSTRUMENT PANEL

FISHING COCKPIT

Ravahine passing Hurst Castle at high speed and showing typical trim of a semi-displacement motor boat

Great Days and the Rambler Class

Builder	J.J. Bickford of Topsham
Date Built	1957
Design No.	Number 255
L.O.A.	35 ft. 0 in. (10.68 m)
L.W.L.	27 ft. 6 in. (8.39 m)
Beam	9 ft. 8 in. (2.96 m)
Draft	4 ft. 3 in. (1.3 m)
Displacement	7.5 tons (7.62 tonnes)
Sail Area	432 sq. ft. (40.18 m²)
Rig	Bermudan Sloop

Great Days was conceived for the owner, who knew exactly what he wanted; an ideal singlehanded motor sailer which would be big enough to live aboard in reasonable comfort. Cost was an important controlling factor which meant that money was to be spent on the best possible construction, but cutting out expensive gear and fancy fittings. By producing a hull with good beam this allowed the draft to be reduced and yet still maintain stability. This was extremely useful for two reasons; first she could put to shore anywhere for scrubbing and maintenance and thus save on such costs, and secondly, she could enter little secluded creeks or sit comfortably on mud. As a singlehander it was necessary that she should be easy to handle, be quick on the helm and be able to look after herself with little assistance.

A great deal of thought was put into *Great Days* with respect to her ease of maintenance and simplicity of equipment. For example, the choice of engine installed in her was a big, slow-running 4 cylinder 20 b.h.p. Brit which was placed amidship in the cabin under a big table. It was housed within a sound-proof box which could be dismantled in a few seconds so that the engine could be fully exposed for repairs. *Great Days'* rig was also extremely simple with no runners or winches, so that the deck was spacious and uncluttered. Single spreaders were considered adequate on her and the mast was stepped on deck, reducing deck leakage and improving the amount of accommodation below. Additional space was acquired by the fact that she had no water tanks but instead used several removable two gallon polythene bottles.

Construction everywhere on her was of the best quality. She had bronze floors, a teak bottom, teak coamings, teak deck trim, stainless steel rigging, and a stainless steel anchor windlass. The internal accommodation was very simple and prior to her launch she was not furnished. Furniture was acquired over a number of years by the owner, saving on the initial costs and making sure of its correct placement.

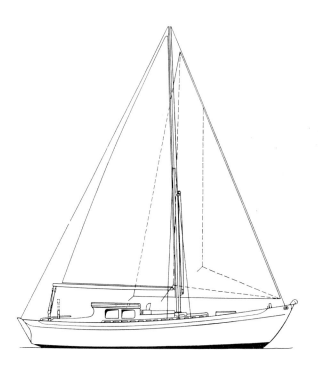

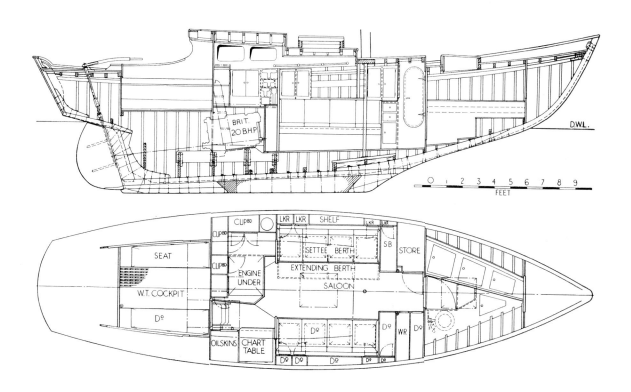

BRI.T.
20 B.H.P.

D.W.L.

0 1 2 3 4 5 6 7 8 9
FEET

CUPᴮᴰ | LKR | LKR | SHELF | LKR | LKR
CUPᴮᴰ
SEAT | SETTEE BERTH | SB | STORE
CUPᴮᴰ | EXTENDING BERTH
ENGINE UNDER | SALOON
W.T. COCKPIT
Dº
OILSKINS | CHART TABLE | Dº | Dº | WR | Dº
Dº | Dº | Dº | Dº | Dº

Star Sapphire

Owner	D.W. Mollins
Builder	Cantiere Navale V. Beltrami, Genoa
Date Built	1957
Design No.	258
L.O.A.	73 ft. 7 in. (22.43 m)
L.W.L.	50 ft. 3 in. (15.33 m)
Beam	16 ft. 9 in. (5.11 m)
Draft	7 ft. 0 in. (2.14 m)
Displacement	35 tons (35.56 tonnes)
Sail Area	1945 sq. ft. (180.89 m²)
Rig	Ketch
Engines	Twin 150 b.h.p. Mercedes

During the 1950s there had been a tendency not only to give auxiliary cruisers more power, but also more sail, while trying to retain the sailing qualities of the vessel. Prior to the design of *Star Sapphire*, such yachts were considered to have poor manoeuvrability and proved difficult to sail, except in strong winds, and it was often necessary to run the motor while sailing. In *Star Sapphire*, built in 1957, Laurent Giles achieved a perfect marriage of the two. The hull profile was almost of a racing yacht yet the deck structure was more like a motor boat, complete with a bridge. There was nearly 2000 square feet of sail, and although not quite comparable with similar sized yachts, it was of a very efficient design.

The full-power motor yacht has many advantages over the sailing yacht as a means of getting from A to B, but, in practice, the uncomfortable motion of the motor yacht had led designers to add more and more sail. In the 1950 Motor Boat Show Laurent Giles introduced the *Taylor Trusty* motor sailer from which he developed a new family of motor sailers, including *Star Sapphire*.

Star Sapphire was designed to provide the best of both worlds since she had almost as much power as would normally be given to a full-power motor yacht. Her engines were a pair of Mercedes O M 315 A diesels each developing 150 b.h.p. at 1800 r.p.m. These were coupled via cardan shafts to Slack and Parr variable pitch propellers. Not only did she have these powerful engines, she also had much more sail than a normal motor sailer yacht of her waterline length and the sail areas were kept to a manageable size by using a cutter rig ketch. Her hull was more like a metre boat than a motor boat, and the superstructure was interesting because not only was there a comfortable deckhouse but, aft of this, there was a raised bridge, a feature which is still considered unusual today. The skill of the design was to reduce the apparent height of the superstructure and the result was very pleasing to the eye.

Below decks the internal arrangement consisted of the owner's suite aft, being behind the engine room, which was located below the centre saloon. In the forward accommodation was the galley together with two guest cabins, and in the foremost cabin there were two separate crew bunks.

The owner was delighted with the result and after a few years with *Star Sapphire* returned to Laurent Giles to commission a new design. This was for the ultimate motor sailer, which would be known as *Blue Leopard*. ,

Photo opposite: *Star Sapphire* being launched in Italy

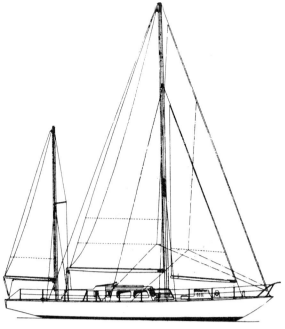

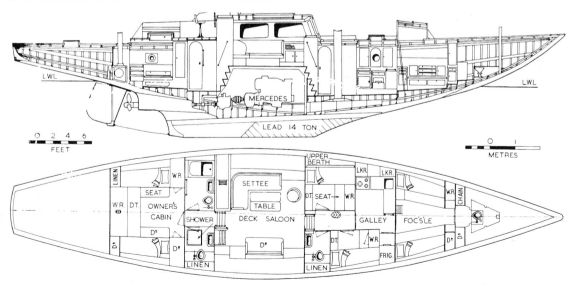

LWL

MERCEDES

LWL

LEAD 14 TON

0 2 4 6
FEET

0 1
METRES

LINEN

W.R.

SEAT

UPPER
BERTH

LKR

LKR

W.R.

CHAIN

W.R. DT.

OWNER'S
CABIN

SHOWER

SETTEE

TABLE

DT SEAT

W.R.

GALLEY

FOC'S'LE

Dº

Dº

DECK SALOON

Dº

DT.

W.R.

Dº

Dº

LINEN

LINEN

FRIG

Donella and the Donella Class

Owner	G.B. Haywood
Builder	Unknown
Date Built	1958
Design No.	279
L.O.A.	43 ft. 0 in. (13.12 m)
L.W.L.	33 ft. 0 in. (10.07 m)
Beam	10 ft. 9 in. (3.28 m)
Draft	6 ft. 0 in. (1.83 m)
Displacement	13.6 tons (13.82 tonnes)
Sail Area	831 sq. ft. (77.28 m²)
Rig	Cutter

From the outset the Donella Class was designed with two different rigs in mind; a cutter and a ketch. The ketch can possibly be described as a motor sailer and the cutter as a yacht with a large auxiliary engine. The lines show a fuller hull form than usual, this being dictated by the owner's original requirements which were for a six-berth interior arrangement with a below-deck passageway running from the aft cabin to the forward cabin. *Donella* was one of the first yachts to establish this feature, which allows access between the forward and aft accommodation without going up over the cockpit.

Another major feature of this boat was the saloon and aft cabin hatches which were double-hinged and could open to face forward or aft. This allowed for much improved ventilation throughout the boat. Supplying light to the interior of a yacht is an important part of the design, and *Donella* and her sisters not only had port holes in the hull, but dead-lights in the cabin top and large windows in the doghouse. In fact the boats were so light and airy that it prompted *Yachts and Yachting* in 1958 to write; 'One of the big differences between a modern and an old-fashioned cruiser is the amount of light below decks. The big improvement which has come about in the last few years is largely as a result of the influence on design of Laurent Giles. Long before the war they were drawing plans of boats that were a joy to live aboard, in strong contrast to some of the dark seagoing dungeons then in vogue.'

The ketch rig version of the design clearly demonstrated Jack Giles's ideas on standing rigging.

This was that the two masts are not joined together by rigging so that should one mast be lost it would not pull down the other. The ketch rig is nowadays underrated and often scoffed at for its apparent loss of efficiency compared to having a larger sloop rig. However, for short handed crews or for larger yachts the splitting of the sail area into smaller more manageable sizes makes for easier sailing. The ability to balance the boat on her sails is also advantageous for long-distance cruising. To many people the difference in performance would be undetectable and comes down to an individual's preference.

Donella the first of the Donella Class

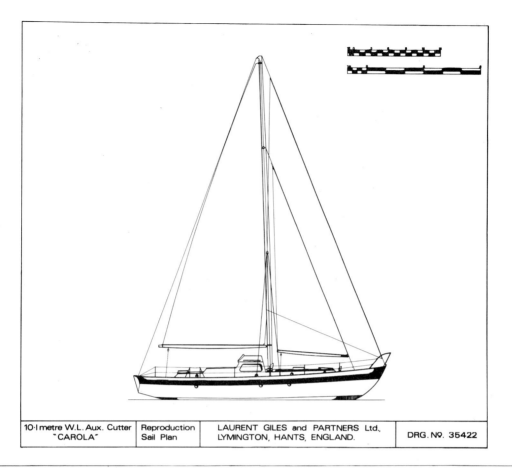

| 10·1 metre W.L. Aux. Cutter "CAROLA" | Reproduction Sail Plan | LAURENT GILES and PARTNERS Ltd., LYMINGTON, HANTS, ENGLAND. | DRG. NO. 35422 |

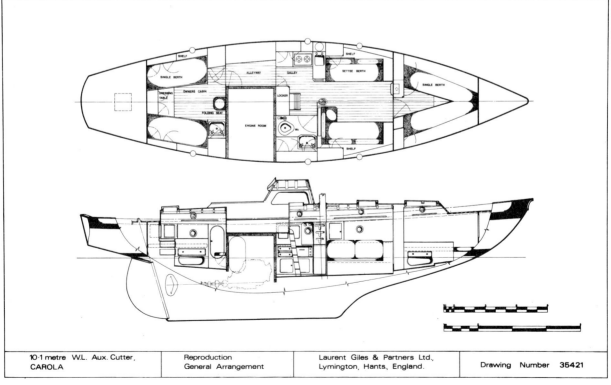

| 10·1 metre W.L. Aux. Cutter, CAROLA | Reproduction General Arrangement | Laurent Giles & Partners Ltd., Lymington, Hants., England. | Drawing Number 35421 |

Normandy Class

Builder	Various
Date Designed	1957
Design No.	304
L.O.A.	27 ft. 10 in. (8.48 m)
L.W.L.	21 ft. 6 in. (6.56 m)
Beam	7 ft. 10 in. (2.38 m)
Draft	4 ft. 3 in. (1.3 m)
Displacement	3.5 tons (3.56 tonnes)
Sail Area	343 sq. ft. (31.90 m²)
Rig	Bermudan Sloop

The following description of the Normandy Class of yacht is taken from an original article written for *Yachting World* by Jack Giles in March 1958.

'Designers always like to imagine themselves able to produce better and better boats. If we did not have this confidence we should die of exhaustion and morbid self-pity. There is also the public which buys the boats which we design: half of them believe that a new boat will be a better boat, bless them, for they give zest to life; the other half are firmly convinced that a new design is a risk only to be eradicated by long and arduous trial (by others); these buy the good old friends, bless them, too, for they give grist to the mill with a minimum of thought, work and anxiety!

So, having a staunch and trusted "good old friend" in the Vertue Class, we decided that it would be nice to start a new line. After all, the original Vertue, *Andrillot*, was put on paper in 1935 and stands in our boat list as number 15. So, after a lapse of twenty years, one felt the urge to try again, to make a fresh start for those who believe in progress. Rather slowly in the midst of considerable preoccupations, a new boat was put on the board. At this time the Vertue numbers were running up to the 80s, they are now up to the 90s (March 1958), and our overall boat numbers gave the first of the new boats the number 304; so it can safely be said that they belong to a different era. After some distasteful class names had been chewed over and spat out we settled for Normandy. It fell with appropriate modesty into our stock design names Biscay, Channel, Brittany and it is also the name of that corner of the parish of Lymington in which I live.

It is difficult then to write of the Normandy without comparison with Vertue. On that basis, however, what do we believe we have achieved?

First, on dimensions, the Normandy is a sensibly bigger boat, she is longer overall and she has more beam: she is of a slightly lower displacement but it has been possible to keep the same floor lines. Internal space is, therefore, better potentially than the Vertue.

Secondly, some slight economy of construction has been possible; for instance, scantlings have been slightly reduced and the basic model has a simple deck edge with foot rail in place of bulwarks.

Thirdly, the sail area has been reduced, and that and the rigging has been simplified. This reflects on first cost, on maintenance and on handling.

One attraction of the Vertues is a reasonable performance on a moderate draft. We decided to design the Normandy with alternative moderate draft of full draft R.O.R.C. limits. This is done on the same wood keel to allow builders' moulds to be used for either. The accommodation has been tackled as a comprehensive range of alternatives. We felt that we could, at any time, revert to any of the well tried variants used in the Vertues but that it was time to offer some rather different ideas. It was our idea that the Normandy would generally lead a less strenuous life than her older and tougher sister, and to begin with we laid her out with a larger cockpit. This is to some extent basic because it has allowed us to incorporate as standard the Parsons "Prawn" power unit, and the bulkhead between doghouse and cockpit which is an essential part of the "standard" design of hull and deck works. This much, at least, in such a conception of stock design must be kept unaltered, or the idea of building to standard plans breaks down.

Within the accommodation space, subject to the essential requirements of mast support (for the mast is stepped on deck) and of the need to pitch bulkheads on the standard timber spacing, certain variations of subdivision are permissible.

The various layouts which we have adopted revolve around lavatory and galley positions. Thus there are forward and midship positions of lavatory; the former generally in conjunction with minor accommodation, forward; the latter where the forward accommodation is more or less of the forecabin type, in which space has been gained by doubling up the galley with the lavatory, which is placed under the cook's seat.

Now this is a fundamental point; should the cook stand or sit ? We have to remember we are dealing with a boat which, if paralleled to bird recognition gauges of size, would be classified as "very small" that is, next to "minute" the smallest of all. The effect of this on the galley is that even if we provide standing headroom in the after part of the doghouse, the side deck is so low that the stove is forced down to a height which no housewife would accept. So it may be argued that the cook has to sit even at the conventional aft galley. Why not then a "sitting"

galley up forward where the ascending and descending angels on Jacob's Ladder neither interfere nor are given in interference?

With the galley at the forward end of the saloon it is still not so forward a position as to render the galley unusable in reasonable weather at sea, nor is the cook any less in and out of the saloon party than in the conventional positon aft. The saloon settees benefit by being less pinched at the fore end. Galley ventilation is possibly better this way, certainly for as long as the forehatch can be kept at work, since the normal airstream goes through the boat from aft.

Finally, we set ourselves determinedly to the solution of the aesthetic problem. The Normandy was to be as handsome a little yacht as we knew how to make her. We had our self-imposed standards of space below decks but these must be fulfilled with yet something better than no offence to the eye.

Two Normandys were afloat last season, *Blue Mink* at Itchenor and *Quasi* at Portofino. Both have won the hearts of their owners. I have sailed *Blue Mink* once or twice and she seems a promising little boat; she may be fast but that remains to be seen.'

Normandy, the fifteenth of the Normandy Class

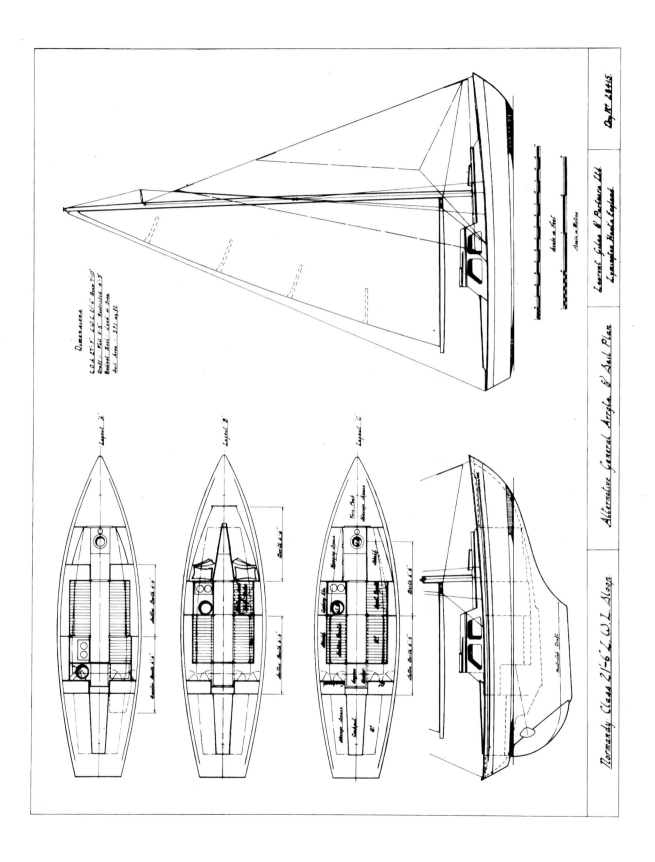

Chapter 4
Post-War Designs (1959–1982)

Introduction

The end of the 1950s marked the end of an era in which wood construction had been almost totally dominant in the building of all small waterborne craft. Aluminium, steel and the infant G.R.P. were becoming more and more popular although wood continued to be a viable building material. In this chapter *Margham Abbey* provides a good example of a boat designed in steel, while yachts like *Stormvogel* and *Blue Leopard* illustrate the high technology and skill that had evolved in design and construction of wooden yachts. Important G.R.P. designs which began life in the 1960s are discussed in a separate chapter, except for the Salmo Salar which started life as a wooden boat before being produced in G.R.P.

The days of post-war austerity were past and there was a notable increase in the demand for large luxury motor yachts like *Aetea*. At the other end of the scale, more families could afford to go sailing and the popularity of the sport was growing dramatically. There was a demand for new types of boat like *Audacity*, a weekend trailer sailer, as well as for new types of motor sailer. These boats, like the Dhorus Mhor Class, were particularly favoured by the weekend yachtsman since the powerful engines made them more dependable and could ensure a return to work on Monday morning after a weekend's sailing.

Margham Abbey

Owner	Port Talbot Pilotage Authority
Builder	Richard Ironworks Ltd
Date Built	1959
Design No.	335
L.O.A.	88 ft. 0 in. (26.84 m)
L.W.L.	80 ft. 0 in. (24.4 m)
Beam	20 ft. 0 in. (6.1 m)
Draft Aft	9 ft. 4 in. (2.85 m)
Displacement	117.19 tons (119.07 tonnes)
Engine	Crossley HRN/4

The name of Laurent Giles is not normally associated with commercial or working craft, but Jack Giles maintained a strong interest in this type of work following his wartime experiences designing the Motor Fishing Vessel (M.F.V.) for the Admiralty.

Margham Abbey was one of the largest projects of this type undertaken by the company and was designed as a pilot vessel for the Port Talbot Authority. One of the main problems for the pilotage service at Port Talbot was the vicious sea encountered at the harbour entrance in the normal onshore southwesterly winds. Seas 100 ft. long and 15 ft. high were often experienced, and very special considerations were necessary in this aspect of the design. For example the hull form had to be dry, stable and free from any tendency to broach, yet be highly manoeuvrable when coming alongside larger vessels.

Tank testing with a self-propelled model was undertaken at the Saunders Roe open basin at Cowes which was, interestingly enough, originally established to test the landing capabilities of flying boats. Her hull form below the waterline was similar to a normal displacement power yacht, but she had been modelled on other advantageous principles. For example, the topsides were flared up to the deck line throughout her length and a double flare was used forward. The bulwarks were tumblehome for most of her length but turned into flare at the bow and stern. Her profile, with bold sheer and the relatively tall superstructure, blended well with the hull and showed that considerable attention had

been given to achieving a pleasing aspect.

The accommodation was divided into the forward section for the pilots and the aft section for crew. The pilots' entrances were by way of the boarding rails at the forward end of the deckhouse port and starboard. In the entrance lobby were several lockers for oilskins and equipment, this area opening out into the wireless room, pilots' galley, toilet, deck lounge and chart room. Access to the crew's quarters was by an entrance in the after end of the superstructure and comprised a messroom together with four double cabins with separate bunks on the lower deck. All of the accommodation was designed to be particularly light and airy.

Margham Abbey was constructed in Cor-Ten high strength low alloy steel to Lloyds 100 A1 classification and to full British Government requirements. Normal methods of construction, at the time, were undertaken with both welding and riveting being used in the steel work. The propeller was designed and manufactured by Manganese Bronze and Brass Co. and the main engine was a Crossley HRN/4 2 stroke, exhaust pulse pressure-charged, direct-reversing marine Diesel with a rated output of 300 b.h.p. at 300 r.p.m.

On trials, *Margham Abbey* achieved a healthy speed of almost 11 knots on full power whilst keeping her decks dry and on successful completion of these and other trials was entered into service in 1959.

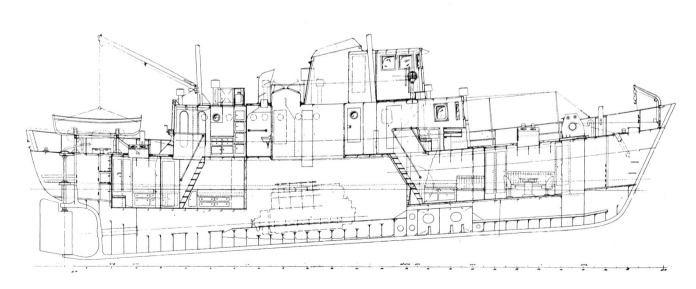

Freelander

Owner	Brigadier P.O.G. Wakeham O.B.E.
Builder	Port Hamble Ltd.
Design No.	358
Date Built	1959
L.O.A.	70 ft. 0 in. (21.35 m)
L.W.L.	65 ft. 0 in. (19.83 m)
Beam	14 ft. 3 in. (4.35 m)
Draft	4 ft. 0 in. (1.22 m)
Displacement	25.29 tons (25.69 tonnes)
Sail	300 sq. ft. (27.9 m²)
Engines	3 Perkins 56m (100 h.p. each)
Max Speed	13.65 knots

Freelander was a direct descendant of *Woodpecker*, being similar in style and having similar lines but with a very light displacement and narrow hull. She was intended to operate at the lower end of the semi-displacement range which is a particularly difficult region to design for. Her length displacement ratio was 92, below the magic 100, and her narrow lines forward and centre of buoyancy well aft, combined with her triple screw installation, gave her a top speed of 13.65 knots. This speed is representative of a speed length ratio of 1.7 which would be hard to beat even with the advancement of today's engines of the same power. *Freelander* demonstrates very clearly the expense of power needed to push a hull faster. The diagram shown illustrates the speeds obtained on trials with first one engine running (10 knots), then two engines (12 knots), and finally all three (13.65 knots). The triple screw arrangement was utilised because she was expected to undertake a lot of canal work. Within such confined conditions a single central engine and rudder was considered to be more efficient and it would also be less likely to be damaged than when running on wing engines. On the engineering side it is interesting to note that the flexibly mounted engines were kept as low as possible in the hull using Hardy Spicer intermediate shafts with universal couplings. This was particularly advantageous in reducing vibration and structural noise.

Freelander is at first sight very similar to *Woodpecker* and was constructed using the by then well-tested, multi-stringer principle with steam bent timbers at six inch centres, and inside of these stringers at twelve inch spacings. The planking was double skin mahogany and the deck single skin teak. This gave her a light but strong structure. Although conserving weight was an important factor, her interior was well furnished with painted bulkheads, furniture of polished makore and cabin soles of holly splined makore.

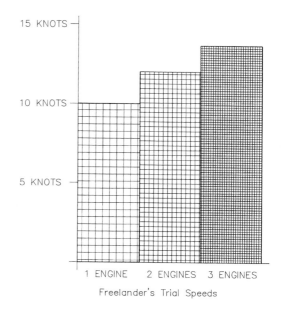

Freelander's Trial Speeds

Freelander slicing through the water

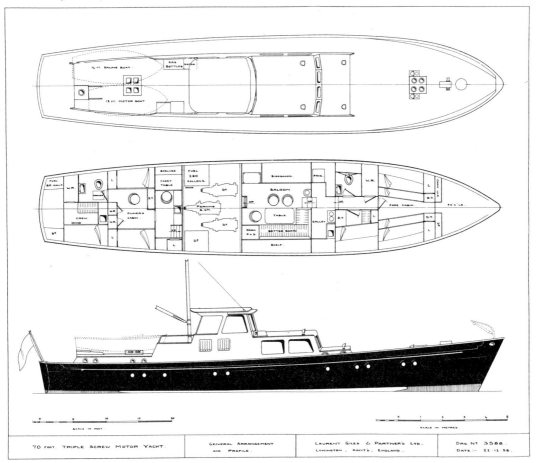

| 70 FOOT. TRIPLE SCREW MOTOR YACHT. | GENERAL ARRANGEMENT AND PROFILE. | LAURENT GILES & PARTNER'S LTD. LYMINGTON, HANTS, ENGLAND. | DRG. Nº 3588. DATE :- 22·12·58. |

Golden Gain and the Pearson Class

Owner	Various
Builder	Charles Pearson (Hull) Ltd
Date Designed	1947
Design No.	362
L.O.A.	33 ft. 10 in. (10.31 m)
L.W.L.	28 ft. 0 in. (8.54 m)
Beam	9 ft. 0 in. (2.75 m)
Draft	4 ft. 0 in. (1.22 m)
Displacement	10.7 tons (10.87 tonnes)
Sail area	225 sq. ft. (20.93 m²)
Rig	Dipping Lug

When Charles Pearson (Hull) Ltd. were intending to build a sturdy little cruiser on the lines of a North Sea fishing boat, they immediately beat a path to Quay Hill. The 61 ft. 6 in. Admiralty Motor Fishing Vessel (M.F.V.) Jack had designed during the war had proved to be an impressive sea boat and here was the chance to transfer its theme into the yachting world. The result was a hull with really beautiful lines, with a good beam of 9ft. and with a firm turn of bilge giving her plenty of stability. The waterlines were drawn into a canoe stern giving her a distinctive fishing boat style yet still maintaining a high displacement. The hull lines had the look of a yacht rather than a motor boat, which is necessary if a motor boat is to be capable of making sea going passages economically and comfortably.

The construction was of the best British timbers with heavy scantlings, since little ballast was required. The hull was planked in $1\frac{1}{8}$ in. oak on grown oak frames with steamed timbers of oak at 9 in. centres, with a larch bilge stringer. The deck was one-inch tongue and grooved pine on oak deck beams with a larch beam shelf and clamp. The coachroof was oak-framed with $1\frac{1}{2}$ in. pine coamings.

The two alternative interior accommodations were arranged so that they would be simple, straightforward and spacious. The first providing only two fixed berths with a dressing room, navigation area and galley. The second had two pipe cots in the fo'c'sle and a toilet compartment in place of the navigation area. Steps then led up to the wheelhouse, with the engine under the sole. Aft of the wheelhouse was a deep cockpit which had plenty of stowage.

There were also two sail plans; one was a Bermudan ketch with a loose-footed mainsail, and the other was a ketch but with a dipping-lug rig on the main mast. Neither rig carried enough sail to justify her as a motor sailer, but there was sufficient canvas to act as steadying sails and produce some forward propulsion in the event of an engine failure. *Golden Gain* was the first of this Pearson Class and proved to be a strong and comfortable boat with great character.

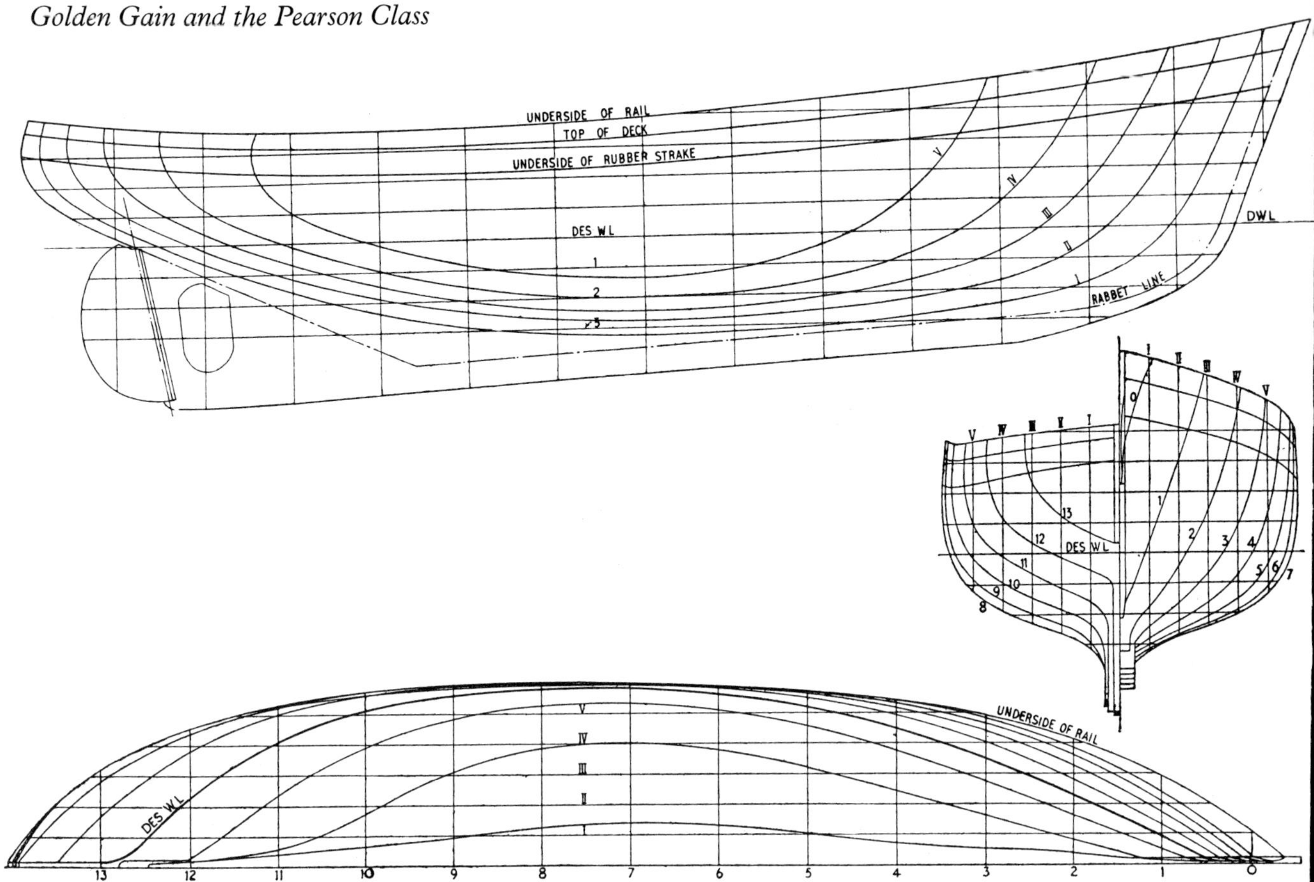

UNDERSIDE OF RAIL
TOP OF DECK
UNDERSIDE OF RUBBER STRAKE

DES WL

RABBET LINE

DWL

UNDERSIDE OF RAIL

DES WL

DES WL

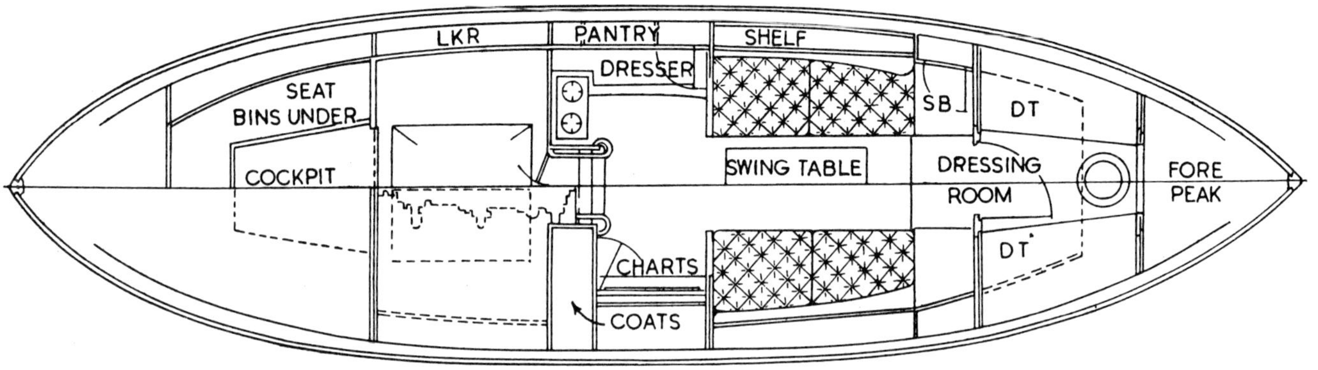

LKR   PANTRY   SHELF
DRESSER
SEAT
BINS UNDER
SB   DT
COCKPIT   SWING TABLE   DRESSING
ROOM   FORE
PEAK
CHARTS   DT
COATS

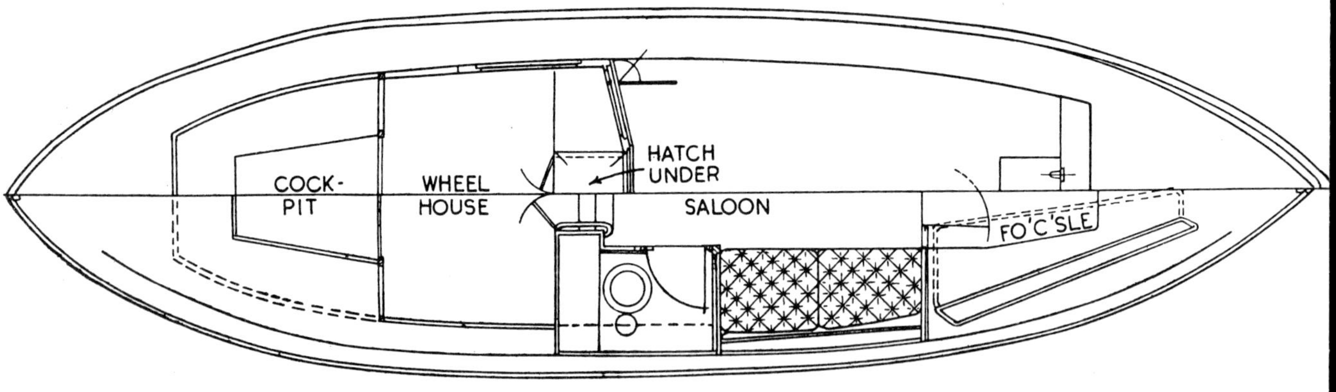

COCK-
PIT   WHEEL
HOUSE   HATCH
UNDER
SALOON   FO'C'SLE

Stormvogel

Owner	C. Bruynzeel
Builder	Lamtico, Stellenbosch, South Africa
Date Built	1961
Design No.	367
L.O.A.	74 ft. 6 in. (22.72 m)
L.W.L.	59 ft. 4 in. (18.10 m)
Beam	16 ft. 0 in. (4.88 m)
Draft	9 ft. 3 in. (2.82 m)
Displacement	31.2 tons (31.7 tonnes)
Sail area	2181 sq ft. (202.83 m²)
Rig	Bermudan Ketch

Stormvogel was one of the more unusual and interesting of Laurent Giles yachts since she extended the concept of light displacement into a size in which it had never before been seen. On a waterline length of 59 ft. 4 in. she had a designed displacement of 31 tons, and in fact achieved this within a very small margin. In terms of her displacement length ratio of 149 she was, therefore, comparable only to certain light displacement small yachts designed for ocean racing and to the Scandinavian square-metre classes of the time.

The design of *Stormvogel* was the result of an unusually close collaboration with her owner, C. Bruynzeel of Bruynzeel Plywood, Jack Giles, Van De Stadt and John Illingworth. Following on from his experience with his previous yacht, *Zeevalk*, the owner started with the idea of a chine hull. A number of such designs were included in the tank tests programme, but failed to make the grade in comparison with round bilge hull forms. The light displacement naturally called for exceptional measures in the hull construction, but with the help of Mr Bruynzeel's knowledge of glue technology, it was possible to work out an extremely strong method based on Laurent Giles' usual lightweight stringer construction but employing a multi-skin glued shell. Plywood, manufactured by the owner's company, was naturally used for the deck, and all other parts of the vessel were studied carefully so that maximum weight reduction could be made and many special measures were taken.

The design team worked together extremely well, Van de Stadt producing a very beautiful set of lines and John Illingworth applying his practical knowledge to the sail plan, mast and rig with, as results have shown, great success. Laurent Giles were able to devote their time and care to the design of the hull and to the general internal work, using their knowledge of light construction and their general experience working with vessels of this size.

In the circumstances it was of the greatest help to the project to have an owner of such great experience and knowledge, and much of the design of the yacht reflects his own ideas and views. Much credit also reflects on the personnel charged with the building of *Stormvogel* at Table Bay, South Africa. To build such a vessel and launch her on time in a yard unaccustomed to large yacht construction was indeed a great achievement.

After the briefest of trials at Cape Town, *Stormvogel* sailed for England on the 3rd May, 1961 with a ship's company of fourteen. She called at Ascension Island and the Azores and arrived at Dartmouth, England, on the 22nd June. In spite of predominantly light winds, the 7660 mile voyage was completed in a good time averaging a speed of 7.6 knots. Her high basic speed was proved time and time again, particularly by her records in the Fastnet and Dinard races.

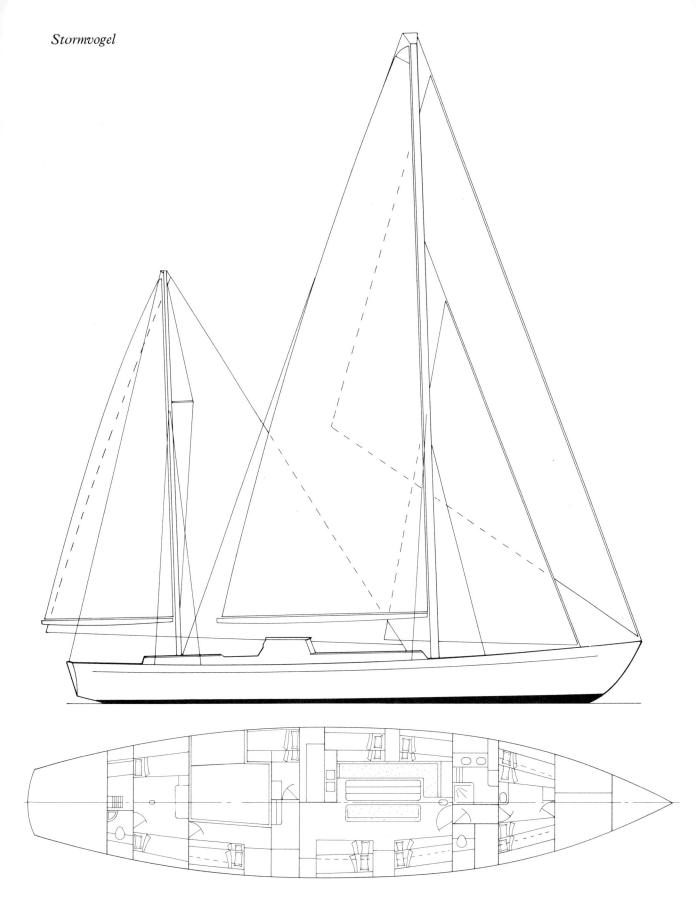

Stormvogel charging through the Solent in the 1961 Cowes Regatta

Tumbelina

Owner	Cartwright and Campbell
Builder	R.J. Prior and Son
Date Built	1960
Design No	371
L.O.A.	38 ft. 0 in. (11.59 m)
L.W.L.	28 ft. 0 in. (8.54 m)
Beam	9 ft. 9 in. (2.97 m)
Draft	6 ft. 6 in. (1.98 m)
Displacement	8.75 ton (8.89 tonnes)
Sail Area	690 sq. ft. (64.17 m²)
Rig	Bermudan Sloop

Tumbelina was designed as a cruiser racer under R.O.R.C. rules. Her hull was fairly standard for her day with moderate overhangs, relatively flat sheer line and high freeboard. For this design Giles chose a generous beam and maximum draft allowance, and surprisingly she was given a sharp toed keel, a detail that Giles liked but many other designers disagreed with. The advantage over a radius toe is that the ballast has a lower centre of gravity and is further forward where it is so often needed. Another convention that Giles did not follow was raking the rudder post to 45 degrees, and *Tumbelina* was given a more vertical rudder which improved her turning moment considerably.

Tumbelina was conventionally constructed with an oak and iroko centre line structure, with main transverse frames of laminated oak and intermediates of steam bent oak. Her decks were pine laid and her superstructure was of mahogany. Although *Tumbelina* had a generous displacement she had a ballast ratio of 55%, which was quite high, and this combined with the powerful hull allowed for a big fractional rig to be carried. The sail plan shows a big mainsail of modest aspect ratio and a small jumper strut foretriangle, a rig not normally associated with Jack Giles. The advantage of this rig is that it provides good performance when cruising without the need for an elaborate wardrobe of headsails.

Down below the accommodation was arranged for four people when cruising in comfort with two occasional berths for racing. There was plenty of stowage space for sails and equipment in the forepeak, the cockpit lockers and the roomy aft peak. In the cockpit *Tumbelina* had the choice of wheel or tiller steering, the latter which could be quickly fitted for those that preferred a tiller.

Tumbelina was regarded as a particularly handsome yacht on the water and was much admired.

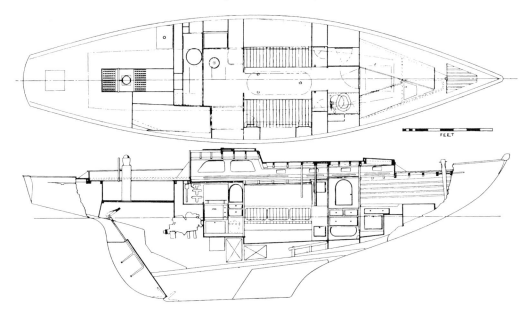

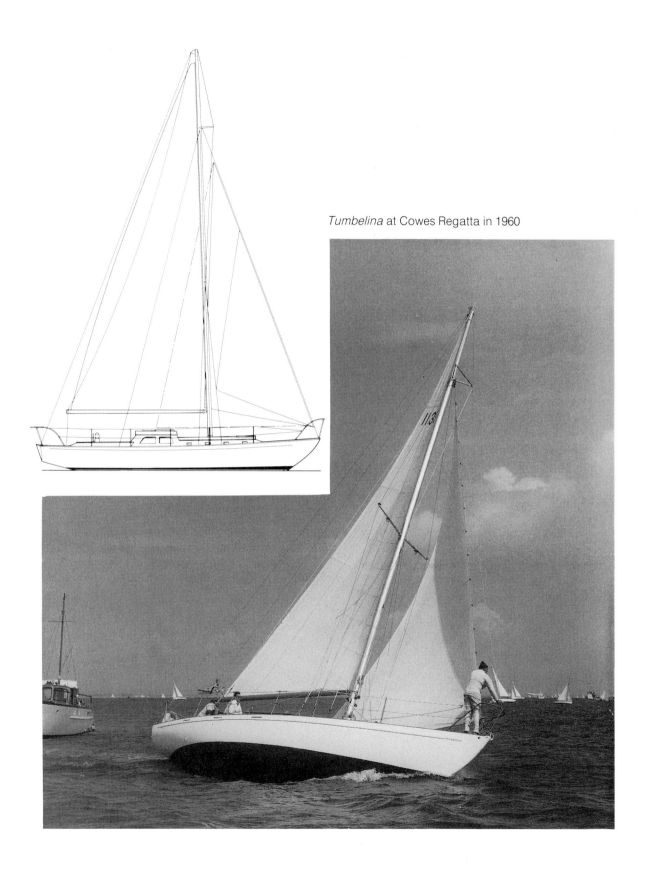

Tumbelina at Cowes Regatta in 1960

Audacity and the Audacity Class

Built for	News Chronicle
Builder	Walter Lawrence and Sons Ltd.
Date of Design	1959
Design No.	376
L.O.A.	21 ft. 5 in. (6.54 m)
L.W.L.	18 ft. 6 in. (5.64 m)
Beam	7 ft. 3 in. (2.21 m)
Draft	1 ft. 7 in. (0.47 m)
Displacement	1.6 ton (1.63 tonnes)
Sail Area	203 sq. ft. (18.88 m²)
Rig	Centre Board Sloop

The development and design of *Audacity* for the *News Chronicle* is best explained by Jack Giles himself, who gave a talk about the background of this class and its 'Evolution of Design' on 11th December, 1959. In his speech it is interesting to discover the history of *Audacity* and to appreciate his ideas and techniques of design, particularly as they are so closely associated with some of his previous designs which are outlined in this book.

'Yacht design is one of the arts of compromise; it is also an empirical art. That is to say that every design has drawn for inspiration on many accounts. Elements may come from larger yachts, from smaller yachts, from generally dissimilar yachts. In the following diagram is the *Audacity* family tree and the leaves growing on this tree are the multitude of boats which we shall see emerging from this factory. A little technicality please.

Sailing yachts are commonly divided into light and heavy displacement, according to whether the part in the water is slim or bulky. It is easy to see that *Audacity*, for all the bulkiness which has been necessary for the comfort of the occupants, is pretty slim in her underwater parts. In other words, we are looking at a yacht of the light displacement type. I have therefore taken for her roots only yachts of that type.

You will see that the main or "tap" root springs from a mere canoe, the reason for which I will come to later. On the left a root comes from *Wapipi* (1939), one of my first light displacement boats and a centre-boarder. That root joins a main root taking inspiration from dinghies in general. Also feeding into that main root is the first trailer-cruiser which we did, *Mousetrap* (1956), her root being itself fed by "trailers". *Mousetrap* is an important forebear of *Audacity*. On the other side of the tap root is *Myth of Malham* (1947), probably the first full blown light displacement ocean racer in the world to be built for the job. From the parentage of *Wapipi*, the dinghies and *Myth*, fertilised by *Theta* and her owner, came *Sopranino* (1950). She was followed by *Barchetta*, a similar but less specialised design, and like *Sopranino* and *Myth* a fixed keel boat. A little later came *L'aghulas*, a centre-boarder, and the world-circling *Trekka*.

All these four were virtually the same size, that is, around 20 foot in overall length. Finally came the proposition of the *News Chronicle* which first produced designs for a close successor to *Trekka*. This is where Walter Lawrence and Sons came into the picture. They supplied the final root for this tree in their great experience of wood-working, and in particular of building wooden aircraft fuselages, the Mosquito, the Hornet and the Vampire.

When Patrick Ellam first came to me he had been trying out the sea-going possibilities of what at first sight would appear to be the most unlikely boat he could find. This was an 18 ft. racing canoe. This in effect is three watertight boxes built into boat shape, the central one having a small foot-well and the centre-board. These craft have little beam and are kept upright by the crew sitting out to windward on hiking boards or hanging out on lines attached to the mast and known as trapezes. *Theta* was fitted with watertight hatches to the forward and after compartments so that clothes, food, and general gear could be carried safely and in the dry. In this craft Ellam cruised around the East coast, made the trip down the Channel to

Audacity number one commissioned by the *News Chronicle*

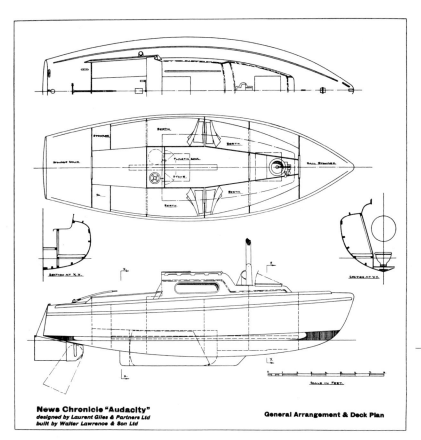

News Chronicle "Audacity"
*designed by Laurent Giles & Partners Ltd
built by Walter Lawrence & Son Ltd*

General Arrangement & Deck Plan

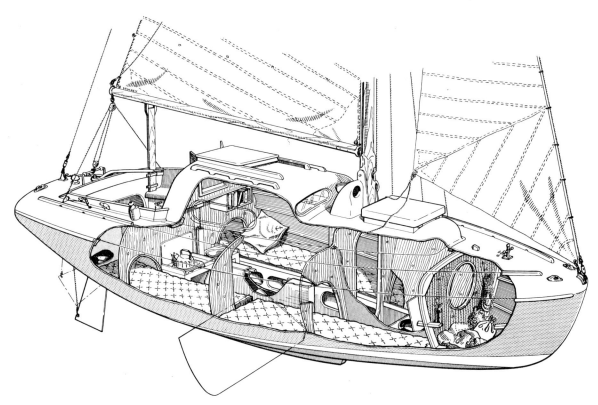

the Isle of Wight, and then crossed to and fro to France a number of times. Like most modern dinghies, *Theta* was unsinkable, and a capsize merely meant that she lay on her side in the water until with sheets eased and the crew on the centreboard she was pulled up again. I am speaking rather without the book, but I seem to remember Ellam reckoned that seven capsizes were about average for a Channel crossing. He seemed to thrive on that, but he found it a little difficult to get his crews to go again. Apart from the lack of accommodation of any sort or kind, and her propensity to capsize, *Theta* had shown herself able and fast.

Ellam therefore came to me with a sound knowledge of the worst possibilities, and very definite ideas of what he wanted. That was the nearest thing to *Theta* in sea-going characteristics and general sailing ability, but with some sort of living quarters and enough inherent stability to eliminate the capsizing habit, even if it still required the trapeze act to get her to windward at speed.

I drew my inspiration from the roots of *Wapipi*, from dinghies, and from *Myth*, threw them with Ellam's specifications into the saucepan, and cooked up *Sopranino*. When I did the design, coastwise cruising and racing was the declared purpose of the boat, but it soon came out that the broad Atlantic was in fact Ellam's Everest. With that in view he staged a try-out in the form of hanging on to the Ocean Racing fleet from Plymouth to Santander and back via La Baule, a trip which the little boat performed with the utmost success. The Atlantic venture was therefore on. The story is told in Ellam's book entitled, in this country, *Sopranino* and in the U.S.A., *Western Crossing*. The major crossing from the Canaries to Barbados was made in 28 and a half days, the second smallest yacht, and one of the fastest voyages irrespective of size recorded for the East-West southern crossing.

But "Soppers" was a specialist boat, and not to my way of thinking a suitable proposition for other Ellams, so I drew up a rather beamier version of which 21 have been built in this country and elsewhere. These we call the Barchettas. Then a client in East Africa wanted one especially for the shallow reefs and river bars of those parts, and we produced a semi-centreboard version, the board being entirely within the fin.

The next move was from John Guzzwell who wanted a strictly sea-going version to build himself. The response to this was *Trekka*. Guzzwell made a wonderful job of her and set off unknown to us for Hawaii, making a remarkable singlehanded trip from San Francisco. Most of you know enough to have no need of a detailed recitation of Guzzwell's circumnavigation, which has indeed been a remarkable performance, not for overall speed from departure to return, but for the consistently high speed of his passage between ports. The oceans of the world seem somehow to divide themselves into stages of about 3,000 miles, and 30 to 35 days seems to have been his regular time. John Guzzwell was Channel Island born, and so becomes the first British singlehanded circumnavigator, and *Trekka* the smallest yacht to have circled the globe.

For a while we worked along the lines of an only slightly modified *Trekka*, but market research and general considerations of the usage for which such a boat would be required caused us in the end to abandon the idea in favour of the centreboard type. It was felt that there would be a wider scope for the shallow draft in inland waters; that errors of navigation resulting in a wait for the tide to turn on a mudbank would be more happily survived at 20 than at 40 degrees of heel; that more often it would be possible to get over the side and push off; that beaching or landing for picnics would be easier. Furthermore, this boat will be an altogether simpler thing to handle off and onto a trailer and much better towing. We have probably sacrificed some performance to windward in a sea-way, but we feel that in general appeal that is less important than the other features which we have gained.'

A number of notable voyages have been made in Audacity Class yachts, including a trip to the Hebrides made by a young family in July 1962 in their boat called *Rona*.

Dhorus Mhor and the Dhorus Mhor Class

Owner	R.E.B. Sergent
Builder	Port Hamble
Design No.	397
Date Built	1961
L.O.A.	49 ft. 3 in. (15.02 m)
L.W.L.	38 ft. 0 in. (11.59 m)
Beam	12 ft. 6 in. (3.84 m)
Draft	6 ft. 6 in. (1.98 m)
Displacement	13.6 tons (13.82 tonnes)
Sail Area	949 sq. ft. (88.26 m²)
Rig	Ketch
Engine	60 h.p. Gardner Diesel

Laurent Giles had, by the end of the 1940s, gained a name for designing motor sailers and *Dhorus Mhor* was yet another successful class of this type. Her hull form was, and still is, unusual in having flair forward and a knuckle at the level of the thickened sheer strake. This would later be seen on the popular Salar Class and became something of a Laurent Giles trademark particularly on the Moody and Westerly production yachts. The hollow flair and knuckle made for a drier boat with a greater amount of reserve buoyancy. *Dhorus Mhor* and her sister ship *Franda* handled exceptionally well under sail with a fine degree of balance even when heavily pressed. The good manners of these boats were quite outstanding, and with the helm set amidships it was possible to steer them by simply adjusting their staysail sheets. Unlike many motor sailers the Dhorus Mhor Class boats were not sluggish under sail. This was due in part to a 33% ballast ratio and well thought out sail plan, intelligently and somewhat unusually derived from their previous ocean racing yacht designs. For example a Genoa, which initially was only used on inshore racing classes and which nearly doubled the working sail area when used with a mizzen staysail, was part of the normal suite of sails carried onboard.

Under motor *Dhorus Mhor* could achieve 8 knots from a 60 h.p. Gardner diesel engine driving a 4-bladed fixed propeller. It was partly due to the improved power-to-weight ratio, a result of the development of the then modern engine, that helped the motor sailers become better sailing boats. Also the size of the engine, for a given power, was much reduced and no longer required large engine compartments. This had a direct result on the internal accommodation, and allowed room for an internal passageway between the aft cabin and the saloon running alongside the engine compartment.

The Dhorus Mhor Class was an extremely attractive design and proved to be a popular yacht. Her sister, *September Moon*, the sixth of this class built, won the prestigious Lloyd's yacht trophy award for 1970. This is given to one yacht each year, built under Lloyd's survey, which is considered the best constructed and engineered.

The original *Dhorus Mhor* has had several owners in her time, one of whom, John Button, recently commissioned Laurent Giles Ltd to design a new 43 ft. yacht *Rapscallion*, a modern U.L.D.B. type described with her sister *Phantom* later in this book. Although designed by the same company it is hard to imagine two more widely differing designs than *Dhorus Mhor* and these new boats.

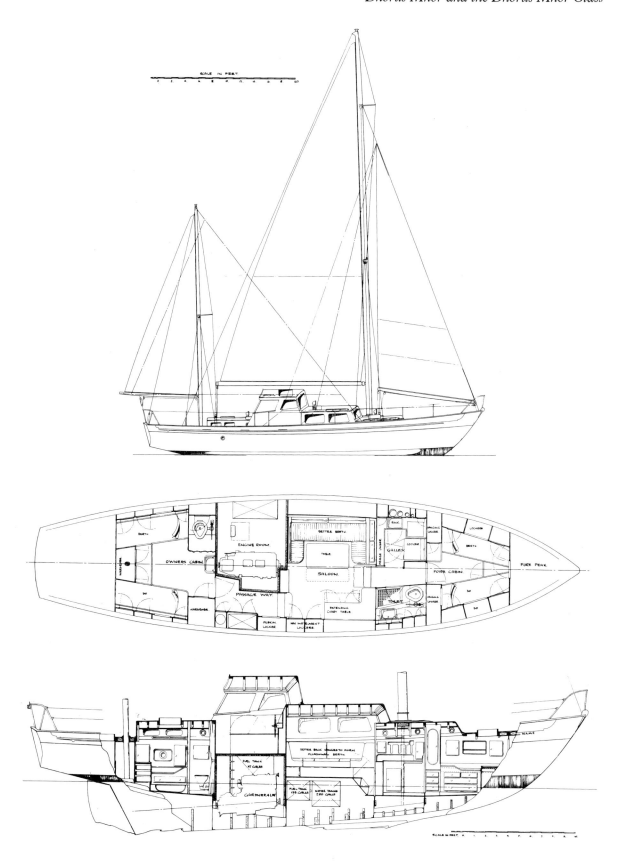

September Moon the sixth of the Dhorus Mhor Class and prestigious holder of the Lloyds Trophy showing her flair and knuckle

Blue Leopard

Owner	Mr Desmond Mollins
Builder	William Osbourne
Date Built	1962
Design No.	430
L.O.A.	111 ft. 9 in. (34.08 m)
L.W.L.	75 ft. 0 in. (22.88 m)
Beam	19 ft. 0 in. (5.8 m)
Draft	9 ft. 6 in. (2.9 m)
Displacement	47.8 tons (48.56 tonnes)
Sail Area	3500 sq. ft. (325.5m²)
Rig	Ketch

If you asked anyone who was knowledgeable about yachting to 'name three Laurent Giles designs' we would bet that *Blue Leopard* would be one of those named, since she is one of the most successful and beautiful boats ever built. *Yachting World* in 1963 wrote: 'She is without question the most successful combination of fully rigged sailing yacht, fast motor yacht and comfortable home afloat ever produced.'

The secret of *Blue Leopard* was her ultra-light displacement, the displacement length ratio being only 113. Her dimensions were much the same as the legendary 'J' class racing yachts, yet her displacement was only one-third of these yachts which were themselves not excessively heavy boats. Laurent Giles had had a great deal of experience in light displacement design and already to their credit had the famous *Myth of Malham*, *Gulvain* and *Stormvogel* to draw on. *Blue Leopard* was, however, to be the ultimate U.L.D.B. and most famous yacht he ever designed.

Blue Leopard was capable of sailing at 15 knots off the wind and 11 knots when going to windward in a Force 5. Under motor her two 380 h.p. Rolls Royce engines were powerful enough to drive her at a comfortable 15 knots. The high speeds attained were the result of an extremely efficient hull which was the product of careful tank testing. This being directly responsible for the creation of long overhangs and it was specifically the stern overhang which allowed *Blue Leopard* to achieve such high speeds, for as she trimmed by the stern, the counter became immersed and dramatically increased her waterline length.

Blue Leopard's light displacement was achieved by her excellently engineered scantlings and by keeping the volume of accommodation down to a comfortable level, something that is rarely seen these days. Vast weight reduction in the hull was obtained by a cold moulded construction method using four skins, glass sheathed, which were laid over the stringers and frames. Extensive use of aluminium alloy for floors and high stress areas helped reduce weight still further, and the decks were designed as a box sandwich construction without beams. Finally the coamings and superstructure minimised weight again employing the extensive use of aluminium alloy.

The ketch rig is considered more suitable for short-handed sailing and was used on *Blue Leopard* mainly for this reason. Unusual for the time were her head sails which were sheeted by hydraulic winches, a novel innovation for her day, but now common practice on any superyacht.

Blue Leopard was designed for Desmond Mollins who had previously commissioned *Star Sapphire*. So pleased was he with *Star Sapphire* that he requested Laurent Giles to design a larger yacht with the same concept but taken several evolutionary steps further. The resultant yacht speaks for herself as the owner kept her until his death in 1988. *Blue Leopard* was undoubtedly the most remarkable yacht of her generation and is still one of the most impressive sailing yachts afloat.

Blue Leopard

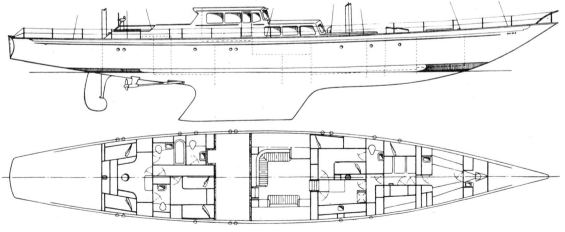

134

The magnificent *Blue Leopard* demonstrating how a small rig can power a light boat at high speed

Diadem of Dewlish

Owner	J.A. Boyden
Builder	Richards Ironworks, of Lowestoft
Date Built	1962
Design No.	431
L.O.A	95 ft. 9 in. (29.20 m)
L.W.L	89 ft. 0 in. (27.15 m)
Beam	21 ft. 6 in. (6.56 m)
Draft	8 ft. 10 in. (2.68 m)
Displacement	139 tons (141.22 tonnes)
Engines	Twin Gardner 8L3B diesels

Diadem of Dewlish, one of Laurent Giles' larger motor yachts, was designed with the role of tender to the 12-Metre yacht *Sovereign* specifically for her owner, Tony Boyden, to watch the *America*'s Cup race in 1962. The main requirement was for a comfortable seaworthy craft which would be able to cross the Atlantic and sail to Australia under her own steam. She also had to be manoeuvrable enough to allow her to obtain strategic positions during the 12-Metre races.

Although she had a fairly high superstructure this was designed with Giles's usual style and flair so that she was pleasing to the eye. She incorporated two unusual features in that she had a wide transom and a knuckle in the topsides forward. Both ideas were borrowed from trawler designs, the latter being practical as a spray deflector and in reducing the overall width at deck level, as well as breaking the vertical lines of the topsides, thus making them appear lower. This ability to reduce the apparent height of topsides and superstructures was one of many of Giles' skills and is well demonstrated on *Diadem*.

Since comfort was a main priority in her design, roll damping fin stabilizers were incorporated and proved most effective. The main engines were twin Gardner 8L3B diesels, each developing 230 b.h.p. at 1150 r.p.m. which drove 4ft. 6in. diameter propellers. A maximum speed of 11.7 knots was attained on trials, but under average cruising conditions speeds of 9.9 knots were usually recorded.

The accommodation on board *Diadem* comprises, on the lower deck, a crew mess and foc's'le with space enough for four, a sail room to carry the 12-Metre's sails, a galley and pantry. Behind these cabins was the owner's stateroom, bathroom and dressing room and aft of this the engine room. In addition, there were four good-sized cabins with a bathroom and separate toilet, with sufficient space for eight people. A notable feature of the design was the observation lounge immediately abaft the wheelhouse, which gave a comfortable sheltered position with all-round visibility for viewing the match racing.

Soon after trials were completed *Diadem* crossed the Atlantic Ocean in good time for the *America*'s Cup Series.

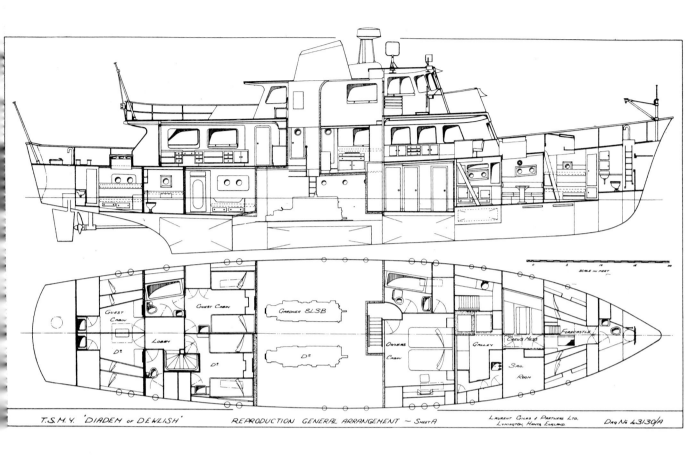

T.S.M.Y. 'DIADEM OF DEWLISH'   REPRODUCTION GENERAL ARRANGEMENT ~ Sheet A   Laurent Giles & Partners Ltd. Lymington, Hants, England.   Drg No 43130/A

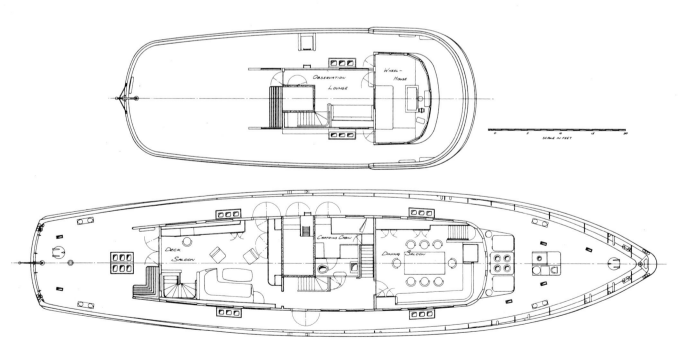

Treasure and the Treasure Class

Owner	J. Guzzwell
Builder	J. Guzzwell
Date Built	1962
Design No.	450
L.O.A.	46 ft. 3 in. (14.11 m)
L.W.L	33 ft. 9 in. (10.29 m)
Beam	12 ft. 0 in. (3.6 m)
Draft	7 ft. 0 in. (2.14 m)
Displacement	16.3 tons (16.56 tonnes)
Sail Area	1087 sq. ft. (101.09 m²)
Rig	Cutter

Treasure under sail

Treasure was designed for John Guzzwell as a much larger and more comfortable replacement for his much travelled *Trekka*. *Treasure* was over twice the length and twelve times the displacement of his former boat and incorporated many features learned from his great experience of ocean sailing. *Treasure*'s construction, which is laid out in detail in John Guzzwell's own book *Modern Wooden Yacht Construction*, was of a cold moulded hull comprising three skins, the inner two diagonal and the outer fore and aft, with longitudinal stringers and a minimum of transverse frames and bulkheads. The deck was a sandwich plywood construction with the upper surface cascover sheathed, which made for a more watertight surface. *Treasure* was built for practicality rather than for beauty, and her well protected cockpit and cuddy were considered an essential feature. She was cutter rigged to allow plenty of room for her wind-vane steering system, and the accommodation was only notable for its large central toilet compartment, the lack of berths in the saloon and its full-height engine room with work bench. Although unusual these were all very sensible considerations for extended cruising.

   Treasure was built in England and after completion was sailed by the owner's family to New Zealand, after which she undertook a round trip to Alaska. She has sailed extensively in the Pacific, her owner being exceptionally pleased with her performance, saying, 'she is an excellent little ship, ideal for a couple to handle, and all our passages have been made without a crew other than our two young sons.' John Guzzwell also built a sister vessel called *Sunrise* on the same principles as *Treasure*, using the cold moulded system, but with four layers of 5/16th diagonal veneer and then sheathed with epoxy resin and Dynel to make for a more water- tight vessel. Laurent Giles introduced this popular and seaworthy design into the company stock plans as the Treasure Class in 1963.

Today *Treasure* is in fine condition and is still sailed by her original owner in America.

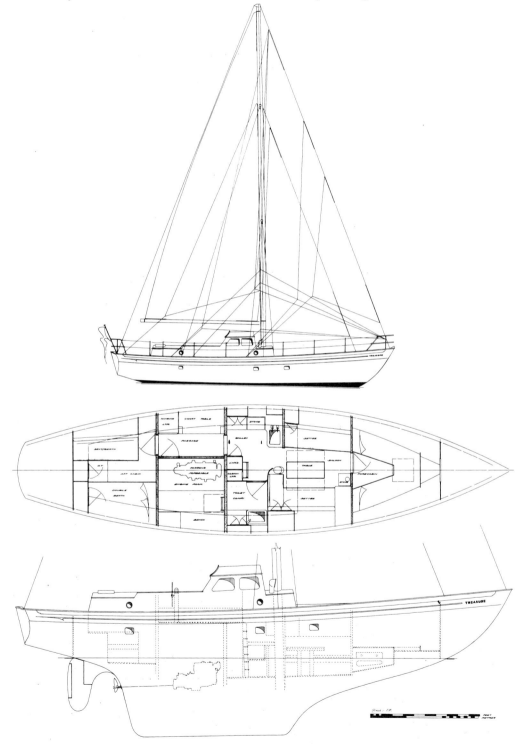

Rose Rambler and the Rose Rambler Class

Owner	Humphrey Barton
Builder	Porter and Haylett Ltd., Wroxham, Norfolk.
Date Built	1963
Design No.	452
L.O.A.	35 ft. 3 in. (10.75 m)
L.W.L	27 ft. 6 in. (8.39 m)
Beam	9 ft. 9 in. (2.97 m)
Draft	4 ft. 9 in. (1.45 m)
Displacement	8.1 tons (8.23 tonnes)
Sail Area	550 sq. ft. (51.15 m²)
Rig	Bermudan Sloop

Rose Rambler was designed by Laurent Giles as a home afloat for Humphrey Barton. The hull was based on a modification of *Great Days* and the measurements were roughly the same except that on this boat the L.O.A. was slightly larger at 35 ft. 3 in. and the draft was a little deeper at 4 ft. 9 in. *Rose Rambler* had a Bermudan slutter rig and carried 550 square feet of sail on a 43 ft. mast which was stepped in a socket on deck. Like her predecessor she was designed to be used for extensive cruising and sailed with a minimum of crew. The interior had a normal four-berth layout with well thought-out ventilation, and the foredeck hatch was hinged both ways to allow for maximum air circulation. Humphrey Barton had wanted everything on her to be as simple as possible so that she would be easy to handle with minimum crew.

Rose Rambler's maiden voyage began on 31st May, 1963, and finished in August 1964 when Humphrey Barton made a unique journey covering over 13,000 miles in fourteen months. It was almost a repeat of a previous voyage he had undertaken in *Rose of York* which took him, in May 1963, from Lowestoft to Rotterdam, Amsterdam, Belgium and up the Meuse. After journeying through the French canals, he sailed to Barcelona in Spain, Algeciras, Tangier, Casablanca, Agadir and on to Arreciffe in Lanzarote. Sailing between the Canary Islands he called into the ports of Santa Cruz, Las Palmas and Tenerife. In his third crossing of the Atlantic (the previous time being in his Laurent Giles Channel Class yacht *Rose of York*), he took 20 days to sail from the Canaries to Barbados. He then cruised throughout the Caribbean and continued on to Bermuda, arriving eventually in Miami in April 1964. He later took 35 days to cover 1200 miles to Cape May, travelling via the inland waterway, and during this journey decided to head for New York. At Newport he met C. Bruynzeel in his 74ft. Laurent Giles designed Bermudan ketch *Stormvogel*. From Rhode Island he continued on to Newfoundland then back across the Atlantic to the Isle of Wight. During a period of 14 months *Rose Rambler* had covered 13,146 miles, having visited 182 ports of call and returned in excellent order.

So successful was the design and so suitable was the yacht as an easy-to-handle family boat that it was developed into the Rose Rambler Class. *Rose Rambler* is still in good condition and is currently based on the River Orwell on England's East coast.

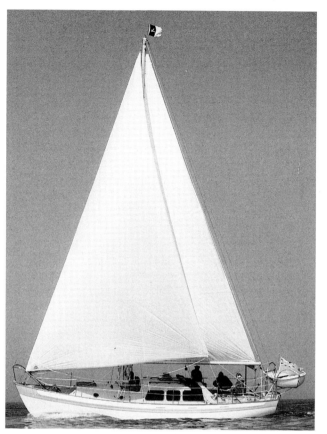

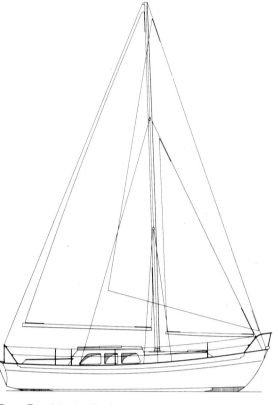

Rose Rambler the first of the successful Rose Rambler Class

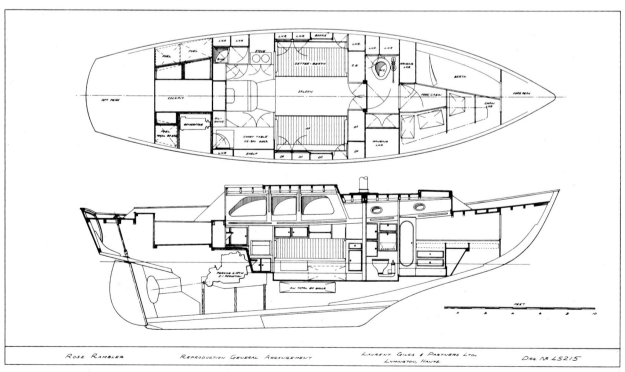

ROSE RAMBLER   REPRODUCTION GENERAL ARRANGEMENT   LAURENT GILES & PARTNERS LTD. LYMINGTON, HANTS.   DRG. Nº L5215

Aetea

Builder	Richards (Shipbuilding) Ltd.
Date Built	1964
Design No.	469
L.O.A.	105 ft. 1 in. (32.03 m)
L.W.L.	96 ft. 0 in. (29.28 m)
Beam	21 ft. 8 in. (6.62 m)
Draft	8 ft. 0 in. (2.44 m)
Displacement	185 tons (187.96 tonnes)
Engines	2 Gardner diesels

The owners' requirements for this vessel were somewhat unusual since they wanted a boat which would house two families and a total of seven people including children. One of the most important requirements was for a playroom on the lower decks, and the sleeping accommodation was arranged so that three large cabins and one small twin cabin were all grouped in the aft of the vessel around several bathrooms and W.C.s. The arrangement of the deck-level accommodation was also unusual since there was a large, lavish, main saloon which also acted as a dining saloon. The smoking room was intended to serve mainly as a sitting room but could also be used as a dining room when entertaining a large number of guests.

Space was available for a crew of six and was arranged in the forward section of the boat. This comprised two single cabins and a foc's'le for four people being grouped around the mess and was close to the galley. Since the yacht was designed for service in the Eastern Mediterranean, it carried an elaborate air conditioning system throughout the lower decks. There was also 30 cubic feet of cold storage and a cold cabinet in the deck saloon.

The yacht was designed for a moderate speed of 12 knots, and as an easy motion was particularly required, Vosper roll-damping fins were fitted. Much attention was applied to the design of the superstructure and hull shape so that a balance could be achieved between the length and height of the vessel. Giles was successful in reducing the apparent height of the superstructure and producing a very pleasing profile. This he managed by placing the stanchions, which support the upper deck, in a straight line with the superstructure and not at the rakish and rather strident angle used on similar boats of the same period, which draws needless attention to the height of the deckhouse.

Aetea's hull was lengthened in 1974 when an additional 6 ft. was added to the aft end. A cabin behind the wheelhouse was also added and the boat deck was extended. In 1986 she was extensively refitted and magnificently redecorated, and renamed *Lady Hoo* by her new owners Draycott Marine Ltd. Today she is operating as a luxury charter boat in the Mediterranean.

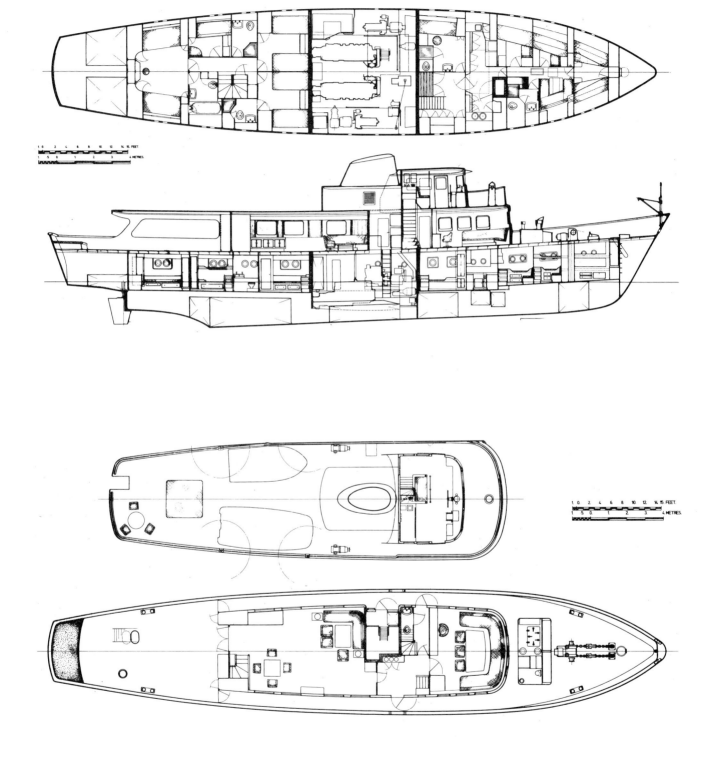

Photo left: *Aetea* after her extensive re-fit

Lamadine

Owner	J. Frye
Builder	Camper and Nicholson
Date Built	1967
Design No.	98
L.O.A.	97 ft. 0 in. (29.59 m)
L.W.L.	68 ft. 0 in. (20.74 m)
Beam	17 ft. 5 in. (5.34 m)
Draft	9 ft. 3 in. (2.82 m)
Displacement	48.3 tons (49.07 tonnes)
Sail Area	2502 sq. ft. (232.69 m²)
Rig	Ketch

Lamadine was designed to the same philosophy as *Blue Leopard* as a lightweight, full-powered motor sailing yacht. Since the owner planned to use her as a world cruising boat, she was designed with a slightly higher displacement/length ratio. She had a range of 2,000 miles under power at an average speed of 10 knots, the engines were twin, light alloy G.M. diesels which could each develop 200 b.h.p. so that a total of 400 b.h.p. was available. Her hull, which was developed from previous Giles's masterpieces such as *Star Sapphire* and *Blue Leopard*, was long and graceful and allowed her to achieve very high speeds. During her trials she reached a maximum of 12 knots under power and showed promise of speeds in excess of this under sail, and in the right conditions has exceeded 15 knots.

The hull was a multi-stringer construction and the shell was made up of four skins glued together and each independently fastened. The centreline reinforcement was made of light alloy together with the whole of the deck and superstructure. The mast step, floors, engine bed and all house coamings were also made of lightweight alloy, and both the deck and the tops of the coachroof consisted of a ply/foam sandwich, which helped to reduce the weight significantly. The shape of the hull was very pleasant having long ends and a pretty looking bow. Under the water *Lamadine* had a fin keel of small lateral area compared with the large area of the balanced rudder. This huge rudder was placed in the best possible position, vertically at the extreme end of the waterline. This arrangement allowed for an extremely efficient engine installation as well as making the boat easier to steer when driven under full power.

On deck the whole emphasis was on ease of handling, with the main windlass being used for hoisting sails and the power capstan for handling the sheets of the large headsails. She had two helm positions, one within the wheelhouse and the other at the after end of the cockpit. On deck the accommodation was arranged so that there was a sizeable area for sunbathing, forward of which was the cockpit. This was fitted out as a cocktail and dining area with access down to the main dining room where there was ample space for six people. Situated on the lower deck was the owners' twin-bedded stateroom with private bathroom. To port there was a twin guest room with wash basin, and to starboard another twin cabin together with a shower room, W.C. and wash basin. In the forward area was a large galley, a foc's'le for four crew members and a separate cabin for the engineer. The engine room, which was placed below the deck saloon, was very generous in size, making it not only easy to work in but also to maintain. The interior of the ship was very luxurious and the joinery being of high quality teak veneer. The galley was exceptionally large, having more space and boasting better fittings than kitchens in many houses of the day.

Since her launch *Lamadine* has cruised extensively in the Mediterranean. She has recently been refitted and now carries a stowaway rig and has satellite communications equipment installed.

A one thirty second scale model of *Lamadine* displaying her fine hull shape

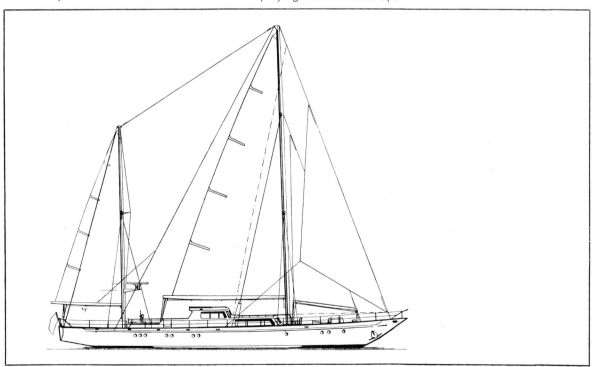

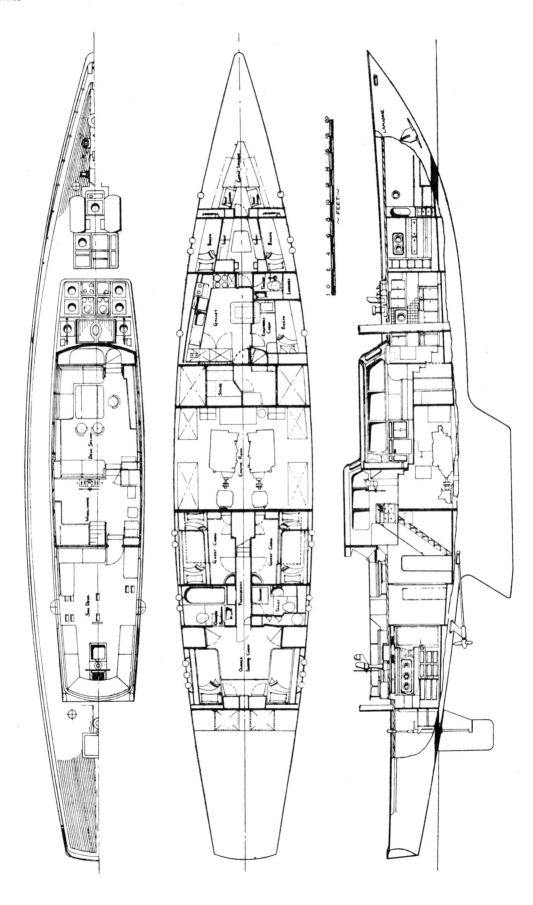

Salmo Salar Class

Built for	Saltons Yacht Agency
Builder	Essex Yacht Builders Ltd.
Date	1965
Design No.	522
L.O.A.	39 ft. 0 in. (11.9 m)
L.W.L.	31 ft. 0 in. (9.46 m)
Beam	11 ft. 3 in. (3.43 m)
Draft	5 ft. 3 in. (1.60 m)
Displacement	10.4 tons (10.57 tonnes)
Rig	Sloop or Ketch
Sail Area	S = 670 sq ft. (62.31 m²)
	K = 642 sq ft. (59.71 m²)

The Salmo Salar was designed to be a family pleasure yacht for sailing within the rugged waters around Britain. Initially the design was drawn for a wooden version; however, using the most up-to-date materials and techniques of the day, a glass-fibre boat was also offered. The name chosen for these boats, Salmo Salar, was derived from the name of the Atlantic Salmon, one of the finest of all deep water fish. The resultant design was also very fine and was admired by many yachtsmen. Having been entered into a *Yachting World* competition, one of the judges said that the Salmo Salar 'was the standard of what a gentleman's yachting is all about.' Her attractive appearance together with her robustness yet elegance gave her 'an almost queenly motion,' as stated in a *Yachting World* report of her at the time.

The Salar really fitted the description of a motor sailer since she had more spacious accommodation, greater initial stability and an engine of above average power. As a basic family boat there was plenty of room for six people, and the interior was arranged in three separate compartments with two occasional berths in the cockpit. A remarkable feature for her size was that she had two toilet heads, one in the fore and one in the aft cabin.

The cockpit comprised the centre compartment and contained all the sheets and engine controls which were arranged for easy handling. The engine was placed below the central cockpit, thus allowing it to be reached quickly, for easy maintenance and keeping noise to an absolute minimum in the living quarters. Two types of rig were offered, a ketch or sloop, the latter being preferred by most people. The Salar was to become a very popular family motor sailer, and in 1966 a complete all-wood Salar cost just £15,500 and the fibreglass version £11,500.

A number of adventurous journeys have been made in Salar's, but one in particular was that made by Robin Collins and his wife in *Wild Wing*. In 1971 they cruised over 2000 miles from the south coast of England to Malta in the Mediterranean in under eight weeks, and during their voyage they encountered severe gale conditions in the Bay of Biscay. Robin Collins commented that they found having a good motor sailer with the capabilities of both a motor boat and yacht extremely beneficial in such conditions. He also said that he 'found her a comfortable family cruiser, but was a very slippery boat which could show her heels not only to other motor sailers, but even to many so-called cruiser racers of a similar size.' One of the reasons for her good speed was her big rig, but her real secret, as Robin pointed out, 'seems to lie in the sweet lines of her hull. No concessions to her motor sailer role have been made below the waterline. She is a sailing yacht with a fine entry, adequate draft, a small propeller aperture and a smooth run aft.' After two years in the Mediterranean, Robin decided to continue and to cross the Atlantic and head for the West Indies. On arriving in Gibraltar he met Humphrey Barton in *Rose Rambler* and together these two Giles designs were moored stern to stern. Taking this opportunity he asked Humphrey Barton's advice about his planned trans-Atlantic crossing, as Barton had at that time crossed the Atlantic seventeen times. In February 1972, Robin and his wife arrived in Antigua and then continued to cruise the Caribbean. At the end of March they then set sail for Bermuda, finally returning home via the Bay of Biscay arriving in June 1972. Perhaps the most pleasing remark made about the Salar by Robin was that 'after two Atlantic crossings and over 8000 miles of sailing in the Mediterranean, if we started again knowing what we know now, we should pick exactly the same vessel.'

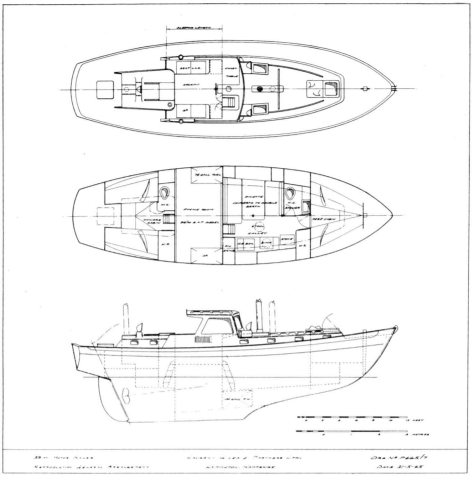

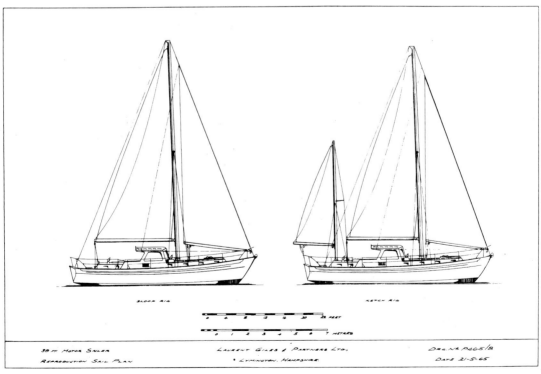

White Gull

Builder	Benetti Franelli of Viareggio
Date Built	1983
Design No.	816
L.O.A.	154 ft. 0 in. (46.97 m)
L.W.L	128 ft. 0 in. (39.04 m)
Beam	30 ft. 0 in. (9.15 m)
Draft C/B up	13 ft. 0 in. (3.97 m)
Displacement	370.0 tons (375.92 tonnes)
Sail area	11500 sq. ft. (1069.5 m²)
Rig	Staysail Schooner

White Gull like *Blue Leopard* can be called a 100/100 motor sailer, but the similarity stops there, for *White Gull* had a large amount of accommodation to the highest standards of luxury and a very full specification with little concession to weight saving. Her hull was made of steel and her superstructure was of aluminium alloy constructed to the Bureau Veritas Plus I 3/3 yacht rules. Her two 520 h.p. main engines were each connected to four-bladed variable pitch propellers which enabled the boat to cruise at 13.5 knots under power. With a total tank capacity of 9300 U.S. gallons she had an impressive cruising range. Under sail she was equally impressive, with her massive staysail schooner rig with its large wardrobe of sails which was balanced underwater by a hydraulically driven centre board that increased the draft by 7 feet when extended. All of her electrical requirements were provided by three 80 kilowatt generators.

The accommodation was laid out on three decks. On the lower deck there were living quarters for eight crew members arranged in three cabins, each with its own adjoining toilet and two separate showers. There was also a crew's mess and space for ten people as well as a large galley, cold storage room, laundry room and the housekeeper's cabin with adjoining bathroom. The domestic equipment, particularly in the kitchen, rivals that of a good hotel having two dishwashers and two washing machines. After the engine room there were three guest cabins with adjoining bathrooms which comprised a bath, wash basin, bidet and toilet. On the main deck was the owner's double stateroom complete with an ensuite bathroom and separate ensuite toilet. Behind this was the steward's pantry connected to the galley via a dumb waiter. This was immediately forward of the large dining room which adjoined the main saloon. Aft of the saloon was a sheltered cockpit which led onto the vast open deck. The wheelhouse with a navigation and radio office was situated on the upper deck, as was the captain's cabin which included an adjoining bathroom. The flying bridge with sheltered sun deck was located behind these cabins.

All of the decks were teak laid in best yacht fashion and for security the walkways were monitored by video cameras. She carried a wide variety of navigation equipment, too numerous to mention, and among her many luxuries was a 20 ft. tender with a 220 h.p. Mercruiser engine which could be launched by a single arm hydraulic davit.

White Gull was sold by her original owner in 1987 when she was re-rigged using a stowaway mast-sail system prior to being sailed around the world.

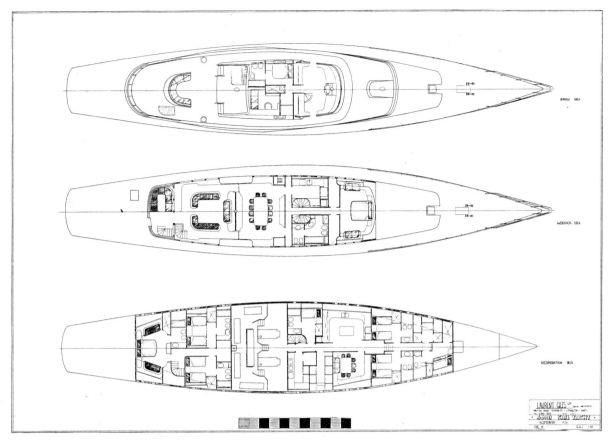

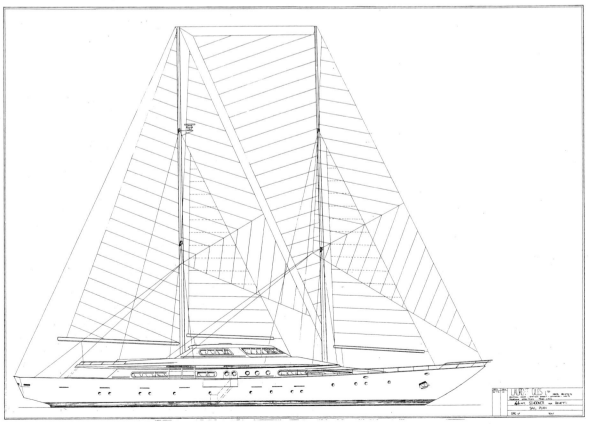

Chapter 5

Production Boats (1962–1982)

Glass Fibre and the Advent of Mass Produced Boats

The development of glass reinforced plastic (G.R.P.) during the post-war years, created new opportunities for boat builders and designers and they were quick to accept the potential of this new building material. The advantages in using G.R.P. in the early days seemed endless since it has many beneficial qualities for sailing boats. For example, it is a very cost effective material being extremely tough and durable, it is rarely affected by changes in temperature or climate which makes it ideal for boats sailing in all parts of the world, and it is light in weight which makes it particularly useful. The methods used in G.R.P. construction mean that fewer inherent leaks occur and in general maintenance costs are lower. Not only this, G.R.P. boats are completely impervious to all marine borers and there are few corrosion problems with this material.

In one-design class racing yachts G.R.P. comes into its own. The use of an accurately manufactured mould ensures a precise hull form which does not require later measurements to be made prior to racing. Also, the weight of the boat can be controlled within close limits and will not change with subsequent soakage, as happens with timber. A further advantage is that the hull has a very smooth finish and therefore superb racing qualities. Perhaps the greatest advantage of G.R.P. boats is that they can be built faster than a boat in any other material using semi-skilled or unskilled labour, thus keeping the costs to a minimum.

The introduction of G.R.P. called for a different approach to design and construction techniques since a production boat is not designed to the requirements of a particular owner but for mass appeal. Some variety and choice has to be provided and maybe offered in the form of different keel configurations, deck mouldings or interiors on the same hull. To a designer, the creation of a mass production boat is quite a difficult problem since he must produce a boat with instant appeal for a wide range of people who have different reasons for buying a boat. Since the internal accommodation is one of the most important factors, and there is only so much that can be placed inside a boat of a particular size, the designer must use his skill and judgement to arrange the interior in the most effective and ergonomic manner. It is perhaps the interior of a production boat which is its most important selling point.

The sixties were a pioneering period as people tried different designs and construction methods, the result sometimes ending in disaster. Laurent Giles, however, was on the production boat scene at an early stage and produced the successful Scimitar one-design day boat in 1962. They then went from strength to strength during the sixties and seventies designing a multitude of production boats for a number of boat building companies which are listed in this chapter. As there were often many variations and updates on a particular hull design, which were given separate model names by their builders, the list may not appear to be complete. A small selection of seven of these distinguished production boats are discussed in detail.

Laurent Giles Designed Production Boats

Production boats designed by Laurent Giles since 1960. The boats are listed under the boatbuilders' names and are ordered chronologically relative to the company's design number.

Westerly Boats

576 Centaur
591 Pageant
600 Jouster
603 Longbow
606 Fastnet 27
610 Warwick
629 Conway
635 Renown/Pentland
662 GK 24
683 Westerley 33
738 Westerley 34
726 Giles 38
760 GK 34 (not built)
761 Konsort
795 GK 29

Moody Boats

575 Carbineer 44
622 Moody 44
637 Carbineer 46
701 Moody 66
762 Moody 48
799 Grenadier 134
805 Grenadier 183
810 Moody 52
821 Moody 146

Seamaster Boats

589 Seamaster 23
611 Seamaster 19

Other Boats

455 Saro Scimitar
646 Buccaneer
650 Aquamarine 40
702 Bowman 40
731 Starlight
733 Azimut 42
783 Benetti 19
792 Benetti 16
817 Bucklers Hard 46

Saro Scimitar

Designed for	SARO, Anglesey Ltd
Date Designed	1962
Design No.	455
L.O.A.	20 ft. 3 in. (6.18 m)
L.W.L.	16 ft. 0 in. (4.88 m)
Beam	6 ft. 0 in. (1.83 m)
Draft	3 ft. 0 in. (0.92 m)
Displacement	1.075 tons (1.09 tonnes)
Sail area	190 sq. ft. (17.67 m²)
Rig	Bermudan Sloop

The *Saro Scimitar* was the first of a long line of G.R.P. production boats designed by Laurent Giles. The company was commissioned in 1962 by Saunders Roe (SARO) to design a dayboat of about 20 ft. overall which would be suitable for one-design class racing as well as family sailing. It was to be made almost entirely of reinforced polyester resin as a three-piece moulding so that the hull, deck and keel could be bolted together. Shown at the London Boat Show in 1962, the Saro Scimitar was then one of the very few new 'day-boat' designs and quite a lot of interest was shown in her. The special qualities of this design lay in the fact that the boat could be easily transported by towing it behind a car on a trailer. Also, the three-part construction meant that they could easily be assembled by keen amateur boat builders and an optional hardtop cover allowed her to be used as a weekend cruiser.

Laurent Giles took the project very seriously spending a great deal of time and effort on her design, even tank testing a model hull at the Saunders Roe Fluid Dynamics Laboratories at Cowes. The resultant boat was considered to be perfect for teaching, fleet hiring, day sailing, for club ownership and even for racing. The *Scimitar* proved to be very popular not only in the U.K. but also overseas, and since they were intended for a worldwide market their three-part moulding had been designed to make them easy to transport.

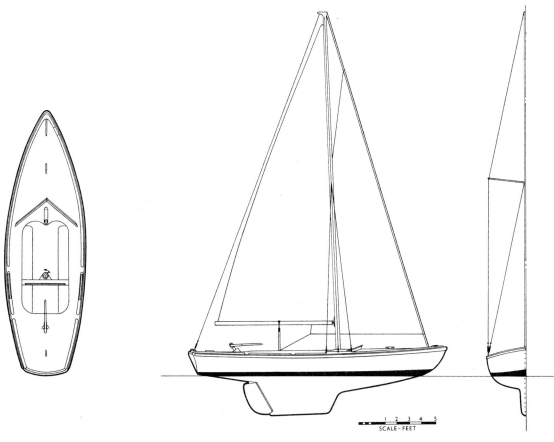

SCALE – FEET

The first Laurent Giles designed GRP production boat Saro Scimitar

Moody Carbineer 44

Designed for	A.H. Moody and Son Ltd.
Date Designed	1968
Design No.	575
L.O.A.	44 ft. 0 in. (13.42 m)
L.W.L.	36 ft. 0 in. (10.98 m)
Beam	12 ft. 2 in. (3.72 m)
Draft	6 ft. 0 in. (1.83 m)
Displacement	16.0 tons (16.26 tonnes)
Sail area	650 sq. ft. (60.45 m²)
Rig	Bermudan Ketch

The Carbineer 44 was designed for Moodys, who saw a demand for a motor sailer with good sailing performance and comfortable accommodation that would be equally suited to Northern Europe as well as hotter climates. It is not surprising that they commissioned Laurent Giles to design this boat since their reputation for motor sailers had become worldwide.

To provide adequate accommodation a high volume hull was required which dictated the use of short overhangs with a full transom complemented by a rounded bow with slight flair. The fin keel was made long and provided good directional stability whilst keeping the draft to a minimum. Three interior options were available in the accommodation catering for up to six people in three cabins with permanent berths. The aft cabin had its own ensuite shower and toilet compartment while the two forward cabins shared similar facilities. The position of the galley was designed either to be down on the same level as the forward accommodation or it could be positioned in the raised saloon. The raised saloon was the main feature of the boat, being teak clad both internally, and externally, providing good all round visibility from inside as well as plenty of room to lounge in. In fact there was enough room for a proper internal helm position to also be included. The saloon was situated only a few steps below the aft deck with a large self-draining cockpit with a pedestal steering position. This cockpit when fitted with canvas dodgers around the taffrail provided a sheltered and secure haven for the crew when in rough seas, or a private area for sun-bathing when the weather permitted.

Externally the timber cladding of the saloon, the timber taffrail, bulwark capping, hatches and grabrails helped, not only to reduce the apparent height and improve the aesthetics of the boat, but gave her a more traditional feel than many production G.R.P. boats. Under sail she was docile and well balanced and in a Force 4 to 5 with the number one jib, main and mizzen, she proved to be a stiff yacht who could keep her decks dry. Any fear of being under-canvassed in light airs could be overcome by the use of a Genoa and mizzen staysail which effectively doubled the sail area.

The Carbineer 44 proved to be very successful and a lengthened version was later introduced, called the Carbineer 46. This was also to become a popular design.

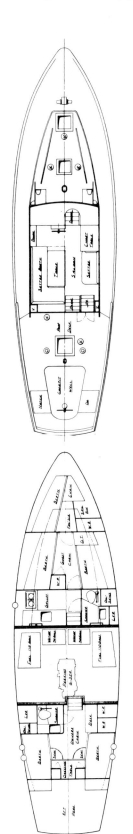

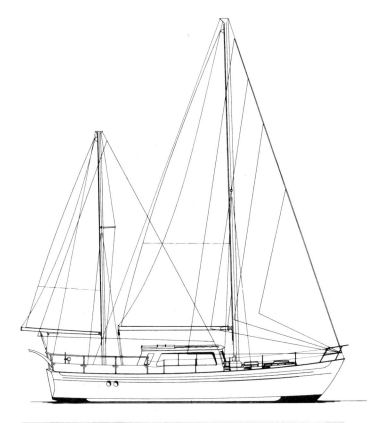

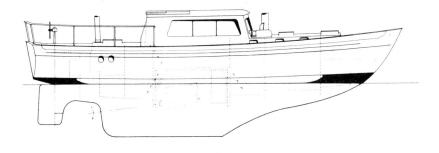

Westerly Centaur

Designed for	Westerly Marine
Date Designed	1968
Design No.	576
L.O.A.	26 ft. 0 in. (7.93 m)
L.W.L.	21 ft. 4 in. (6.53 m)
Beam	8 ft. 5 in. (2.58 m)
Draft	3 ft. 0 in. (0.92 m)
Displacement	2.8 tons (2.84 tonnes)
Sail area	294 sq. ft. (27.34 m²)
Rig	Sloop

The Centaur is of particular interest not only because of her tremendous popularity, approximately 2,500 have been built over the years, but also because of her many innovations. The Centaur was designed from the start as a bilge keeler. Laurent Giles had, over the years, conducted much research and tank testing with bilge keels and decided to tank test the Centaur at Southampton University's Woolfson Unit. This is thought to be the first time such work had been undertaken on a production boat. Her hull was beamy with a low knuckle forward to improve interior volume, a characteristic which was to become a virtual trademark of Laurent Giles designed Westerlys. The knuckle helped to disguise her high freeboard and the bilge keels were handed port and starboard with a 2 degree toe-in. She started production with a spade rudder although later the rudder and the keels were to be modified to reduce production costs.

The Centaur came with a range of interior layouts, and later a range of rig and keel configurations sporting the name Pembroke as a fin keel variant and Chieftain as an aft cabin version. Most, however, were sold as Centaurs. The variety of options was to be another first for this range.

The accommodation was arranged in two cabins with the usual V-berth cabin forward being separated from the main cabin by the head and hanging locker. One of the first production boats to take advantage of G.R.P. mouldings for the interior, providing bright easy-clean surfaces, this together with the large saloon windows provided a much lighter interior.

Originally designed with a small engine, she soon had a 23 h.p. diesel which was much larger than necessary and gave her a name as a motor sailer, though in fact she sails nicely with a good turn of speed and points well. Her deep cockpit and good shelter, provided by the coachroof, makes for a secure feeling when sailing this rugged and surprisingly comfortable little yacht. During the seventies the *Centaur* was responsible for introducing more people to cruising than possibly any other yacht.

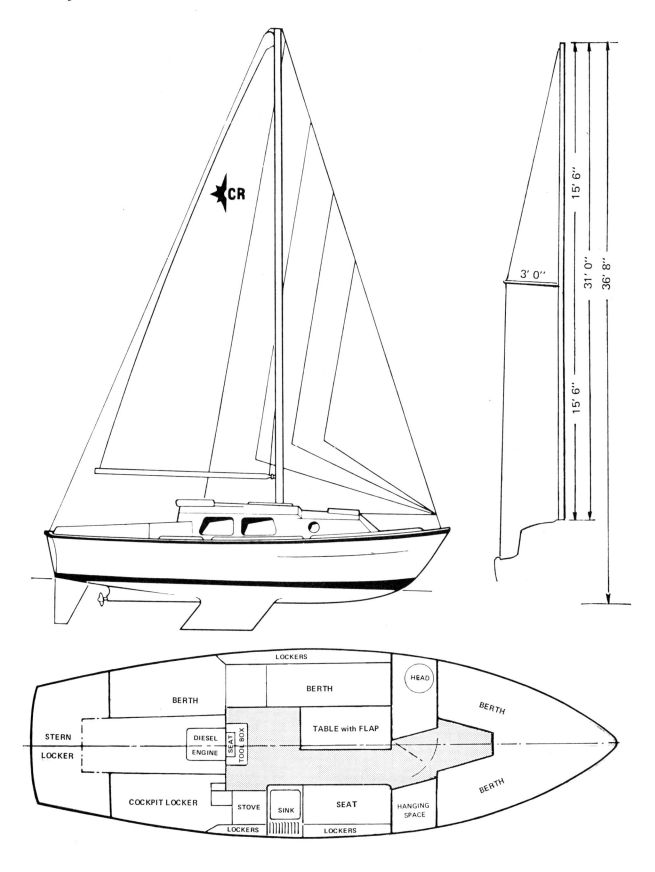

One of the most prolific yachts, the Westerley Centaur

Seamaster Sailer 23

Designed for	Seamaster Ltd.
Date Designed	1971
Design No.	589
L.O.A.	23 ft. 0 in. (7.02 m)
L.W.L.	19 ft. 9 in. (6.02 m)
Beam	8 ft. 3 in. 2.52 m)
Draft	2 ft. 6 in. (0.76 m)
Displacement	2.21 tons (2.25 tonnes)
Sail area	250 sq. ft. (23.25 m²)
Rig	Bermudan Sloop

The boat building firm Seamaster Ltd had been a well established firm producing motor cruisers, but in 1971 decided to change tack and commissioned Laurent Giles to design a new 23 ft. production yacht. This was to be a very interesting assignment since this new boat's main rival would be the Westerly Pageant which had also been designed by Laurent Giles. A shallow draft was considered to be an important factor and was always in demand since it eased the launching of the boat from a trailer and allowed for sailing within shallow waters. The designers minimised the draft by using bilge keels on the Pageant but elected for a centre board on the Seamaster Sailer 23. This centre board was totally enclosed inside a shallow keel, which had two advantages: firstly the centre board did not intrude into the accommodation and the yacht could still beat to windward with the board up, and secondly, the centre board, an uncommon feature in production boats at that time, gave a performance edge to the Sailer 23 that the Pageant could not match. By comparison, the Pageant had a draft of 2 ft. 10 in. and the Sailer 23 with its board up, reduced the draft by a further 4 inches, and with the board down increased the draft to 5ft. 6 in. The added lift produced by the centre board when down helped give the Sailer a sparkling performance whilst remaining well mannered.

Perhaps the hardest part of designing a cruising boat of this size is to arrange the accommodation in such a way that the exterior of the boat does not look out of proportion. Excessive freeboard and high cabin tops can often be the result. Laurent Giles achieved a good proportion and style by raising the deck forward of the cockpit to the same height as the cockpit coaming whilst maintaining a single sheerline and by utilising a stepped coachroof. Inside this 23 ft. envelop Laurent Giles fitted five berths in two separate cabins, a separate W.C. compartment, a hanging locker, galley, an inboard engine and a 6-foot long cockpit.

The Sailer 23 received very favourable reviews from the yachting press who had not expected such a good sailing yacht from a company renowned for building motor boats. Part of her success was due to the tremendous attention to detail which came, not only from the designers, but also from the yard who built a prototype and incorporated many ideas learnt from their production motor boats. Another reason for her acceptability was the high standard of equipment and fittings that came as standard on the boat. *Yachting Monthly* in 1972 said of her: 'The Sailer 23 is a comfortable, well balanced and well behaved little boat with a pocketful of good points and advantages.' Following the success of the Sailer 23, Laurent Giles was soon asked to design a smaller version, the Seamaster Sailer 19.

The popular Seamaster Sailer 23

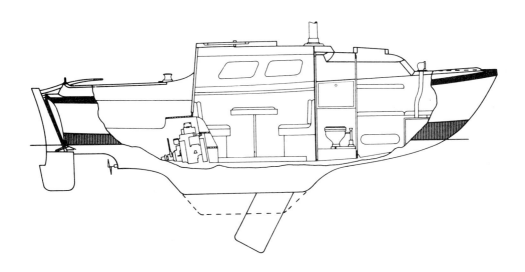

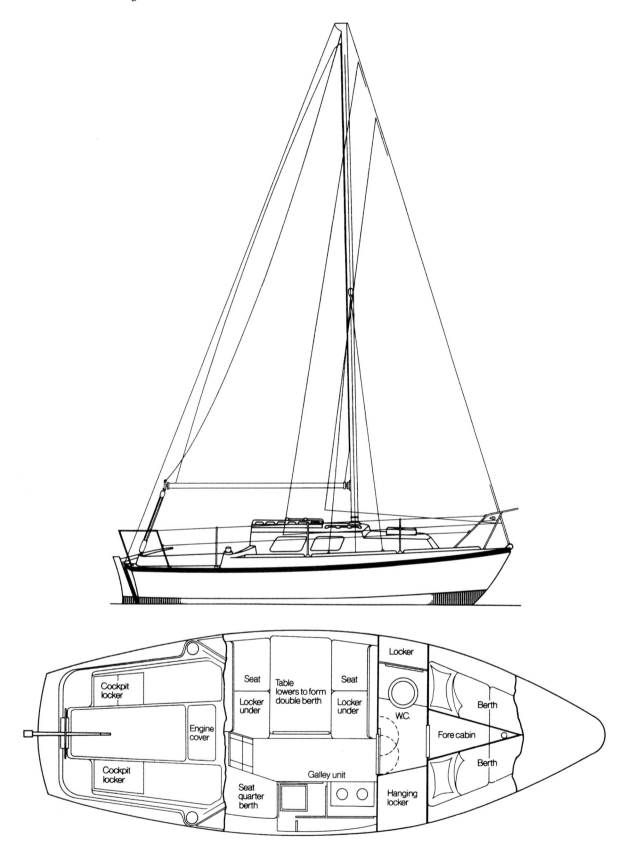

Cockpit locker

Cockpit locker

Engine cover

Seat

Table lowers to form double berth

Seat

Locker under

Locker under

Locker

W.C.

Berth

Fore cabin

Berth

Seat quarter berth

Galley unit

Hanging locker

Westerly GK24

Designed for	Westerly Marine
Date Designed	1974
Design No.	662
L.O.A.	24 ft. 0 in. (7.32 m)
L.W.L	19 ft. 7 in. (5.96 m)
Beam	9 ft. 3 in. (2.82 m)
Draft	5 ft. 0 in. (1.53 m)
Displacement	1.6 tons (1.63 tonnes)
Sail area	221 sq. ft. (20.55 m²)
Rig	Bermudan Sloop
I.O.R. Rating	18 ft. 0 in

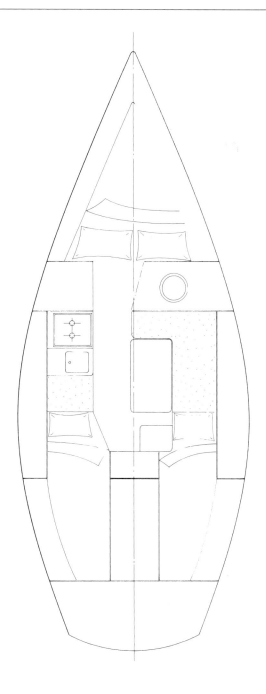

Westerly Marine were well known for their solid cruising boats and it caused a certain amount of surprise that they asked Laurent Giles to design an uncompromising I.O.R. racing yacht. The prototype *Ebblake IV* proved to be successful in races over the following two years and from this yacht the final version, GK24, was developed using all the information gained over two seasons campaigning with *Ebblake IV*. The GK24, was designed to be a sailing yacht, but with a performance good enough to attract the attention of the racing enthusiast and at a price that would make it accessible to as many people as possible. To this end the GK24 was marketed in three standards of fit-out, including a stripped out standard boat, a fully equipped racing boat, and a cruising version which had more concessions to comfort.

With the evolution of the I.O.R. rule, the designer's aim was to manipulate design parameters and thus to bend the rules so as to achieve an advantage over the competition. This resulted in yachts which were initially meant for cruising moving further away from the cruising ideal and becoming true racers. The GK24, like so many yachts, was not really suited as a cruising boat being less comfortable and losing balance to racing quality. This did not, however, deter many designers and boat yards from turning their successful racing machines into so-called cruisers. The GK24 went on to become a popular club racer, and encouraged by sales Westerly commissioned Laurent Giles to design the larger GK29. After this preliminary designs were

drawn for a GK34, but because of a change in demand for stripped-out cruiser racers, which the specifications of the GK34 did not fit, this boat was never built.

The popular club racer the Westerly GK24

Giles 38

Designed for	P.P. Marine Sales
Date Designed	1972
Design No.	726
L.O.A.	38 ft. 10 in. (11.83 m)
L.W.L	30 ft. 7 in. (9.32 m)
Beam	11 ft. 0 in. (3.36 m)
Draft	5 ft. 4 in. (1.63 m)
Displacement	10.8 tons (10.97 tonnes)
Sail area	754 sq. ft. (70.12m²)
Rig	Bermudan Sloop

The Giles 38 is unashamedly a powerful, heavy displacement, long keeled cruising yacht. She is very much in the style of the Vertue, with many of her distinctive characteristics. The first boat built was to a very high standard by Moody's for P.P Marine Sales. Her accommodation was spacious with the normal V-berth forward cabin, this was followed by the toilet compartment and behind this the saloon. The saloon had a large dining area which could accommodate eight or more people at the table, and still have room for a traditional pilot berth. Aft of the saloon was the galley to port and opposite this there was a good chart table, quarter berth and wet locker. The cockpit was large and deep with cavernous lockers beneath the seats, which were designed so that crew could sleep in the cockpit on balmy nights. A great deal of stowage space was made available as well as copious fuel and water tankage considering the number of people she was intended to carry, the sign of a well thought out interior for a serious cruiser.

The coachroof had been kept narrow thus giving a greater width of side deck, this coupled with the shallow bulwark gave a tremendous feeling of safety when moving about the decks. Underway she was remarkably well balanced with a solid feel to her motion and was considered an ideal family cruising boat. *Yachting World* described her in 1972 as 'A comfortable fast cruising yacht and one of the best I have ever seen.' Several customised versions of the Giles 38 were commissioned and built and hull moulds are still available.

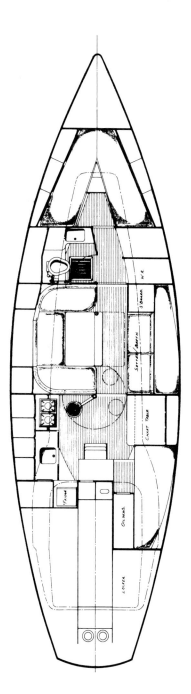

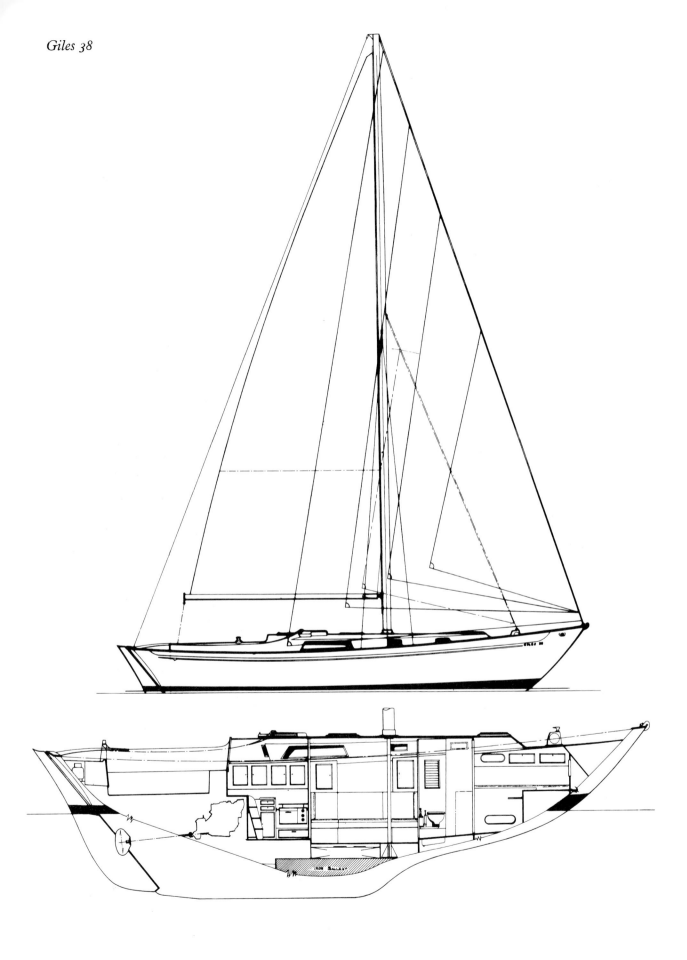

Grenadier 183

Designed for	A.H. Moody and Son Ltd.
Date Designed	1979
Design No.	821
L.O.A.	60 ft. 0 in. (18.3 m)
L.W.L.	48 ft. 0 in. (14.64 m)
Beam	16 ft. 3 in. (4.96 m)
Draft	8 ft. 0 in. (2.44 m)
Displacement	35.5 tons (36.07 tonnes)
Sail area	1492 sq. ft. (138.76 m²)
Rig	Bermudan Ketch

The Grenadier 183 was one of the biggest yachts designed for Moody and was based on the earlier Moody 63 which at the time was one of the largest production boats ever built. Designed as a high quality, deep sea cruising yacht with a powerful auxiliary engine, the Grenadier's hull profile shows a moderate length fin keel and skeg hung rudder with relatively short overhangs. Her decks were protected by a shallow bulwark and remained uncluttered with only the centre cockpit and saloon coachroof encroaching onto the teak laid decks. Sensibly, the Grenadier was rigged as a ketch, which is so much more practical than a sloop for this size of yacht despite all the advances in self-stowing sails and power-driven winches.

The accommodation illustrates how unobtrusive a centre cockpit can be on a large yacht. A number of interior design options were available depending on how the boat was to be used, for example as a charter boat with crew, a private yacht with crew or a family boat. One lay-out, shown in the interior plan drawing, consists of, from bow to stern, a V-berth cabin forward, aft of this a double-bunk cabin to port and a shower and toilet to starboard. Immediately behind the toilet there is a large galley and to port a double berth cabin, steps then lead up to the main saloon which has L shaped settees on both sides. Behind the port settee there is a large navigation area with lockers on the opposite side. Steps then lead down to the aft accommodation which comprises a double-bunk guest cabin with shower and toilet. In the stern of the boat is the double-berth master cabin with ensuite shower and toilet.

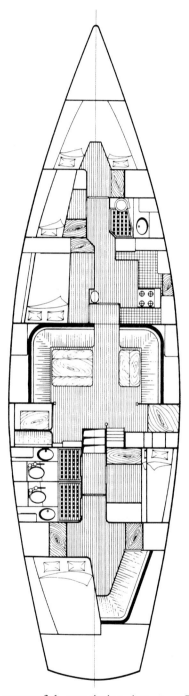

The successful association between Laurent Giles and Moody's was to continue for many years, and two further production boats were designed and built by this team, the Moody 52 and 146.

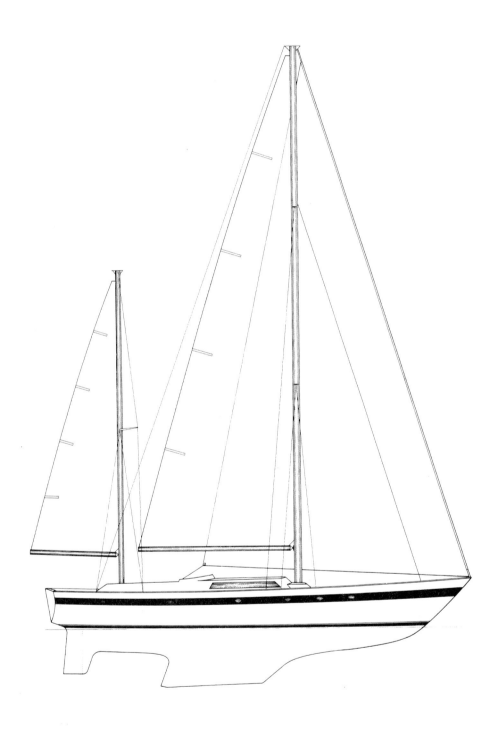

Chapter 6

Laurent Giles Ltd Designs (1982–1990)

Introduction

This final chapter brings the Laurent Giles story into the 1990s with the formation of the new firm and entry into the computer-aided design era. The company has maintained the traditions as well as the wide span of diverse designs from racers to cruisers to motor and work boats. They still follow Jack Giles's quest for lightweight construction and improved all round performance, as illustrated by their successful series of U.L.D.B. yachts such as *Phantom* and *Flying Boat*. They also find many new challenges to face from the requests from ever more demanding owners, as some of the boats described, like *The Other Woman* and a Survival Craft, will

show. The seven boats chosen for this chapter represent a few from a large range of designs produced during this short period and make for interesting comparisons with their ancestors. It will be interesting to see which of these new designs will stand the test of time and become classic boats to be mentioned in the same breath as *Dyarchy*, the Vertues and *Blue Leopard*.

Shipwright 70 Class

Owner	Ocean Youth Club
Builder	Various
Date Design	1984
Design No.	D 111
L.O.A.	69 ft. 0 in. (21.05 m)
L.W.L.	53 ft. 6 in. (16.32 m)
Beam	17 ft. 9 in. (5.41 m)
Draft	8 ft. 6 in. (2.59 m)
Displacement	38.5 tons (39.12 tonnes)
Sail Area	2120 sq. ft. (197.16 m^2)
Rig	Bermudan Ketch

When it was announced that the Ocean Youth Club were looking for a new design for a sail training yacht to gradually replace their existing ageing fleet, Laurent Giles Ltd were keen to win the commission. After stiff competition with other designers Laurent Giles Ltd was finally awarded the contract. The O.Y.C. had very specific ideas of the vessel they wanted, having considerable experience in sail training with yachts of this size. The yachts were to be very different from their existing boats in a number of ways. They were to be steel hulled instead of G.R.P., have considerably more internal space and be much more sophisticated being built to Lloyds 100 A1 plus classification.

The final design shows a powerful 70 ft. cruising ketch of elegant proportions with a large cockpit and ample deck space. The yacht has an easily driven hull with a long fin keel and spade rudder. The keel ballast is internal and full advantage of the steel construction is taken with the use of integral tanks for fuel and water. To reduce excessive weight and loss in stability, the superstructure is constructed from G.R.P. and bolted to a carlin on the steel deck.

Accommodation is for 12 cadets in triple-bunked pipe cots forward, who share two toilets and shower compartments with the two double-bunked cabins for the watch leaders. Aft of these cabins is the main saloon which is raised for good visibility and includes two large settees and tables. Behind this dining area, the galley is situated to port and a large navigation area to starboard. Below the saloon is a central engine room with a workshop area and pantry on opposite sides. In the aft end of the boat is the captain's cabin comprising two berths, a desk and an ensuite toilet and shower compartment.

Two boats have been built in Newcastle by Amarc using Youth Opportunities and training scheme labour, providing valuable experience in many different trades to the unemployed. During the construction of the first boat *James Cook*, a square-rigged sail training ship *The Marquez* was lost at sea with a large loss of life. This disaster brought sail training ships into the headlines and many questions were raised concerning the lack of proper rules for such vessels. It was realised that the rules that existed were very much open to interpretation, so much so that the Department of Trade started to formulate a new set of design and building regulations. These were to take some time to finalise and be approved by the Ministry, since consultation with sail training organisations and designers was necessary, and the result would affect both old and new boats in different ways. Trying to guess what these new rules might be, and so avoid a possible major refit, caused many delays on the project; however, *James Cook* was finally launched in 1988 by Princess Alexander. The yacht has proved to be a good sea boat with a performance far better than most yachts she encounters in the sail training fleets. Just prior to her launch the second of the shipwright class began construction, *Sir John Laing*. Since these yachts are built from donations made to the organisation, assuming such funds are forthcoming then eight further yachts will be built to this design.

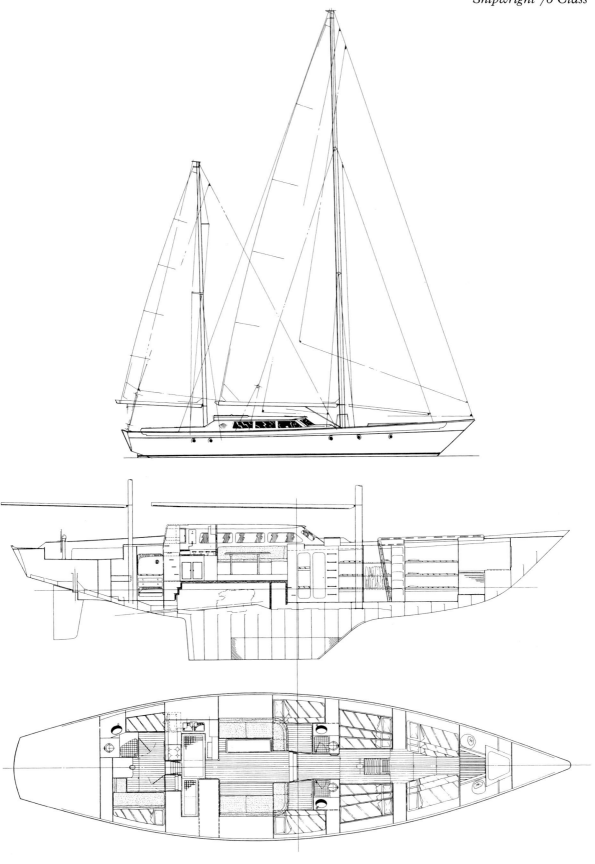

Crusader II

Owner	British *America*'s Cup Challenge
Builder	Cougar Marine
Date Design	1985
Design No.	D 121
L.O.A.	71 ft. 5 in. (21.79 m)
L.W.L.	44 ft. 0 in. (13.42 m)
Beam	12 ft. 6 in. (3.81 m)
Draft	8 ft. 10 in. (2.68 m)
Rig	Sloop

The success of *Australia II* in finally wrestling the *America*'s Cup from the clutches of the New York Yacht Club fired new enthusiasm for this trophy. The fact that it was won by a yacht with a radical winged keel was to have a great influence on all of the contenders for the Perth series.

When Graham Walker was putting a syndicate together the idea was for two radical boats. As fund raising progressed this changed to one radical and one conventional 12-Metre. The conventional 12-Metre was to be a Howlit design and the radical yacht by a design triad of Dave Hollom, a highly successful model yacht designer with many exciting and innovative yacht design ideas; Herbert Pearcy, of British Aerospace, a specialist in aerodynamics; and finally Laurent Giles Ltd. Dave Hollom was primarily responsible for the hull shape, Herbert Pearcy for the winged bulb and keel, and Laurent Giles Ltd. for the structural design.

A great deal of time was spent in tank testing, computer simulation and free model sailing trials. The final design was '*Hippo*' this nickname coming unfairly from her hull shape. She was in fact a very long and narrow 12-Metre with a forward bustle and aft bustle. She had a long flat run to the transom with a very tight turn of bilge in the counter.

The keel was all aluminium and the entire ballast weight of some 17 tons was in the cast lead warped bulb. This bulb gave the boat a very low centre of gravity and was held in place by a single transverse pivot bolt. This allowed the bulb's angle of attack to be changed between sailing trials. Winglets were also tried on the bulb, as was an alternative bulb.

Unfortunately for *Hippo* the syndicate decided to build the conventional 12-Metre first. It soon became apparent that *Hippo* would arrive very late in Perth and would only have a short work-up time before the start of the Round-Robin races. Although she proved at times to have an inspired performance it was felt that the conventional boat, *Crusader I*, should be entered as the crew had more experience of this yacht. Although *Hippo* was rarely seriously campaigned she, on several occasions, gave people a glimpse of what she might be capable of. One such time was in the 1988 12-Metre world championships in Sweden where she finished 4th in the fleet races, and won the midnight sun race against a fleet that included *Australia III* and *Kookaburras II* and *III*.

Hippo had an unlucky life which included falling off the deck of a cargo ship into the North Sea whilst in transit. She was later salvaged, only to be scrapped by the insurance company.

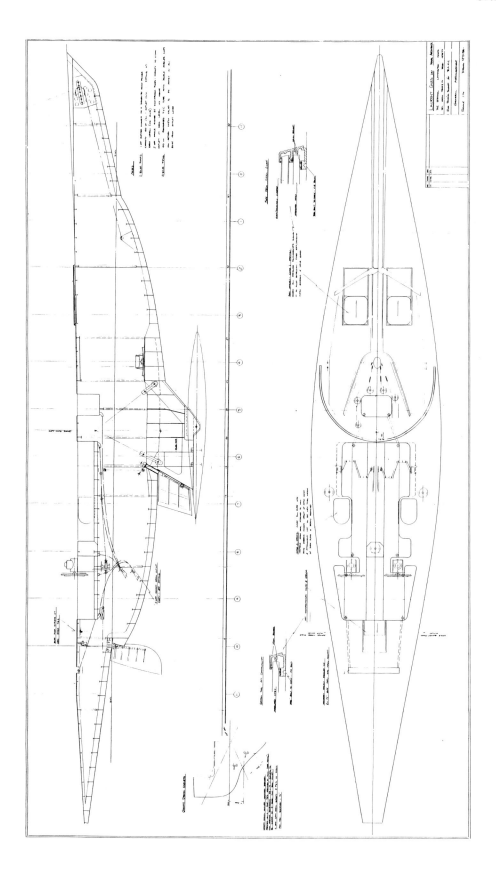

Flying Boat

Owner	Warwick Collins
Builder	West Custom Marine
Date Design	1984
Design No.	D 125
L.O.A.	25 ft. 3 in. (7.7 m)
L.W.L.	23 ft. 0 in. (7.02 m)
Beam	7 ft. 9 in. (2.36 m)
Draft	2 ft. 11 in. (0.88 m)
Displacement	1.13 tons (1.15 tonnes)
Sail Area	300 sq. ft. (27.9 m²)
Rig	Bermudan Sloop

Flying Boat was designed for Warwick Collins, who wanted a yacht that would show his new keel design off to its best advantage. Since the keel could not be rated under the International Offshore Racing rules (I.O.R.) it was decided that they should abandon any ideas of racing rules and design a U.L.D.B. which would race under a channel handicap with whatever rating they would see fit to give her.

In her design the beam was kept narrower than might be expected, as the low centre of gravity of the keel meant that form stability was not as important a factor as on a conventional keel. *Flying Boat* has long waterlines with a fine entry and a flat run aft. Her sections show a tight turn of bilge to help initiate planing and surfing.

Her construction was kept simple and light, the hull shell being strip planked cedar laid over plywood web frames and stringers, the outside then being sheathed with a single layer of glass fibre rovings and epoxy resin. The accommodation is simple because she was conceived as a lightweight racer, and comprises V-berths forward with a small galley area with settee berths both port and starboard.

The cockpit takes up a large proportion of her length and is open at the transom. The fractional rig is also simple with single swept-back spreaders and an adjustable backstay. *Flying Boat* lived up to her name and was highly successful in the races she entered. In the Lymington town sailing clubs Solent Circuit Series, racing in class 8, she was never beaten by a monohull and sometimes she proved faster than many trimarans. In her very first race she finished 6 minutes ahead of the nearest trimaran and 16 minutes ahead of the next monohull. In the final race the crew volunteered to sail in class 7 and she still managed to finish third. So delighted was he with the boat's performance, the owner commissioned Laurent Giles Ltd to design a larger U.L.D.B. called *Fighter*, which also proved to be very successful.

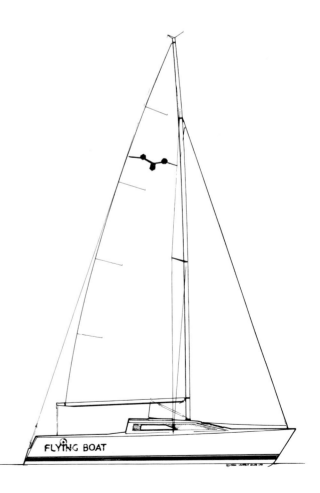

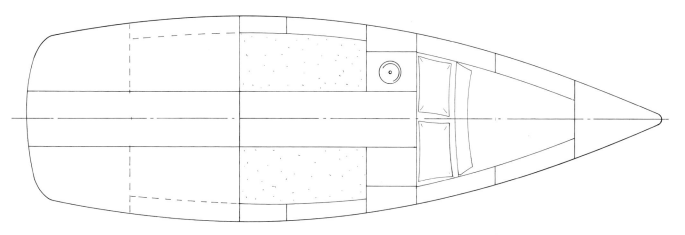

The Other Woman

Builder	Runmere Shipyard in Brisbane, Australia.
Date Design	1984
Design No.	D 144
L.O.A.	190 ft. 6 in. (58.1 m)
L.W.L.	149 ft. 0 in. (45.45 m)
Beam	34 ft. 0 in. (10.37 m)
Draft	6 ft. 6 in. (1.98 m)
Displacement	500 tons (508 tonnes)
Sail Area	10,480 sq. ft. (974.64 m²)
Rig	Schooner

The owner's requirements for this megayacht read like a challenge of immense proportions to any naval architect. She was to be 190 ft. overall, a motor sailer with a draft of only 6 ft. 6 in., and to be capable of 15 knots under sail and 20 knots under power with a range of 5000 miles. The accommodation was to be as luxurious as a small stately home and both the interior and exterior had to be designed to accommodate a wheelchair.

After much thought, tank testing and free model sailing trials, Laurent Giles Ltd proved to themselves that there was a feasible design solution. The yacht would have to carry a schooner rig with over 10,480 sq. ft. of working sail with an additional two 6000 sq. ft. spinnakers. All of the working sails would be hydraulically furled and trimmed using captive sheet winches, an idea pioneered by Laurent Giles Ltd, and the sail plan would be balanced by two immense lifting keels in tandem. To achieve the draft requirements, two low aspect ratio rudders would be used for steering at slow speed and under sail. These could be locked on the fore and aft direction when under power. The main propulsion would be provided by two engines producing 5600 h.p. and driving a pair of steerable water jets.

Her vast accommodation comprises four decks which are linked by a lift and a spiral staircase. The lower deck comprises the crew's accommodation, with space for nine including a lounge, dining room and the main galley. There are also four double guest suites, each one containing an ensuite bath-

room with spa bath. On the main deck is the owner's suite incorporating a sitting room, two bathrooms, a dressing room and a fully equipped office with centralised communication. There is a further double guest cabin and bathroom next to the owner's suite, as well as a second large galley. The owner's day rooms include a dining room and an enormous lounge with grand piano. The bridge and adjoining captain's cabin is situated on the weather deck together with a large cocktail lounge and bar. On the flybridge there is a swimming pool, and adjacent to this is an outdoor bar and seating area. The weather deck has two sports boats of approximately 30 ft. length, and a landing craft which can take ashore the limousine or a small runabout car which are to be carried onboard.

She is presently being built in Brisbane, Australia, and constructed to American Bureau of Shipping class A 1 yacht standard. When completed she will be the largest aluminium yacht ever built.

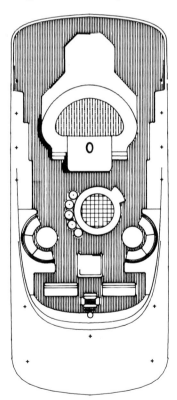

Flying Bridge

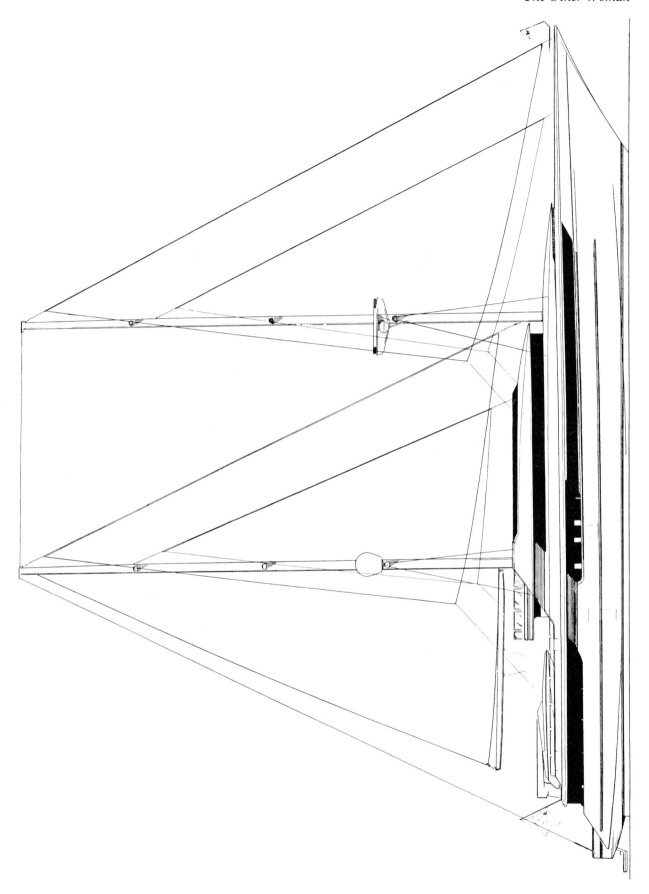

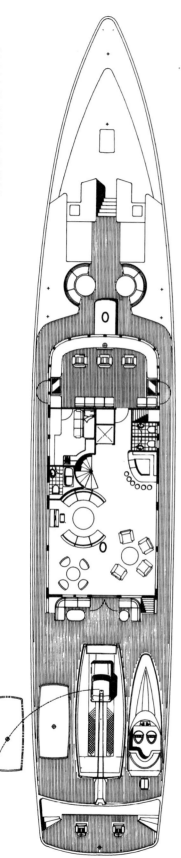

Boat and Promenande Deck

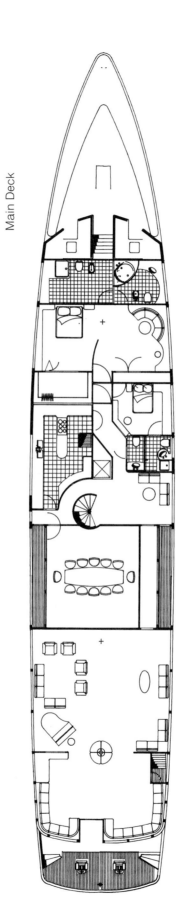

Main Deck

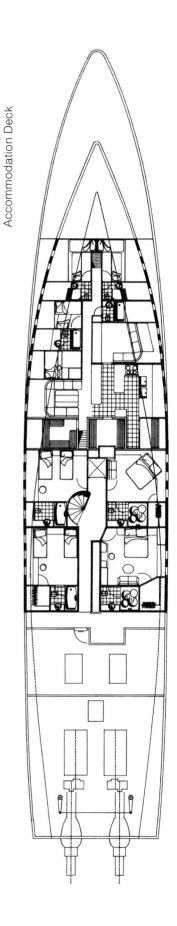

Accommodation Deck

Survival Craft

Builder	Blue Sea
Date Design	1986
Design No.	D 159
L.O.A.	27 ft. 5 in. (8.37 m)
L.W.L.	22 ft. 10 in. (6.95 m)
Beam	9 ft. 9 in. (2.97 m)
Draft	3 ft. 5 in. (1.05 m)
Displacement	6.25 tons (6.35 tonnes)

Every now and again Laurent Giles Ltd are faced with an unusual challenge. For example, a request made by Blue Sea for a small survival craft to I.M.O. (International Maritime Organisation) regulations was something out of the ordinary. Most ships' lifeboats are built and designed by companies who specialise in this field and have evolved their designs over many years, making sure they conform to the ever tighter international regulations. Laurent Giles Ltd, ever eager to enter new design fields, produced from scratch a brand new lifeboat. Since such a project involves the construction of three boats, the initial wooden version, the G.R.P. mould and finally the finished hull, they had to make sure the design worked first time.

The stringent requirements for lifeboats call for a very careful review of all aspects of design. The craft was to be a 7.3-Metre self-righting lifeboat with a double ended hull and able to carry 30 people. A further requirement was that the boat must achieve a minimum speed of 6 knots, which is relatively high for a displacement vessel of this size. In addition to this the craft was to be launched using hydrostatically released davits, which was one of the most recent safety regulations for lifeboats.

On completion, the lifeboat had to pass a series of very strenuous tests which were to be witnessed by the world's major classification societies. The tests in the fully laden condition included:

i) A side impact test to simulate swinging against a ship's side whilst being lowered in rough weather. This was carried out by suspending the lifeboat on 20 ft. hawsers and hauling her out sideways 8 feet, and releasing her so that she swung against a concrete wall.

ii) A drop test to simulate an emergency release of the boat if the falls jammed before the craft reached the water. For this test the vessel is raised so that its keel is 7.5 feet above the sea's surface and then released.

iii) Self-righting trials to simulate a 180 degree knockdown. For this trial the vessel is forcibly rolled over and then released and the amount of time required for the vessel to right itself is recorded.

iv) Fire tests to simulate launching into a burning sea. A dock is flooded with kerosene and the lifeboat is anchored in the centre of the dock with recording instruments inside to measure the temperature. The engine is started, the propeller engaged and its deck washing pump and oxygen cylinders activated. The kerosene is then ignited and left to burn for five minutes. When the test is over and the smoke clears everyone looks to see what remains. Hopefully this is a fully intact and seaworthy craft which would, under real conditions, have a warm but uncooked crew.

There are many less exciting tests which are carried out, including embarkation and evacuation of the vessel in an emergency which must be performed in less than a certain prescribed time.

Some of the design features specific to this lifeboat include the hull which was designed as a heavy displacement form but with an aft knuckle and flattened buttocks to prevent excessive trim when at full speed. The superstructure was shaped to ensure the boat would self-right from a 180 degrees knockdown, and that water would flow smoothly over the entire surface when sprayed from the boat's integral fire-fighting system. Space had to be found inside for 30 survivors and regulation supplies of fuel, food, water, emergency equipment, survival suits and many more items specified by I.M.O., and yet remain within a strict T.D.L. (Total Davit Load).

The craft was constructed using three major G.R.P. mouldings; hull, deck and interior with sub-mouldings for watertight doors, engine case and stowage compartments. The space between the interior moulding and the hull was foam filled to produce positive buoyancy when the lifeboat was swamped in the fully laden condition. The mouldings were designed using a relatively simple lay-up as the vessel was to be built and mass-produced in Taiwan.

It was with a certain amount of relief that Laurent Giles Ltd received a telex on the 21st August 1987 saying that the prototype had passed all its tests and was fully certified for use on commercial shipping.

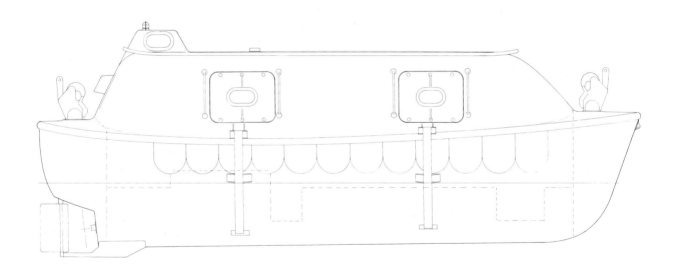

Phantom and Rapscallion

Owner	Chris Hatton and John Button
Builder	West Custom Marine
Date Built	1986
Design No.	D182
L.O.A.	43 ft. 0 in. (13.12 m)
L.W.L	36 ft. 1 in. (11.13 m)
Beam	12 ft. 6 in. (3.81 m)
Draft	6 ft. 6 in. (1.98 m)
Displacement	13,560 lbs (6.16 tonnes)
Sail Area	825 sq. ft. (76.73 m²)
Rig	Sloop

In 1986 Chris Hatton asked Laurent Giles Ltd to design a lightweight cruiser/racer for channel handicap racing. During the previous Cowes Week he had chartered *Fighter*, the 33 ft. Ultra-light Displacement Boat (U.L.D.B.) that the company had recently designed, and had been impressed by her performance. Chris had decided that he wanted something more exciting than his present Sigma 41, and thus began the design for *Phantom*. West Custom Marine, who had been responsible for building *Fighter*, were appointed to build the new yacht and work started in October that year.

The brief was to design a yacht that was capable of beating *Barracuda of Tarrant*, a boat whose fame had been made on the B.B.C.'s T.V. series 'Howards Way', and in which Chris could take his family on holiday to Brittany. Laurent Giles had always been keen supporters of the U.L.D.B. concept, but felt that in this case this design type would be too light and additional displacement would be required for this all-round boat. These boats suffer in light air, due to lack of canvas and relatively high wetted surface area, and also in heavy weather windward work, due to lack of stability and flat fore foot causing bad slamming. Off wind, in moderate to heavy going conditions, however, they are untouchable. The designers' experience with *Flying Boat* and *Fighter* convinced them that it would be possible to maintain outstanding off wind performance whilst at the same time reducing the inherent weakness of a true U.L.D.B. From the outset it was important to generate stability from a low centre of gravity rather than excess beam. More beam would have been an advantage for racing where the effect of crew on the rail is very significant, but undesirable when cruising. The hull lines were developed closely from *Fighter*, which has a long waterline, with flat run aft and broad transom with hard turn of bilge for good surfing and planing. This was coupled to a fine waterline entry with a little bow flare to keep the decks dry when running into a big sea. Displacement length was slightly higher to account for the well fitted, open plan interior, and sail area displacement was slightly down, which would make her a better windward boat particularly offshore. Laurent Giles were also keen not to make *Phantom* too much of a handful when cruising, which was a mistake since she has only cruised for one weekend. It turned out that the owner preferred racing.

The owner was also intrigued by the possibilities of moderate draft and new keel technology. Having worked closely with Dave Hollam on the design of the 12-Metre *Crusader 88* there were some strong ideas about the avenues to explore. *Phantom* was tank tested at Liverpool University with four keel derivatives, a conventional fin keel of 7 ft. 7 in. draft as the base, an undistorted fish tail bulb, a warped and cambered bulb, and a highly developed bulb/wing form with a high sweep back. The tests clearly showed that the simple fish tail bulb was a very good all-round design; however, the wing/bulb also showed promise. Unfortunately the one characteristic that could not be tested was position of the centre of lateral resistance (C.L.R.). This closely affects the balance and feel of the yacht and from the previous 12-Metre work it had been shown that these developed wing forms could cause significant shifts of C.L.R. In practice the wing keel worked tolerably well on *Phantom* but the C.L.R. prediction was not quite right. *Phantom* suffered from a lack of 'feel' making her difficult to keep in the 'groove'. Nevertheless she showed heself to have a good performance particularly to windward in a moderate breeze, and convincingly beat *Barracuda* in the inshore races and the offshore races, except when it blew hard and the course was downwind. With a new suite of sails *Phantom* turned in some excellent results in the Lymington spring series. Her performance suffered in light airs and it was decided this was due to the increased wetted surface of the wing/bulb. Her keel was changed to a conventional fin keel of 7 ft. 9 in. draft, the original being 6 ft. 6 in., which although some 300 kg. heavier still does not achieve the low centre of gravity of the previous configuration. Since she is hardly ever used for cruising she always has plenty of crew for the weather rail and the reduction in stability goes almost unnoticed.

Her victories for 1988 and 1989 include the following R.O.R.C. races; Cowes to Ouistreham 1st in class and 1st overall; Channel Race 1st to finish; Lymington to La Rochelle 1st in class and 1st overall; Cowes to Le Havre 1st in class, 1st to finish, 1st overall; Overall Points Champion 1st in class; Cowes to St Vaast 1st in class and 1st overall.

Other races include: W.S.C.R.A Round the Island 1st to finish (1988 and 1989); Royal Lymington Yacht Club, Lymington to Jersey 1st to finish and 1st in class. She has also won a whole host of trophies including; Hugh Astor Salver, De Vere Hotels Salver, La Rochelle Prize, Lekeito Cup, L'Horizon Trophy, Moët et Chandon Methuselah, Jamarella Trophy, Ouistreham R.O.R.C. Trophy, S.R.C.O. Trophy and the Loujaine Cup.

A sister ship, *Rapscallion*, was built the following year but had several major differences since her whole design was orientated to cruising. Her keel had a fish tail bulb and her rig boasted a blade jib with a fully battened mainsail and simplified standing rigging. Her cockpit and interior were laid out in an uncompromising cruising style. *Rapscallion* has recorded 12 to 13 knots close reaching with just three crew onboard with one reef in the mainsail and jib set. Although a cruising boat *Rapscallion* easily took line honours in the Guernsey to Jersey race shortly after her launch.

Phantom on a close spinnaker reach.

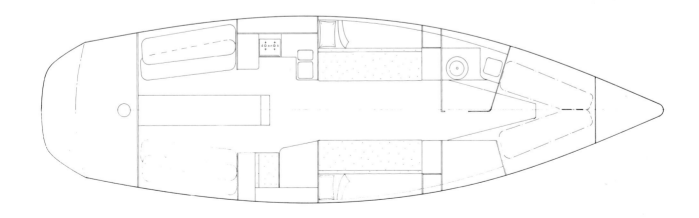

Dalvina

Owner	R. Iliffe
Builder	Berthon Boat Company
Date Design	1987
Design No.	D 194
L.O.A.	80.0 ft. 0 in. (24.4 m)
L.W.L	69.0 ft. 9 in. (21.27 m)
Beam	21.0 ft. 0 in. (6.41 m)
Draft	6.0 ft. 0 in. (1.83 m)
Displacement	75 tons (76.2 tonnes)
Engines	Twin V8 M.T.U. Diesels.

As production boats get larger and larger one finds that customers who come to Laurent Giles Ltd for a one-off design do so because they have very specific requirements that cannot be fulfilled by the often inflexible mass-production boatyards. The 80 ft. Twin Screw Diesel Yacht (T.S.D.Y.) Dalvina is a case in point. The owner wanted a gentleman's motor yacht which looked like a trawler yacht but would achieve a cruising speed of 18 knots when fully laden in a 10 knot head wind and with the associated sea state. In addition she was to have a range of 1000 miles and be very quiet, especially in harbour or at anchor. The owner also wanted a robust sea boat with all modern conveniences and duplication of all systems. This all pointed to a semi-displacement hull of moderate beam. The semi-displacement hull form has been much neglected in recent years, especially in larger private yachts. It was therefore thought essential, because of the heavy displacement, that a model testing programme should be undertaken. A model was tested at Liverpool University's re-circulating water channel to optimise a hull wedge and spray knuckle and to sight the underwater exhausts. The model was then run at the British Maritime Technology's half-mile long tank at Feltham in Middlesex, to obtain accurate resistance figures and to test the model in waves. It was at this point that an additional spray rail was added to the fore part of the vessel. This was the last ever model to be tested at Feltham before the tank was closed due to lack of funding.

The hull and superstructure were constructed of aluminium alloy and built by Cougar Marine. The hull was framed using a system of longitudinal stringers and deep webbed frames. The hull and superstructure were built separately and were later joined at the finishing yard in Lymington.

From the tank test data it was decided to install a pair of V8 M.T.U. diesel engines developing 1300 h.p. each and driving four-bladed propellers on monel shafts. For manoeuvring in restricted waters a 40 h.p. retractable hydraulic bow thruster was installed. To reduce rolling, especially at anchor, a computer-controlled moving weight stabiliser was also fitted. Electrical power was supplied by twin generators in acoustic housings, while other systems included reverse heat centralised air conditioning, a hot water central heating system and centralised toilet flushing system.

A great deal of attention to detail was made to reduce noise levels, the more uncommon features being the use of floating soles to all major cabins and resiliantly mounted bulkheads. To save weight all the bulkheads and joinery were constructed from balsa cored teak veneered panels.

The accommodation consists, from bow to stern on the lower deck, a fore peak followed by a three-berth cabin with shared toilet and shower, a laundry room to port with an occasional berth and a handed pair of guest cabins with ensuite bathrooms, which are separated from the owner's suite by the engine room. The owner's suite comprises several cabins which are interconnecting. These include a large day-cabin with office communication equipment and a settee that can convert to two single beds. The

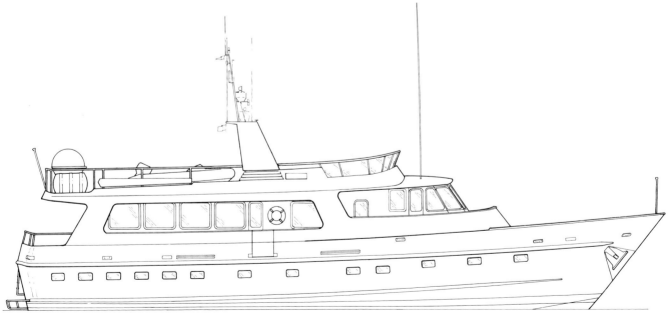

owner's night cabin which includes a large double bed, walk-in wardrobe, dressing table and settee, also has an ensuite bathroom with bidet and a full sized bath. Between this and the day cabin's W.C. is a shower compartment which is accessible from either bathroom.

On the main deck is a fully double-glazed, large wheelhouse with seating for six and all imaginable electronic aids. There is access from the wheelhouse to the bridge wings which have duplicate docking controls port and starboard. Aft of the wheelhouse

is a deck toilet and wet locker to port, and fully fitted kitchen to starboard. Access to the engine room can be gained from the side deck immediately behind the toilet compartment. The rest of the deck house is an open-plan lounge and dining room with large patio doors which lead onto the aft deck.

The large fly bridge can comfortably sit twelve people, and aft is the boat deck with two deck lockers for stowing equipment. There is ample space for two 13 ft. fast launches, which are raised and lowered by hydraulically operated low profile davits styled into the flybridge coamings.

Dalvina achieved and surpassed her design brief. She easily met her required speed with power to spare and has proved to be highly manoeuvrable and impressive in a seaway. Unlike many semi-displacement boats *Dalvina* exhibits very little change of trim throughout her speed range. The owner is very pleased with her and they can be regularly seen cruising the waters around her home port of Lymington.

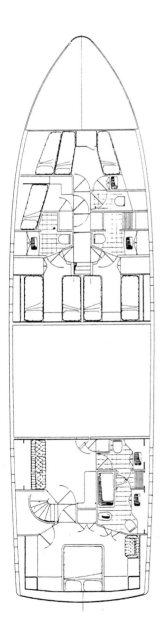
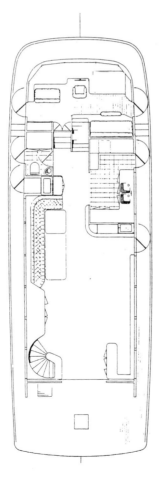
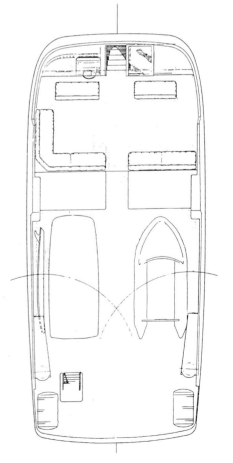

Appendix

The following list comprises a complete collection of the yachts, motor sailers and motor boats designed by Laurent Giles from the beginnings of the company Laurent Giles and Partners Ltd in 1927 to the formation of the present-day company Laurent Giles Ltd set up in 1982. The list has been compiled from old design books, index cards, sail plan drawings and company literature. The boat list is ordered according to a company Boat Number, which appears to have been given to one-off designs as well as designs for a class of boat and to production boats. Unfortunately, after much research and cross referencing of the material available some data could not be found. Although most of the information is available some boat names are missing, and where this occurs the owner's name has been entered where this is known. It is more common for the boat names to be missing where there have been many produced for a particular class of boat, for example for the Vertues, Columbias and Peter Ducks. It appears that not all of the boats produced from one particular design have been registered by a separate boat number and so the complete list can never be reconstructed from the records available. For the production boats, only the prototype or production names have been given since there have been thousands produced. Where a boat has been registered with more than one name during its life, its original name has been used. The list also contains length overall L.O.A., length at the water line L.W.L., beam, draft, sail area and displacement. All of the dimensions are in imperial units, i.e. feet, square feet and tons. Some of these data have been lost or were never recorded and these are marked by a dashed line. Where displacement values could not be found, a Thames tonnage measurement was calculated using the width of the beam and L.O.A. values.

Where there are blank entries in the list the following notation is used:

No name	... No boat name or owner name can be found
+Name	... More than one name has been recorded; first name is shown
—	... Information lost
Not built	... Boat was designed but not built
Displacement T	... Calculated Thames Tonnage
N.A.	... Not applicable

After the name of the boat the list comprises columns where the class name of the boat is listed together with the type of vessel design and rig. A list of the abbreviations used to describe this information is given below.

Class Names and Type of Boat

AU	Audacity Class
BR	Brittany Class
BA	Bachetta Class
BS	Biscay Class
CC	Channel Class
CO	Columbia Class
DY	Dyarchy Class
DO	Donella Class
DM	Dhorus Mhor Class
DR	Dragon Class
G7	Giles 37 Class
G8	Giles 38 Class
GC	Gull Class
GK	GK Class
IN	Infanta Class
JB	National Jolly Boat RMYC
LA	Launch
LU	Luce Class
LY	Lymington Class
M44	Moody 44 Class
M63	Moody 63 Class
MBU	Modified Buccaneer
MCA	Modified Carbineer
MCO	Modified Columbia
MWA	Modified Wanderer
MV	Modified Vertue
MY	Motor Yacht
NCC	New Channel Class
OD	One Design
NO	Normandy Class
PB	Production Boat
PD	Peter Duck Class
PT	Pearson Type
RC	Rambler Class
RL	Revised Lymington Class
RN	RNSA 24 Class
RO	Rosette Class
RR	Rose Rambler Class
RY	RUYC Class
SA	Salar Class
SI	Scimitar Class
TE	Treasure Class
TR	Trusty Class
TS	Tesse Class
V	Vertue Class
WA	Wanderer Class
WP	Whooper Class
8M	Eight Meter Class

Type of rigging or type of boat

BC	Bermudan Cutter
BK	Bermudan Ketch
BS	Bermudan Sloop
BY	Bermudan Yawl
CT	Catamaran
CU	Cutter
DI	Dinghy
DL	Dipping Lug
FL	Fishing Launch
GA	Gaff
GC	Gaff Cutter
GY	Gaff Yawl
KE	Ketch
LA	Launch
MC	Motor Cruiser
PC	Pilot Cutter
SB	Service Boat
SC	Schooner
TN	Tender
TR	Triple Screw
TW	T.S.D.Y
YW	Yawl

No.	Name	Class	Rig	LOA (ft)	LWL (ft)	Beam (ft)	Draft (ft)	Sail (Sq ft)	Disp (Tons)
1	*Clymene*	OD	GY	52.0	40.0	12.3	6.1	1717	25.3
2	*Etain*	OD	CU	46.0	31.0	9.0	6.5	814	10.0
3	*Kanga*	OD	MC	26.0	—	—	—	—	—
4	*Argo*	OD	BY	33.0	28.0	9.1	6.0	550	8.6
5	*Cypris*	OD	TW	62.5	59.3	—	—	NA	—
6	*Faeire*	OD	SL	22.5	17.0	6.2	3.3	250	1.7
7	*Samaki*	OD	MC	45.0	39.0	—	—	NA	—
8	*Isabella*	LY1	SL	23.3	19.5	6.8	3.9	275	2.7
9	*Browne*	OD	—	25.6	—	—	—	—	—
10	*Tamahine +*	OD	TW	63.0	60.3	13.1	4.3	NA	25.0
11	*Pinkus*	OD	SL	30.0	19.8	5.5	4.8	256	1.8
12	*Daphne*	OD	FL	38.0	—	—	—	—	—
13	*Helen*	OD	BC	41.0	31.5	9.8	6.0	700	10.8
14	*Jolly Boat*	JB	SL	14.0	—	—	—	—	—
15	*Andrillot*	V1	GC	25.5	21.5	7.2	4.2	366	4.3
16	*Roan*	OD	SL	20.0	—	—	—	—	—
17	*Cleomene +*	OD	BS	26.0	19.5	6.5	4.5	380	2.6
18	*Wanderer II*	OD	GC	24.0	21.0	7.1	4.9	395	4.5
19	*Verity A*	CC1	BC	38.4	26.0	8.8	5.5	624	6.9
20	*Black Pearl*	OD	LA	—	—	—	—	—	—
21	*Sally II*	V2	GC	25.5	21.5	7.2	4.2	386	4.5
22	*Shonagen*	OD	CU	40.0	33.0	—	—	—	—
22B	*Maid of Tesa*	V34	BS	25.3	21.5	7.2	4.5	366	4.3
23	*Maid of Malham*	OD	BC	48.5	35.0	10.7	7.5	955	13.5
24	*English Lass*	CC2	BC	38.1	26.0	8.8	6.0	624	6.9
24B	*Searigs*	OD	BS	30.0	22.0	—	—	—	—
25	*Phemie +*	OD	BC	42.0	30.5	9.4	6.2	806	9.1
26	*White Bear +*	OD	TW	46.0	45.0	—	—	NA	—
27	*Farida*	OD	BC	35.3	28.5	9.3	5.7	569	8.4
28	*Triune of Troy*	CC3	BC	37.9	26.0	8.8	6.0	624	6.9
29	*Kayak*	CC4	BC	37.9	26.0	8.8	6.0	624	6.9
30	*Monie*	V3	CU	25.3	21.5	7.2	4.5	366	4.3
31	*Wapipi*	WP1	BC	38.8	28.0	9.5	3.5	490	5.4
32	*Cerida*	OD	BC	43.0	35.0	10.8	6.5	877	16.1
33	*Valfreya*	OD	BC	34.0	28.0	9.8	6.3	683	8.5
34	*Motihari III*	OD	BC	34.4	24.5	7.3	5.5	442	3.3
35	*Prelude*	OD	BC	36.1	25.0	7.5	6.0	505	4.1
36	*Flotsam*	OD	LA	33.7	32.8	8.8	2.5	NA	3.4
37	*Dyarchy*	DY1	GC	45.8	38.0	12.3	7.5	1410	24.2
38	*Greetings +*	OD	BC	39.0	32.0	10.5	7.0	600	12.1
39	*Kalliste*	OD	BC	28.2	24.5	8.2	5.0	371	6.5
40	*Charis*	V4	BS	25.3	21.5	7.2	4.5	366	4.3
41	*Flotsam II*	OD	LA	36.0	25.0	—	—	—	—
42	*Fairlight*	OD	BC	39.0	32.0	10.8	6.0	600	13.0
43	*Flying Gull*	GC1	BS	26.5	21.5	7.7	4.3	400	3.9
44	*Flica II*	OD	BS	67.0	46.4	11.8	9.0	1914	26.9
44B	*Tryphena*	CC5	BC	39.0	26.0	8.8	6.0	624	6.9

No.	Name	Class	Rig	LOA (ft)	LWL (ft)	Beam (ft)	Draft (ft)	Sail (Sq ft)	Disp (Tons)
45	*Questing*	OD	BC	41.3	31.0	10.8	5.5	732	11.7
46	*Marie Victoire*	OD	BC	39.9	27.0	9.0	6.3	656	7.6
46A	*Whooper*	WP1	BS	39.0	28.0	9.5	3.5	490	5.4
47	*Coryi*	DR	BS	29.2	22.5	6.5	3.9	286	1.7
48	*Bettine*	BR1	BC	33.5	25.3	8.3	5.3	502	6.4
49	*Kawan*	V7	BS	25.3	21.5	7.2	4.5	366	4.3
50	*Caupona*	V8	BS	25.3	21.5	7.2	4.5	366	4.3
51	*Epeneta*	V5	BS	25.3	21.5	7.2	4.5	366	4.3
52	*Francolin*	V6	BS	25.3	21.5	7.2	4.5	366	4.3
52A	*Candy*	V9	BS	25.3	21.5	7.2	4.5	366	4.3
52B	*Almena*	V10	BS	25.3	21.5	7.2	4.5	366	4.3
53	*Dalua*	BR2	BS	33.5	25.3	8.3	5.3	463	5.9
54	*Peter Duck*	PD1	BK	28.0	25.0	9.0	3.5	293	5.6
55	*Peeky*	CC6	BC	39.0	26.0	8.8	6.0	610	6.9
56	*Maid Meriel*	V11	BS	25.3	21.5	7.2	4.5	366	4.3
57	*Kishti*	V12	BS	25.3	21.5	7.2	4.5	366	4.3
58	*+ Atlantis of Rhur*	OD	BC	41.3	31.0	10.8	5.5	732	8.5
59	*Meulette*	V16	BS	25.3	21.5	7.2	4.5	366	4.3
60	*Teresa*	V17	BS	25.3	21.5	7.2	4.5	366	4.3
61	Teasdale	OD	LA	16.0	—	—	—	—	—
62	*Woodpecker*	OD	TW	70.0	65.0	14.0	4.0	NA	24.8
63	*Tilly Whim*	OD	BS	38.3	27.0	9.1	5.8	639	8.0
64	*Myth of Malham*	OD	BC	37.5	33.5	9.3	7.3	626	7.6
65	*Petronella*	OD	BS	34.0	28.0	Not built		—	—
66	*Serotina*	V14	BS	25.3	21.5	7.2	4.5	366	4.3
67	*Frea*	V13	BS	25.3	21.5	7.2	4.5	366	4.3
67A	*Virtue*	V29	BS	25.3	21.5	7.2	4.5	366	4.3
68	*Margurite of Poole*	V15	BS	25.3	21.5	7.2	4.5	366	4.3
69	*Surf Boat*	OD	—	—	—	—	—	—	—
70	Pearson	PB	MC	33.9	28.0	9.0	4.0	225	10.7T
71	*Wapipi II*	WP2	SL	39.0	28.0	9.5	3.5	490	5.4
72	C.P.L. Co.	PB	LA	12.5	—	—	—	—	—
73	*Ruthean*	OD	BY	54.3	40.0	—	—	—	—
74	Not built	PD	BK	28.0	25.0	9.0	3.5	293	5.6
75	*Orcadian +*	OD	CU	46.0	33.5	—	—	—	—
76	*Iska*	OD	BK	54.4	42.5	13.1	8.3	1259	29.0
77	Not built	RN	BS	30.9	24.0	7.5	5.9	465	4.3
78	*Salmo*	V20	BS	25.3	21.5	7.2	4.5	366	4.3
79	*Bettine Jnr*	V18	BS	25.3	21.5	7.2	4.5	366	4.3
80	*Droleen II*	BR4	BS	33.5	25.3	8.3	5.3	463	5.9
81	*Pocahontas*	RN1	BS	31.0	24.0	7.5	5.8	465	4.3
82	*Ceara*	BR3	BS	33.5	25.3	8.3	5.3	463	5.9
83	*Woodpeckers*	OD	TN	12.5	—	—	—	—	—
84	*Cardinal Vertue*	V19	BS	25.3	21.5	7.2	4.5	366	4.3
85	*Wraith +*	V23	BS	25.3	21.5	7.2	4.5	366	4.3
86	*Eleanor of Poole*	V24	BS	25.3	21.5	7.2	4.5	366	4.3
87	*Katrianne*	V26	BS	25.3	21.5	7.2	4.5	366	4.3

No.	Name	Class	Rig	LOA (ft)	LWL (ft)	Beam (ft)	Draft (ft)	Sail (Sq ft)	Disp (Tons)
88	*Melusine*	V25	BS	25.3	21.5	7.2	4.5	366	4.3
89	*Kuniang +*	BR6	BS	33.5	25.3	8.3	5.3	463	5.9
90	*Overdraft +*	V22	BS	25.3	21.5	7.2	4.5	366	4.3
91	*Sabrina*	OD	BS	37.8	24.0	7.0	5.8	415	3.5
92	C.P.L. Co.	PB	DI	9.0	—	—	—	—	—
93	*Bunting*	OD	KE	31.8	28.0	—	—	—	—
94	*Chrunest*	OD	BS	46.8	36.0	9.8	7.7	800	10.0
95	No name	OD	DI	12.5	—	—	—	—	—
96	*Maid of York*	BR5	BS	33.5	25.3	8.3	5.3	463	5.9
97	Not built	OD	MV	—	—	—	—	—	—
98	*Samuel Pepys*	RN5	BS	31.0	24.0	7.5	5.8	465	4.3
99	*Suvretta*	OD	BS	25.0	18.0	—	—	—	2.2
100	*Blue Disa*	RN4	BS	31.0	24.0	7.5	5.8	465	4.3
101	*Minx of Malham*	RN2	BS	31.0	24.0	7.5	5.8	465	4.3
102	C.P.L. Co.	OD	LA	20.5	—	—	—	—	—
103	*Ben's Choice*	RN3	BS	31.0	24.0	7.5	5.8	465	4.3
104	*Gulvain*	OD	BC	55.0	43.0	11.5	8.7	1100	16.0
105	*Patsy*	BS1	BC	47.5	31.0	10.4	7.0	870	10.0
106	*Easy Vertue +*	V27	BS	25.3	21.5	7.2	4.5	366	4.3
107	*Hussar*	V21	BS	25.3	21.5	7.2	4.5	366	4.3
108	*Fandango*	OD	BS	43.3	33.0	9.2	7.3	640	7.2
109	*Four Freedoms*	OD	SL	36.0	33.0	9.5	7.0	600	3.5
110	*Little Otter*	OD	MC	32.8	28.0	—	—	NA	—
111	*Serif*	V28	BS	25.3	21.5	7.2	4.5	366	4.3
112	*Monoleen +*	OD	BY	46.3	33.5	10.7	5.8	1000	21.6T
113	*Cangrejo*	OD	BS	56.0	38.5	—	—	—	9.8
114	*Wellow Maid*	V31	BS	25.3	21.5	7.2	4.5	366	4.3
115	*Galway Blazer*	RN6	BS	31.0	24.0	7.5	5.8	465	4.3
116	*Sylphide*	RN7	BS	31.0	24.0	7.5	5.8	465	4.3
117	Not built	OD	—	—	—	—	—	—	—
118	Le Mare	OD	SL	—	26.3	—	—	—	—
119	*Lahli Lou*	CC7	BC	39.0	26.0	8.8	6.0	624	6.9
120	*Bacchante*	OD	BS	50.6	35.0	10.8	7.6	950	12.5
121	*Island Spell*	V30	BS	25.3	21.5	7.2	4.5	366	4.3
122	*Vive*	OD	BS	32.7	24.0	—	—	—	3.6
123	*Donita*	V32	BS	25.3	21.5	7.2	4.5	366	4.3
124	*Vertue XXXV*	V35	BS	25.3	21.5	7.2	4.5	366	4.3
125	*Andrillot II*	RN8	BS	31.0	24.0	7.5	5.8	465	4.3
126	*Not built*	OD	DI	—	14.0	—	—	—	—
127	*Harvesta*	OD	BS	37.3	28.0	9.9	4.5	650	7.0
128	C.P.L. Co.	PB	LA	20.5	—	—	—	—	—
129	Not built	OD	SL	—	18.0	—	—	—	—
130	*Sopranino*	BA1	BC	19.7	17.5	5.3	3.7	208	0.35
131	*Kongoni II*	TR1	KE	36.3	31.0	10.1	5.0	380	8.6
132	*Rana*	OD	KE	34.3	29.2	9.9	4.1	540	7.8
133	*Beyond*	OD	BC	43.1	32.0	10.6	6.3	690	10.8
134	*Gondolier*	V37	BS	25.3	21.5	7.2	4.5	366	4.3

No.	Name	Class	Rig	LOA (ft)	LWL (ft)	Beam (ft)	Draft (ft)	Sail (Sq ft)	Disp (Tons)
135	*Salamander*	V36	BS	25.3	21.5	7.2	4.5	366	4.3
136	*Kandy*	V39	BS	25.3	21.5	7.2	4.5	366	4.3
137	No name	OD	BS	25.0	18.0	—	—	—	—
138	*Aldyth*	V33	BS	25.3	21.5	7.2	4.5	366	4.3
139	*No name*	BR7	BS	33.5	25.3	8.3	5.3	463	5.9
140	*Levriere*	RN10	BS	31.0	24.0	7.5	5.8	465	4.3
141	*Orsa Minore*	RN9	BS	31.0	24.0	7.5	5.8	465	4.3
142	*Phrynie*	RN11	BS	31.0	24.0	7.5	5.8	465	4.3
143	C.P.L. Co.	PB	DI	7.6	—	—	—	—	—
144	*Maid of Malin*	BR8	BS	33.5	25.3	8.3	5.3	463	5.9
145	Fitzgerald	OD	BS	25.0	18.0	—	—	—	—
146	*Miranda IV*	OD	BS	52.5	39.0	11.4	7.5	1060	13.0
147	*Endeavour +*	V42	BS	25.3	21.5	7.2	4.5	366	4.3
148	*TadorneIII*	OD	KE	33.8	28.0	—	—	—	—
149	*Virtue*	V38	BS	25.3	21.5	7.2	4.5	366	4.3
150	*Festival Vertue +*	V40	BS	25.3	21.5	7.2	4.5	366	4.3
151	*Asali*	BR9	BS	33.5	25.3	8.3	5.3	463	5.9
152	*Cigno +*	RN12	BS	31.0	24.0	7.5	5.8	465	4.3
153	*Tilly Twin*	*OD*	BC	35.5	32.0	8.9	7.0	635	7.7
154	*Cardinal Bird +*	BA2	BC	19.7	17.5	5.3	3.7	208	0.4
155	*Water Music +*	OD	BC	35.5	32.0	8.9	7.0	635	7.7
156	*Gay Vertue*	V43	BS	25.3	21.5	7.2	4.5	366	4.3
157	*Cooinda*	RN13	BS	31.0	24.0	7.5	5.8	465	4.3
158	*Atlanta*	OD	DI	14.0	—	—	—	—	—
159	*Smiley*	V41	BS	25.3	21.5	7.2	4.5	366	4.3
160	*Flum II*	OD	SL	36.5	29.5	9.8	4.5	564	7.7
161	Clark	BA3	BC	19.7	17.5	5.3	3.7	208	0.4
162	*Southern Myth*	OD	BS	41.3	30.0	9.5	6.5	715	7.6
163	*Lutine*	OD	BY	58.5	41.5	13.2	8.6	1400	26.5
164	*Wanderer III*	OD	BC	30.3	26.5	8.5	5.0	423	8.0T
165	*Even*	OD	BS	57.3	39.4	10.3	7.8	1200	26.5T
166	*Artemis II +*	OD	BS	39.0	33.0	—	—	—	—
167	*Davalan*	V48	BS	25.3	21.5	7.2	4.5	366	4.3
168	*Atlanta II*	OD	DI	14.0	—	—	—	—	—
169	*De Wit*	BA4	BC	19.7	17.5	5.3	3.7	208	0.4
170	*Coimbra*	OD	CU	40.0	32.0	10.5	6.3	685	11.6
171	No information	—	—	—	—	—	—	—	—
172	*Thomas*	BA5	BC	19.7	17.5	5.3	3.7	208	0.4
173	*Electron*	BA3	BC	19.7	17.5	5.3	3.7	208	0.4
174	*La Bretonne*	V52	BS	25.3	21.5	7.2	4.5	366	4.3
175	*Lady Marguerite*	BR10	BS	33.5	25.3	8.3	5.3	463	5.9
176	*Speedwell*	V44	BS	25.3	21.5	7.2	4.5	366	4.3
177	*Morris*	V51	BS	25.3	21.5	7.2	4.5	366	4.3
178	*Eliza*	BA6	BC	19.7	17.5	5.3	3.7	208	0.4
179	Not built	WA	BC	30.3	26.5	8.5	5.0	423	8.0T
180	*Minion*	RY	BS	21.0	17.5	6.1	3.0	175	2.9T
181	*Draconis*	NCC1	CU	40.3	27.0	9.3	6.0	627	14.3T

No.	Name	Class	Rig	LOA (ft)	LWL (ft)	Beam (ft)	Draft (ft)	Sail (Sq ft)	Disp (Tons)
182	*Nina V*	OD	BC	47.7	34.8	10.8	7.0	1036	25.0T
183	*Rose of York*	NCC2	CU	38.4	27.0	9.1	6.0	627	12.9
184	*Taylor Trusty*	TR1	BS	36.3	31.0	10.0	5.0	380	8.6
185	D'Ornellas	OD	CU	—	33.0	—	—	—	—
186	*Fey Long*	OD	YW	29.0	26.0	—	—	—	—
187	*Doone*	V46	BS	25.3	21.5	7.2	4.5	366	4.3
188	*Merganser*	V47	BS	25.3	21.5	7.2	4.5	366	4.3
189	*Blue Jenny*	V49	BS	25.3	21.5	7.2	4.5	366	4.3
190	*Bettina +*	V58	BS	25.3	21.5	7.2	4.5	366	4.3
191	*Icebird*	V45	BS	25.3	21.5	7.2	4.5	366	4.3
192	*Cypsela*	OD	BC	48.0	38.0	11.0	8.2	1175	26.0T
193	*Jurgen +*	V50	BS	25.3	21.5	7.2	4.5	366	4.3
194	*Marna*	BR16	BS	33.5	25.3	8.3	5.3	463	5.9
195	*Morag Mhor*	OD	KE	72.3	60.4	16.0	7.0	1408	45.0
196	*Dante*	BA8	BC	19.7	17.5	5.3	3.7	208	0.4
197	Pearson	OD	MC	32.8	28.0	—	—	—	—
198	Scott	V53	BS	25.3	21.5	7.2	4.5	366	4.3
199	Not built	V57	BS	25.3	21.5	7.2	4.5	366	4.3
200	*Saga II*	BR11	BS	33.5	25.3	8.3	5.3	463	5.9
201	*Brits*	BA7	BC	19.7	17.5	5.3	3.7	208	0.4
202	*Dragonera*	DY2	GC	46.0	38.0	12.3	7.5	1410	24.2
203	*Chianti*	RL1	SL	23.3	19.5	6.8	3.9	275	2.7
204	*Valencia*	BA9	BC	19.7	17.5	5.3	3.7	208	0.4
205	*Pamela Jean*	V54	BS	25.3	21.5	7.2	4.5	366	4.3
206	*Lotus*	V55	BS	25.3	21.5	7.2	4.5	366	4.3
207	*Gleam*	OD	SB	30.0	26.3	—	—	—	—
208	*Pinna II*	OD	KE	43.9	34.0	11.6	5.6	—	23.1T
209	Not built	OD	—	—	37.0	—	—	—	—
210	*Anre Hulten*	BA10	BC	19.7	17.5	5.3	3.7	208	5.9
211	*Stella Mattutina*	RN14	BS	31.0	24.0	7.5	5.8	465	4.3
212	*Rakoa*	V56	BS	25.3	21.5	7.2	4.5	366	4.3
213	*L'Aghulas*	IN1	BC	20.0	17.8	6.0	2.5	172	2.7T
214	*Allan*	BA12	BC	19.7	17.5	5.3	3.7	208	0.4
215	Halford	BA11	BC	19.7	17.5	5.3	3.7	208	0.4
216	*Saraband*	BA14	BC	19.7	17.5	5.3	3.7	208	0.4
217	*Fitzgerlad*	BA13	BC	19.7	17.5	5.3	3.7	208	0.4
218	*Zulu*	OD	BS	47.8	35.0	11.2	7.0	1035	12.0
219	*Maid of Mourne*	NCC9	CU	40.3	27.0	9.3	6.0	627	14.2T
220	Not built	G7/1	YW	37.0	26.5	9.5	6.0	450	8.7
221	*Bora +?*	OD	BS	45.9	36.1	10.8	7.6	1000	21.7
222	*Austral Vertue*	V59	BS	25.3	21.5	7.2	4.5	366	4.3
223	Not built	V60	BS	25.3	21.5	7.2	4.5	366	4.3
224	*Odyssey*	OD	BC	42.0	32.0	11.0	5.0	785	11.0
225	Phibbs	OD	MY	43.0	—	—	—	—	—
226	*Penthi Sileia +*	V61	BS	25.3	21.5	7.2	4.5	366	4.3
227	*Shyraga*	OD	TW	95.0	88.0	19.5	7.0	NA	100.0
228	*Aryba*	LY3	SL	23.3	19.5	6.8	3.9	275	4.0T

No.	Name	Class	Rig	LOA (ft)	LWL (ft)	Beam (ft)	Draft (ft)	Sail (Sq ft)	Disp (Tons)
229	*Jen*	OD	BY	40.0	32.0	11.1	3.8	750	18.9T
230	*Ciaccona*	OD	BS	46.6	32.9	10.6	7.2	1000	21.5T
231	*Trekka*	CO1	YW	21.2	18.5	6.5	4.5	197	1.4
232	*Mouse Trap*	OD	CU	24.0	21.5	7.2	3.0	254	2.0
233	*Easterling*	BR13	BS	33.5	25.3	8.3	5.3	463	5.9
234	*Blackburn*	V62	BS	25.3	21.5	7.2	4.5	366	4.3
235	*Pazienza +*	OD	BS	59.1	43.5	14.0	8.8	1588	27.0
236	*Hamal III*	OD	CU	59.1	43.5	14.0	8.8	1588	27.0
237	Van Heygen	BA15	BC	19.7	17.5	5.3	3.7	208	0.4
238	Soton Boat Co.	PB	DI	—	7.6	—	—	—	—
239	Mills	V63	SL	25.3	21.5	7.2	4.5	366	4.3
240	*Araok +*	V66	SL	25.3	21.5	7.2	4.5	366	4.3
241	*Sofong*	V64	SL	25.3	21.5	7.2	4.5	366	4.3
242	Bennet	V65	SL	25.3	21.5	7.2	4.5	366	4.3
243	*Ninfea*	OD	CT	33.0	30.1	17.0	1.3	—	—
244	*Ravahine*	OD	TW	48.0	44.6	12.0	3.5	NA	10.5
245	Ciampi	OD	LA	14.0	—	—	—	800	23.4T
246	*Catriona +*	OD	BY	44.8	35.0	11.5	10.7	—	—
247	*Calypso*	OD	CU	—	24.0	—	—	—	—
248	Lodding	V69	BS	25.3	21.5	7.2	4.5	366	4.3
249	*Eos*	BR14	BS	33.5	25.3	8.3	5.3	463	5.9
250	*Kukri*	V74	BS	25.3	21.5	7.2	4.5	366	4.3
251	Christian	V70	BS	25.3	21.5	7.2	4.5	366	4.3
252	*Betsinda*	V67	BS	25.3	21.5	7.2	4.5	366	4.3
253	*Nora Sheila*	V71	BS	25.3	21.5	7.2	4.5	366	4.3
254	McIver	CO2	YW	20.5	18.5	6.5	4.5	199	1.4
255	*Great Days*	RC1	BS	35.0	27.5	9.7	4.3	432	7.5
256	Ciampi	OD	DI	14.0	—	—	—	—	—
257	*Khwab*	RL2	SL	23.3	19.5	6.8	3.9	275	2.7
258	*Star Sapphire*	OD	BK	73.7	50.3	16.7	7.0	1945	35.0
259	Molisset	CO3	YW	20.5	18.5	6.5	4.5	199	1.4
260	*Girl Pippa +*	OD	TW	40.3	36.9	11.6	4.5	95	14.7
261	*Santa Anna III*	OD	CU	40.O	34.1	—	—	—	—
262	*Sterna II*	OD	CU	—	24.0	—	—	—	—
263	Daldio	OD	SB	—	30.7	—	—	—	—
264	No information	—	—	—	—	—	—	—	—
265	*Golden Poppy +*	BA16	BC	19.7	17.5	5.3	3.7	208	0.4
266	*Kimwana +*	IN2	BC	20.0	17.8	6.0	2.5	172	2.7T
267	*Davis*	BA17	BC	19.7	17.5	5.3	3.7	208	0.4
268	*Gannet IV*	V73	BS	25.3	21.5	7.2	4.5	366	4.3
269	*Wanderer II*	WA	CU	39.0	28.0	9.5	3.5	490	25.5
270	*Dandy*	V72	BS	25.3	21.5	7.2	4.5	366	4.3
271	*Rosette of York*	OD	CU	32.0	24.0	8.4	5.3	468	5.0
272	Harvey	OD	DI	7.5	—	—	—	—	—
273	No name	OD	YT	18.0	—	—	—	—	—
274	Scott	IN4	BC	20.0	17.8	6.0	2.5	172	2.7T
275	King	IN5	BC	20.0	17.8	6.0	2.5	172	2.7T

No.	Name	Class	Rig	LOA (ft)	LWL (ft)	Beam (ft)	Draft (ft)	Sail (Sq ft)	Disp (Tons)
276	Barker	BA18	BC	19.7	17.5	5.3	3.7	208	0.4
277	*Areil II +*	RO	SL	—	24.0	—	—	—	—
278	*Jabounic II*	OD	CU	36.4	27.2	10.7	4.9	700	6.8
279	*Donella*	DO1	BC	43.0	33.0	10.8	6.0	831	13.6
280	Not built	OD	CU	—	32.0	—	—	—	—
281	*Kantread*	V68	BS	25.3	21.5	7.2	4.5	366	4.3
282	*Shandy*	BA19	BC	19.7	17.5	5.3	3.7	208	0.4
282A	*Boomerang*	BR12	BS	33.5	25.3	8.3	5.3	463	5.9
283	Crags	BA20	BC	19.7	17.5	5.3	3.7	208	0.4
284	No name	NO	BS	27.8	21.5	7.8	4.3	343	3.5
285	McCloud	BA21	BC	19.7	17.5	5.3	3.7	208	0.4
286	*Scampi*	G7/2	SL	37.0	26.5	9.5	6.0	450	8.7
287	*Famalu*	OD	BC	52.2	41.5	12.4	6.6	1157	21.4
288	*Seamiste +*	V78	BS	25.3	21.5	7.2	4.5	366	4.3
289	*Westerly*	V76	BS	25.3	21.5	7.2	4.5	366	4.3
290	*Susanna*	OD	BY	48.0	32.0	10.7	6.9	980	10.5
291	*Rosette*	OD	SL	32.0	24.0	—	—	—	—
292	Walker	V82	BS	25.3	21.5	7.2	4.5	366	4.3
293	*Maggie* D	V77	BS	25.3	21.5	7.2	4.5	366	4.3
294	*Jason +*	V75	BS	25.3	21.5	7.2	4.5	366	4.3
295	Frandsen	V79	BS	25.3	21.5	7.2	4.5	366	4.3
296	*Tamvakis*	V80	BS	25.3	21.5	7.2	4.5	366	4.3
297	Bryant	V81	BS	25.3	21.5	7.2	4.5	366	4.3
298	*Sula*	NO3	BS	27.7	21.5	7.8	4.3	343	3.5
299	No information	—	—	—	—	—	—	—	—
300	*Vega of Bosham*	V83	BS	25.3	21.5	7.2	4.5	366	4.3
301	*Quasi*	NO2	BS	27.7	21.5	7.8	4.3	343	3.5
302	Not built	—	—	—	—	—	—	—	—
303	*Nobito*	OD	LA	31.8	28.0	9.1	4.1	NA	10.0T
304	*Blue Mink*	NO1	BS	27.7	21.5	7.8	4.3	343	3.5
305	*Rimouski*	V86	BS	25.3	21.5	7.2	4.5	366	4.3
306	*Foresight*	V85	BS	25.3	21.5	7.2	4.5	366	4.3
307	*Thea*	OD	CU	41.3	31.0	10.8	5.5	800	18.9T
308	*Mafre*	OD	BK	61.3	42.1	13.9	6.9	1455	23.1
309	*Bettina*	G7/3	SL	37.0	26.5	9.5	6.0	450	8.7
310	*Seamouse*	RL3	SL	23.3	19.5	6.8	3.9	275	2.7
311	*Cheoy Lee*	V87	BS	25.3	21.5	7.2	4.5	366	4.3
312	*Kohala*	V88	BS	25.3	21.5	7.2	4.5	366	4.3
313	Not built	NO2	BS	27.7	21.5	7.8	4.3	343	3.5
314	*Riwaru*	OD	KE	48.7	33.5	11.3	5.8	1004	15.0
315	Not built	NO3	BS	27.7	21.5	7.8	4.3	343	3.5
316	*Rumpus*	RL6	SL	23.3	19.5	6.8	3.9	275	2.7
317	No name	BA22	BC	19.7	17.5	5.3	3.7	208	0.4
318	*Kestel*	NO4	BS	27.7	21.5	7.8	4.3	343	3.5
319	*Black Witch II*	NO6	BS	27.7	21.5	7.8	4.3	343	3.5
320	*Mea*	V89	BS	25.3	21.5	7.2	4.5	366	4.3
321	Bush	TR2	BS	36.3	31.0	10.0	5.0	380	8.9

No.	Name	Class	Rig	LOA (ft)	LWL (ft)	Beam (ft)	Draft (ft)	Sail (Sq ft)	Disp (Tons)
322	Not built	G7/4	SL	37.0	26.5	9.5	6.0	450	8.7
323	*Gilliflower*	NO5	BS	27.7	21.5	7.8	4.3	343	3.5
324	*Wanita*	BR15	BS	33.5	25.3	8.3	5.3	463	5.9
325	*Ariel*	V90	BS	25.3	21.5	7.2	4.5	366	4.3
326	Sainsbury	OD	BS	38.0	28.0	9.8	4.4	500	8.8
327	*Sphinx*	RL4	SL	23.5	19.5	6.8	3.9	275	2.7
328	*Caprice*	CO4	YW	20.5	18.5	6.5	4.5	199	1.4
329	Not built	OD	BK	72.1	58.4	17.4	7.3	1860	55.1
330	*Popey Duck+*	CO5	YW	20.5	18.5	6.5	4.5	199	1.4
331	*Bravade*	NO7	BS	27.7	21.5	7.8	4.3	343	3.5
332	*Kelda*	V91	BS	25.3	21.5	7.2	4.5	366	4.3
333	*Catspaw*	RC2	BS	34.6	27.5	9.7	4.3	403	7.5
334	Branch	OD	BS	34.0	27.0	10.8	3.9	400	7.0
335	*Margam Abbey*	OD	PC	88.0	80.0	20.0	9.5	NA	117.2
336	*Calvados*	NO8	BS	27.7	21.5	7.8	4.3	343	3.5
337	*Alcor+*	OD	BY	75.0	50.0	17.0	10.3	2385	48.5
338	*Maalish*	NO9	BS	27.7	21.5	7.8	4.3	343	3.5
338A	*Goulandris*	OD	BK	72.5	52.0	16.6	8.0	1850	46.2
339	*Spindryft*	CO6	SL	20.5	18.5	6.5	4.5	199	1.4
340	Pritchard	V92	BS	25.3	21.5	7.2	4.5	366	4.3
341	*Clemi*	OD	SL	29.5	22.5	9.0	4.3	380	4.5
342	*Alcyone*	RL5	SL	23.3	19.5	6.8	3.9	275	2.7
343	Davidson	BA23	BC	19.7	17.5	5.3	3.7	208	0.4
344	*Mousetrap*	OD	CU	—	21.5	—	—	—	—
345	*Fibreclad*	OD	LA	17.3	15.3	—	—	—	—
346	Padilla	BA22	BC	19.7	17.5	5.3	3.7	208	0.4
347	*Vale of York*	OD	BS	36.1	24.0	9.7	3.8	495	5.8
348	*Puritan*	V93	BS	25.3	21.5	7.2	4.5	366	4.3
349	Bourne	V94	BS	25.3	21.5	7.2	4.5	366	4.3
350	*Lady Margaret*	RC3	BS	34.5	27.5	9.7	4.3	450	8.1
351	Not built	OD	BY	—	—	—	—	—	—
352	*Venitia*	OD	MY	40.9	36.3	12.0	3.9	NA	13.1
353	Not built	NO	BC	27.7	21.5	7.8	4.3	343	3.5
354	*Carola*	DO5	BC	44.0	33.1	11.7	6.0	889	15.2
355	*Butler*	NO10	BC	27.7	21.5	7.8	4.3	343	3.5
355A	*Crissa*	DO6	BC	44.0	33.1	11.7	6.0	889	13.6
356	Not built	V96	BS	25.3	21.5	7.2	4.5	366	4.3
356A	*Rebecca*	DO7	BC	44.0	33.1	11.7	6.0	889	13.6
357	Challinor	V95	BS	25.3	21.5	7.2	4.5	366	4.3
358	*Freelander*	OD	TW	70.0	65.0	14.3	4.0	300	25.3
359	*Tern II*	V97	BS	25.3	21.5	7.2	4.5	366	4.3
360	*Coryphaena*	DO4	BC	44.0	33.1	11.7	6.0	889	13.6
361	*Mia*	DO2	BC	43.0	33.0	10.9	6.0	831	13.8
362	*Goldern Gain*	PT1	DL	33.9	28.0	9.0	4.0	255	10.7
363	*Amitie*	NO11	BS	27.7	21.5	7.8	4.3	343	3.5
364	*Charity+*	V98	BS	25.3	21.5	7.2	4.5	366	4.3
365	*Cocola*	OD	BS	32.4	24.0	9.3	4.8	446	6.2

No.	Name	Class	Rig	LOA (ft)	LWL (ft)	Beam (ft)	Draft (ft)	Sail (Sq ft)	Disp (Tons)
366	*Corio Vertue*	V99	BS	25.3	21.5	7.2	4.5	366	4.3
367	*Stormvogel*	OD	BK	74.5	59.3	16.0	9.3	2181	31.2
368	No name	V102	BS	25.3	21.5	7.2	4.5	366	4.3
369	*Alaria*	V101	BS	25.3	21.5	7.2	4.5	366	4.3
370	*Endeavour*	V103	BS	25.3	21.5	7.2	4.5	366	4.3
371	*Tumbelina*	OD	BS	38.0	28.0	9.8	6.5	690	8.8
372	Turner	OD	BY	25.8	23.0	8.0	5.3	380	2.8
373	Jolly	V104	BS	25.3	21.5	7.2	4.5	366	4.3
374	Hallywell	CO7	YW	20.5	18.5	6.5	4.5	199	1.4
375	No name	DO	BC	44.0	33.1	11.7	6.0	889	13.6
376	*Audacity*	AU1	SL	21.5	18.5	7.3	1.7	203	1.6
377	*Tango*	CO8	SL	20.5	18.5	6.5	4.5	199	1.4
378	*Sheesmyne II+*	NO12	BS	27.7	21.5	7.8	4.3	343	3.5
379	*Gay Gander*	RC4	BS	34.6	27.5	9.7	4.3	403	8.1
380	*Return*	V100	BS	25.3	21.5	7.2	4.5	366	4.3
381	*Polara*	DO11	BY	44.0	33.1	11.7	6.0	889	13.6
382	*Manita*	OD	BY	66.5	47.5	14.1	9.5	1978	33.0
383	*Concerto*	V105	BS	25.3	21.5	7.2	4.5	366	4.3
384	*Chlaloca*	CO9	SL	20.5	18.5	6.5	4.5	199	1.4
385	*Lobie II*	DO3	BC	44.0	33.1	11.7	6.0	889	13.6
386	*Querida*	OD	SL	40.0	28.0	9.0	5.7	800	5.6
387	*Kainui*	V106	BS	25.3	21.5	7.2	4.5	366	4.3
388	*Greylag of Arklow*	CC10	BC	38.4	26.0	8.8	5.5	624	6.9
389	*Prince Neufchatel*	OD	CU	33.1	27.0	9.5	5.8	611	8.6
390	*Neptune*	NO13	BS	27.7	21.5	7.8	4.3	343	3.5
391	Not built	OD	—	—	—	—	—	—	—
392	Porter	CO10	YW	20.5	18.5	6.5	4.5	199	1.4
393S	*Scythe*	OD	YW	42.0	29.5	10.0	6.7	500	10.4
394	*Reefer*	CO11	YW	20.5	18.5	6.5	4.5	199	1.4
395	*Sea Fox*	CO12	YW	20.5	18.5	6.5	4.5	199	1.4
396	*Serlio*	TR3	BS	36.3	31.0	10.0	5.0	380	8.6
397	*Dhorus Mhor*	DM1	KE	49.3	38.0	12.5	6.5	949	13.6
398	Arney	V107	BS	25.3	21.5	7.2	4.5	366	4.3
399	*Fabella*	OD	KE	52.3	41.8	13.0	6.0	1000	24.0
400	*Micia*	DO8	BC	44.0	33.1	11.7	6.0	889	13.6
401	*Fialar*	V110	BS	25.3	21.5	7.2	4.5	366	4.3
402	*Porto Gaio II*	DO9	BC	43.0	33.0	10.8	6.0	831	13.6
403	*Surf+*	NO14	BS	27.7	21.5	7.8	4.3	343	3.5
404	*Pinna II*	OD	KE	43.0	34.0	—	—	—	—
405	*Kerilos*	OD	KE	78.1	54.8	17.8	10.7	2500	56.5
406	*Marial*	PD	BK	28.0	25.0	9.0	3.5	293	5.6
407	*Quetacotl*	DO10	BC	43.0	33.0	10.8	6.0	831	13.6
408	*Marie Galante*	TR2	BS	36.3	31.0	10.0	5.0	380	8.6
409	Mackie	IN6	BC	20.0	17.8	6.0	2.5	172	2.7T
410	*Franda*	DM2	KE	49.3	38.0	12.2	6.5	949	16.9
411	*Normandy*	NO15	BS	27.7	21.5	7.8	4.3	343	3.5
412	*Dodder*	OD	PC	43.8	40.0	11.3	3.1	144	8.6

No.	Name	Class	Rig	LOA (ft)	LWL (ft)	Beam (ft)	Draft (ft)	Sail (Sq ft)	Disp (Tons)
413	*Bonaventure of Lyes*	V108	BS	25.3	21.5	7.2	4.5	366	4.3
414	Playdon	BA23	BC	19.7	17.5	5.3	3.7	208	0.4
415	Not built	RN	BS	31.0	24.0	7.5	5.8	465	4.3
416	*Reprieve*	PD	SL	28.0	25.0	9.0	3.5	293	5.6
417	*Pavan*	V115	BS	25.3	21.5	7.2	4.5	366	4.3
418	Not built	DO12	BC	43.0	33.0	10.8	6.0	831	13.6
419	*Kaliste*	OD	SL	28.0	24.5	8.2	5.0	371	6.4
420	*Raumati*	V112	BS	25.3	21.5	7.2	4.5	366	4.3
421	*Tom Thumb*	V111	BS	25.3	21.5	7.2	4.5	366	4.3
422	*Amitie*	NO11	BS	27.7	21.5	7.8	4.3	343	3.5
423	*Glad II*	CO14	YW	20.5	18.5	6.5	4.5	199	1.4
424	Vida	BA24	BC	19.7	17.5	5.3	3.7	208	0.4
425	*Simo*	V113	BS	25.3	21.5	7.2	4.5	366	4.3
426	*China Bird*	OD	SL	37.8	27.9	9.8	6.3	580	8.8
427	Not built	V	BS	25.3	21.5	7.2	4.5	366	4.3
428	*Transit*	OD	SL	54.0	43.0	15.0	5.3	1450	28.6
429	*Giga*	OD	KE	55.0	39.0	12.7	8.1	1260	21.2
430	*Blue Leopard*	OD	KE	111.8	75.0	19.0	9.5	3500	47.8
431	*Diadem of Dewlish*	OD	TW	95.7	89.0	21.5	8.8	NA	139.5
432	*Karis*	NO17	BS	27.7	21.5	7.8	4.3	343	3.5
433	*Favorita*	NO18	BS	27.7	21.5	7.8	4.3	343	3.5
434	Not built	—	—	—	—	—	—	—	—
435	*Camay*	NO16	BS	27.7	21.5	7.8	4.3	343	3.5
436	*Aldebaran*	V114	BS	25.3	21.5	7.2	4.5	366	4.3
437	*Albertine Cornelia*	DO14	BC	43.0	33.0	10.8	6.0	831	13.6
438	*Les Six Marie*	NO19	BS	27.7	21.5	7.8	4.3	343	3.5
439	*Cardhu*	OD	CU	41.3	31.0	10.8	6.3	771	11.8
440	Barret	BA25	BC	19.7	17.5	5.3	3.7	208	0.4
441	Vos	BR17	BS	33.5	25.3	8.3	5.3	463	5.9
442	*Alessio*	OD	TW	—	76.3	—	—	NA	—
443	*Paralos*	OD	SL	32.0	24.0	—	—	—	—
444	*Ate Logo*	DM3	KE	49.3	38.0	12.2	6.5	949	16.9
445	*Hoitak*	V116	BS	25.3	21.5	7.2	4.5	366	4.3
446	*Etesea*	DM4	KE	49.3	38.0	12.2	6.5	949	16.9
447	Falkenberg	DO13	BC	43.0	33.0	10.8	6.0	831	13.6
448	*Aitor*	OD	KE	72.2	58.4	17.4	7.2	1823	55.1
449	*Julia Jane*	V127	BS	25.3	21.5	7.2	4.5	366	4.3
450	*Treasure*	TE1	CU	46.3	33.8	12.0	7.0	1087	16.3
451	*Raggio Verde*	OD	CU	33.1	32.0	9.5	5.8	500	11.3T
452	*Rose Rambler*	RR	SL	35.3	27.5	9.8	4.8	550	8.1
453	*Rose Fleur*	DM5	KE	49.3	38.0	12.2	6.5	949	16.9
454	*Susanna II*	OD	YW	63.5	45.3	14.6	9.2	1849	31.3
455	*Saro Scimitar*	SC1	BS	20.3	16.0	6.0	3.0	190	1.1
456	*Cresta of Wight*	NO20	BS	27.7	21.5	7.8	4.3	343	3.5
457	*Friska*	V129	BS	25.3	21.5	7.2	4.5	366	4.3
458	*Quan Yin*	OD	CU	36.0	27.0	—	—	—	—
459	*Valere*	LY8	SL	23.3	19.5	8.8	3.9	275	2.7

No.	Name	Class	Rig	LOA (ft)	LWL (ft)	Beam (ft)	Draft (ft)	Sail (Sq ft)	Disp (Tons)
460	*Kotimu*	V117	BS	25.3	21.5	7.2	4.5	366	4.3
461	*Veritas*	V118	BS	25.3	21.5	7.2	4.5	366	4.3
462	*Melita*	OD	TW	58.3	53.5	14.0	4.7	NA	26.4
463	*Eastern Wanderer*	WA1	SL	29.6	24.5	9.3	5.0	438	6.5
464	*Chinita*	V119	BS	25.3	21.5	7.2	4.5	366	4.3
465	*Stelda*	V120	BS	25.3	21.5	7.2	4.5	366	4.3
466	*Christina Ann*	OD	GC	25.3	21.5	7.2	4.5	366	4.3
467	*Jan Gilda +*	V123	BS	25.3	21.5	7.2	4.5	366	4.3
468	*Axel +*	V124	GC	25.3	21.5	7.2	4.5	366	4.3
469	*Aetea*	OD	TW	105.1	96.0	21.7	8.0	NA	185.0
470	No name	RR2	SL	35.3	27.5	9.8	4.8	500	3.6
471	Not built	OD	MY	60.7	—	—	—	—	—
472	*Irene*	NO21	BS	27.7	21.5	7.8	4.3	343	3.5
473	*Nellieday*	PD17	BK	28.0	25.0	9.0	3.5	293	5.6
474	*Christmas Rose*	TR3	BS	36.3	31.0	10.0	5.0	380	13.0
475	*Fram*	OD	SL	38.8	26.0	10.3	4.5	700	7.2
476	*Magadisen*	OD	KE	53.6	42.0	14.0	6.8	1230	25.7
477	*Madifre*	OD	CU	38.0	32.2	—	—	—	—
478	MacDonald	BA27	BC	19.7	17.5	5.3	3.7	208	0.4
479	*Drumler*	V125	BS	25.3	21.5	7.2	4.5	366	4.3
480	*Cavalier*	LY2	SL	23.3	19.5	6.8	3.9	275	2.7
481	*Calluna*	NO22	BS	27.7	21.5	7.8	4.3	343	3.5
482	Steven	WA2	SL	29.6	24.5	9.3	5.0	438	9.2
483	*Contessina*	V121	BS	25.3	21.5	7.2	4.5	366	4.3
484	Ribecto	CO	YW	20.5	18.5	6.5	4.5	199	1.4
485	Not built	NO23	BS	27.7	21.5	7.8	4.3	343	3.5
486	Parrat	BA28	BC	19.7	17.5	5.3	3.7	208	0.4
487	Petersen	BA29	BC	19.7	17.5	5.3	3.7	208	0.4
488	*Leonoreta*	CO15	YW	20.5	18.5	6.5	4.5	199	1.4
489	*Santa Lucia II*	OD	KE	64.3	50.5	16.5	7.5	1425	42.0
490	*Pittulie Pride*	OD	KE	48.0	33.5	11.3	6.3	902	15.1
491	*Dolly*	V132	BS	25.3	21.5	7.2	4.5	366	4.3
492	*Verena Rose*	V128	BS	25.3	21.5	7.2	4.5	366	4.3
493	*Fab*	V126	BS	25.3	21.5	7.2	4.5	366	4.3
494	Cartwright	WA3	SL	29.6	24.5	9.3	5.0	438	9.2
495	*Havssula*	RC2	BS	35.0	27.5	9.7	4.3	403	8.1
496	*Tresco*	OD	SL	37.4	31.3	10.6	5.0	440	9.0
497	Minchin	WA4	SL	29.6	24.5	9.3	5.0	438	9.2
498	*Lamadine*	OD	KE	97.0	68.0	17.5	9.3	2502	48.3
499	*Tesse*	TS	SL	30.0	22.5	9.0	4.3	399	5.3
500	*Klompen*	WA6	SL	29.6	24.5	9.3	5.0	438	9.2
501	*Widgee*	WA7	SL	29.6	24.5	9.3	5.0	438	9.2
502	*Sekyd*	V131	BS	25.3	21.5	7.2	4.5	366	4.3
503	*Baltic Wanderer*	WA5	SL	29.6	24.5	9.3	5.0	438	9.2
504	*Sululu*	OD	KE	41.7	33.0	11.0	5.5	1325	13.9
505	*Shelmalier*	OD	CU	58.4	41.5	13.6	8.6	1423	25.3
506	*Topolina*	WA8	SL	29.6	24.5	9.3	5.0	438	9.2

No.	Name	Class	Rig	LOA (ft)	LWL (ft)	Beam (ft)	Draft (ft)	Sail (Sq ft)	Disp (Tons)
507	*Tomada*	WA9	SL	29.6	24.5	9.3	5.0	438	9.2
508	*Tarema*	CO16	YW	20.5	18.5	6.5	4.5	199	1.4
509	*Sainte Agnes*	NO24	BS	27.7	21.5	7.8	4.3	343	3.5
510	Pecklerd	V133	BS	25.3	21.5	7.2	4.5	366	4.3
511	*Dufresne*	OD	TW	64.9	59.0	16.3	4.5	740	30.6
512	*Tamborella*	OD	CU	42.8	34.0	11.6	5.6	698	12.4
513	Karremaly	OD	CU	—	33.1	—	—	—	—
514	Teece	BA30	BC	19.7	17.5	5.3	3.7	208	0.4
515	Not built	OD	SL	44.3	33.3	11.5	7.2	817	11.6
516	*Aotea*	V134	BS	25.3	21.5	7.2	4.5	366	4.3
517	Clark	WA12	SL	29.6	24.5	9.3	5.0	438	9.2
518	*Clamar*	CO17	YW	20.5	18.5	6.5	4.5	199	1.4
519	*Patience*	V136	BS	25.3	21.5	7.2	4.5	366	4.3
520	Leach	OD	TN	18.0	16.0	7.5	1.9	17	1.4
521	Corrao	CO18	SL	20.5	18.5	6.5	4.5	199	1.4
522	*Salar*	PB	S/K	39.0	31.0	11.3	5.3	642	10.3
523	*Alchemilla*	WA10	SL	29.6	24.5	9.3	5.0	438	9.2
524	McClelland	CO19	SL	20.5	18.5	6.5	4.5	199	1.4
525	*Shaheen*	LY9	SL	23.3	19.5	6.8	3.9	275	2.7
526	*Arwen*	OD	SL	35.0	28.5	10.2	5.3	536	8.6
527	*Calvados*	V	BS	25.3	21.5	7.2	4.5	366	4.3
528	*Fionn*	V140	GC	25.3	21.5	7.2	4.5	366	4.3
529	Rene	CO23	YW	20.5	18.5	6.5	4.5	199	1.4
530	*Albacore*	OD	CU	60.4	45.3	14.6	9.2	1669	31.3
531	*Aries II*	V138	BS	25.3	21.5	7.2	4.5	366	4.3
532	*Dorcelle*	SA2	S/K	39.0	31.0	11.3	5.3	618	10.3
533	*Kea*	V142	BS	25.3	21.5	7.2	4.5	366	4.3
534	Pedersen	RR3	BS	35.0	27.5	9.5	4.3	403	13.0
535	*Ilaria +*	OD	CU	51.5	37.5	12.0	8.0	1166	17.2
536	No name	BA31	BC	19.7	17.5	5.3	3.7	208	0.4
537	Hill	CO20	YW	20.5	18.5	6.5	4.5	199	1.4
538	Basson	CO21	YW	20.5	18.5	6.5	4.5	199	1.4
539	Blucher'alton	CO22	YW	20.5	18.5	6.5	4.5	199	1.4
540	*Druiana*	WA13	GC	29.6	24.5	9.3	5.0	438	9.2
541	*Coppelia*	V137	BS	25.3	21.5	7.2	4.5	366	4.3
542	*Dawn*	V143	BS	25.3	21.5	7.2	4.5	366	4.3
543	Not built	V	BS	25.3	21.5	7.2	4.5	366	4.3
544	*Shenandoah*	WA15	GC	29.6	24.5	9.3	5.0	438	9.2
545	*Chinook*	CO24	BS	20.5	18.5	6.5	4.5	199	1.4
546	*Amitie II*	FR2	SL	38.8	26.0	10.3	4.5	750	7.2
547	Monrome	CO25	YW	20.5	18.5	6.5	4.5	199	1.4
548	*September Moon*	DM6	KE	49.3	38.0	12.2	6.5	949	16.9
549	*Tiki*	CO26	YW	20.5	18.5	6.5	4.5	199	1.4
550	*Phoenix*	V145	BS	25.3	21.5	7.2	4.5	366	4.3
551	*Tilda*	CO27	YW	20.5	18.5	6.5	4.5	199	1.4
552	*Quo Vadis*	DO16	BC	43.0	33.0	10.8	6.0	831	13.6
553	Not built	CO28	BS	20.5	18.5	6.5	4.5	199	1.4

No.	Name	Class	Rig	LOA (ft)	LWL (ft)	Beam (ft)	Draft (ft)	Sail (Sq ft)	Disp (Tons)
554	*Storm Petrel II*	BA34	BC	19.7	17.5	5.3	3.7	208	0.4
555	Debus	BA33	BC	19.7	17.5	5.3	3.7	208	0.4
556	*Redos*	OD	KE	54.2	48.0	13.5	7.0	1253	24.0
556A	*Crislen III*	OD	KE	54.2	48.0	13.5	7.0	1253	24.0
557	*Tangimoana*	CO29	YW	20.5	18.5	6.5	4.5	199	1.4
558	Stadelfeld	CO30	YW	20.5	18.5	6.5	4.5	199	1.4
559	Dotter	AU	SL	21.4	18.5	7.3	1.7	203	1.6
560	*Randax*	OD	YW	54.5	40.0	13.7	8.4	1324	21.5
561	*Airedale*	WA16	SL	29.6	24.5	9.3	5.0	438	9.2
562	Fehringer	CO31	YW	20.5	18.5	6.5	4.5	199	1.4
563	*Treasure*	TE1	SL	46.3	33.8	12.0	7.0	1175	16.1
564	Hordern	WA17	SL	29.6	24.5	9.3	5.0	438	9.2
565	*Swala*	OD	BS	46.8	35.3	12.0	7.6	930	14.9
566	Ozenne	WA18	SL	29.6	24.5	9.3	5.0	438	9.2
567	Wilson	CO32	YW	20.5	18.5	6.5	4.5	199	1.4
568	*La Gallaire II*	DM7	KE	49.3	38.0	12.2	6.5	949	16.9
569	Stevens	OD	SL	36.0	28.0	—	—	—	—
570	*Sea Laughter III*	OD	KE	61.5	46.0	14.4	6.7	1422	25.0
571	Halliwell	BA35	BC	19.7	17.5	5.3	3.7	208	0.4
572	*Sails of Dawn*	OD	YW	56.3	40.0	13.5	7.0	1219	25.5
573	*Martru Wanderer*	WA19	SL	29.6	24.5	9.3	5.0	438	9.2
574	*Tanera*	V146	BS	25.3	21.5	7.2	4.5	366	4.3
575	*Carbineer 44*	PB	KE	44.0	36.0	12.2	6.0	650	16.0
576	*Centaur*	PB	SL	26.0	21.4	8.4	3.0	294	2.8
577	*Enteara*	OD	KE	63.4	47.6	14.8	7.6	1530	23.5
578	Kemp	V147	BS	25.3	21.5	7.2	4.5	366	4.3
579	*Lucina*	DO15	BC	43.0	33.0	10.8	6.0	831	16.9
580	*Airin*	OD	KE	99.5	74.0	21.0	7.2	3023	66.6
581	*Salar 60*	PB	KE	59.7	50.0	15.1	7.0	1350	28.0
582	Bruveris	V148	BS	25.3	21.5	7.2	4.5	366	4.3
583	Brimson	CO33	YW	20.5	18.5	6.5	4.5	199	1.4
584	Not built	DY	GC	45.8	38.0	12.3	7.5	1410	24.2
585	*Yacabba*	V149	BS	25.3	21.5	7.2	4.5	366	4.3
586	*Gulliver Girl +*	SA21	SL	39.0	31.0	11.3	5.3	618	10.3
587	*Fargo II*	SA19	SL	39.0	31.0	11.3	5.3	618	10.3
588	Butland	PB	—	22.0	—	—	—	—	—
589	*Seamaster 23*	PB	BS	23.0	19.8	8.3	2.5	250	2.2
590	Katransky	CO34	YW	20.5	18.5	6.5	4.5	199	1.4
591	*Pageant*	PB	SL	23.0	19.0	8.0	2.8	236	2.0
592	*Arwen II*	OD	KE	56.0	43.5	14.3	7.8	1285	33.0
593	Gillis	RR4	BS	35.0	27.5	9.7	4.3	403	13.0
594	Ross	BA36	BC	19.7	17.5	5.3	3.7	208	0.4
595	Not built	OD	TW	—	119.0	—	—	NA	—
596	Melling	CO34	YW	20.5	18.5	6.5	4.5	199	1.4
597	*Timari*	TS2	SL	30.0	22.5	9.0	4.3	399	5.3
598	Barns	CO35	SL	20.5	18.5	6.5	4.5	199	1.4
599	Jensen	BA37	BC	19.7	17.5	5.3	3.7	208	0.4

No.	Name	Class	Rig	LOA (ft)	LWL (ft)	Beam (ft)	Draft (ft)	Sail (Sq ft)	Disp (Tons)
600	*Jouster*	PB	SL	21.0	17.0	7.4	3.5	181	1.0
601	*Leone*	V150	BS	25.3	21.5	7.2	4.5	366	4.3
602	Perreault	V151	BS	25.3	21.5	7.2	4.5	366	4.3
603	*Longbow*	PB	S/K	31.0	25.0	9.5	4.5	383	4.5
604	*Via Maris*	OD	KE	51.0	37.1	12.5	6.5	944	16.6
605	*Sa Sheer*	CO37	SL	20.5	18.5	6.5	4.5	199	1.4
606	*Fastnet 27*	PB	MB	27.1	24.0	9.5	2.0	NA	2.5
607	*Cadama*	OD	KE	72.0	54.1	16.8	7.5	1914	35.2
608	No information	—	—	—	—	—	—	—	—
609	No name	MCA	KE	45.0	35.0	12.0	6.0	800	12.5
610	*Warwick*	PB	BS	21.5	18.8	7.8	2.8	196	1.7
611	*Seamaster 19*	PB	BS	19.0	16.5	7.2	3.3	184	1.5
612	Tideman	CO38	SL	20.5	18.5	6.5	4.5	199	1.4
613	Not built	V152	BS	25.3	21.5	7.2	4.5	366	4.3
613	*Ebbutt*	OD	KE	70.0	54.0	14.3	9.3	1485	23.0
614	*Esperanto*	MCO	SL	24.0	20.5	7.4	4.5	240	1.9
615	*Goldfarb*	CO39	SL	20.5	18.5	6.5	4.5	199	1.4
616	Dodd	V153	BS	25.3	21.5	7.2	4.5	366	4.3
617	*D'Urville*	OD	TW	70.4	63.0	18.3	5.5	NA	45.0
618	Smith	CO42	SL	20.5	18.5	6.5	4.5	199	1.4
619	Plant	AU	SL	21.5	18.5	7.3	1.7	203	1.6
620	*Fionn Choire*	G8/	SL	38.8	30.6	11.0	5.3	745	10.8
621	*Loch Garth*	V154	BS	25.3	21.5	7.2	4.5	366	4.3
622	*Moody 44*	PB	KE	44.0	34.0	12.6	5.8	760	11.4
623	*Halcyon II*	V155	BS	25.3	21.5	7.2	4.5	366	4.3
624	*Manuita II*	MCO	SL	24.0	21.4	—	—	—	—
625	Bernardi	V157	BS	25.3	21.5	7.2	4.5	366	4.3
626	No name	OD	KE	68.0	60.0	—	—	—	—
627	Hitchman	CO40	SL	20.5	18.5	6.5	4.5	199	1.4
628	*Solveig*	DO17	BC	43.0	33.0	10.8	6.0	831	12.0T
629	*Conway & Solway*	PB	S/K	35.8	30.4	11.2	6.0	553	7.9
630	T/T Fishery Prot	OD	TW	111.5	—	—	—	—	—
631	Young	V156	BS	25.3	21.5	7.2	4.5	366	4.3
632	Dry	V158	BS	25.3	21.5	7.2	4.5	366	4.3
633	*Sallust*	BR18	BS	33.5	25.3	8.3	5.3	463	5.9
634	Elsperson	BR19	BS	33.5	25.3	8.3	5.3	463	5.9
635	*Renown*	PB	S/K	31.0	24.0	9.5	4.5	440	4.2
636	*Running Tide of Avon*	G8/4	KE	38.8	30.6	11.0	5.3	745	10.8
637	*Carbineer 46*	PB	KE	46.5	36.0	12.2	6.0	850	16.3
638	*Ferro Ketch*	OD	KE	45.5	33.5	12.0	7.0	1087	16.3
639	*Wind Jammer*	SAW3	SL	39.0	31.0	11.3	5.3	618	18.8T
640	*Salmo Salar*	SAW1	SL	39.0	31.0	11.3	5.3	618	18.8T
641	*Dorcelle*	SAW2	KE	39.0	31.0	11.3	5.3	618	18.8T
642	Jiskooy	SAW4	SL	39.0	31.0	11.3	5.3	618	18.8T
643	*Leizaola*	V159	BS	25.3	21.5	7.2	4.5	366	4.3
644	*Pumpkin*	CO43	SL	20.5	18.5	6.5	4.5	199	1.4
645	*Seychelles*	PB	KE	50.0	38.0	14.0	6.0	959	22.0

No.	Name	Class	Rig	LOA (ft)	LWL (ft)	Beam (ft)	Draft (ft)	Sail (Sq ft)	Disp (Tons)
646	*Buccaneer*	PB	KE	39.0	31.0	11.3	5.3	618	10.3
647	*Selchie*	CO44	SL	20.5	18.5	6.5	4.5	199	1.4
647A	*Moody 44*	MPB	KE	44.0	34.0	12.6	5.8	760	11.0
648	*Sunrise*	TE2	SL	46.3	33.8	12.5	7.0	1087	16.3
649	Schmidt	CO41	SL	20.5	18.5	6.5	4.5	199	1.4
650	*Aquamarine*	PB	KE	39.6	30.5	11.5	5.6	542	11.4
651	*Mistral*	M44/1	KE	44.0	34.0	12.7	6.5	294	11.0
652	Cowper	OD	CU	41.6	31.1	12.1	6.0	753	12.6
653	*Sussanna V*	M63	KE	63.0	48.0	16.4	8.0	1621	35.5
654	*Sululu*	OD	KE	56.0	43.3	14.0	7.0	1235	33.3
655	Ferdinandez	M44/2	SL	44.0	34.0	12.7	6.5	345	11.0
656	Barnum	TE3	SL	46.3	33.8	12.5	7.0	1087	16.3
657	*Isolde of Hamble*	M44/3	KE	44.0	34.0	12.7	6.5	294	11.0
658	*Mudjimba*	V160	BS	25.3	21.5	7.2	4.5	366	4.3
659	Cooper	CO45	SL	20.5	18.5	6.5	4.5	199	1.4
660	No information	—	—	—	—	—	—	—	—
661	No information	—	—	—	—	—	—	—	—
662	*Ebblake IV*	GK24	BS	24.0	19.7	9.3	5.0	221	1.6
663	Bungay	OD	CU	44.5	33.5	11.7	6.0	869	12.2
664	Faggioli	TS	SL	30.0	22.5	9.0	4.3	399	5.3
665	*Xenois*	M63	KE	63.7	50.5	16.3	8.0	1464	35.1
666	*Candida*	M44/7	SL	44.0	34.0	12.7	6.5	345	11.0
667	Erwood	V161	BS	25.3	21.5	7.2	4.5	366	4.3
668	*Temeraire*	SAW6	SL	39.0	31.0	11.3	5.3	618	18.8T
669	Sommers	V162	BS	25.3	21.5	7.2	4.5	366	4.3
670	MacMeekn	G8/9	KE	38.8	30.6	11.0	5.3	745	10.8
671	Smith	CO46	SL	20.5	18.5	6.5	4.5	199	1.4
672	*Luce*	LU1	YW	36.3	20.0	10.8	6.0	498	6.5
673	Not built	GK24	BS	24.0	19.7	9.3	5.0	320	1.8
674	Rosin	MCO	SL	20.5	18.5	6.5	4.5	199	1.4
675	Jagdamann	RR5	BS	35.0	27.5	9.7	4.3	403	3.6
676	Migge	CO47	SL	20.5	18.5	6.5	4.5	199	1.4
677	Crossland	CO48	SL	20.5	18.5	6.5	4.5	199	1.4
678	No information	—	—	—	—	—	—	—	—
679	*Princess Irene*	OD	KE	60.0	46.0	15.6	7.8	1477	31.1
680	Lemon	V160	BS	25.3	21.5	7.2	4.5	366	4.3
681	*Mozzie*	GK24	BS	24.0	19.7	9.3	5.0	320	1.8
682	Ramsden	GK24	BS	24.0	19.7	9.3	5.0	320	1.8
683	*Westerly 33*	PB	SL	32.7	26.0	10.5	5.5	435	6.3
684	Abbot	V164	BS	25.3	21.5	7.2	4.5	366	4.3
685	Buczynski	V165	BS	25.3	21.5	7.2	4.5	366	4.3
686	Waller	WA20	SL	29.6	24.5	9.3	5.0	438	9.2
687	*Rockhopper*	SA	SL	39.0	31.0	11.3	5.3	618	10.3
688	Lyda	CO49	SL	20.5	18.5	6.5	4.5	199	1.4
689	McRobbie	SA	SL	39.0	31.0	11.3	5.3	618	10.3
690	*Moody 52*	PB	KE	52.0	39.0	14.2	6.8	1069	19.1
691	Schmidt	V166	BS	25.3	21.5	7.2	4.5	366	4.3

No.	Name	Class	Rig	LOA (ft)	LWL (ft)	Beam (ft)	Draft (ft)	Sail (Sq ft)	Disp (Tons)
692	Lucas	GK24	BS	24.0	19.7	9.3	5.0	320	1.8
693	Craig	LU2	YW	36.3	20.0	10.8	6.0	498	6.9
694	Morely	V167	BS	25.3	21.5	7.2	4.5	366	4.3
695	*KEA*	M44/6	SL	44.0	34.0	12.7	6.5	345	11.0
696	Waterhouse	V168	BS	25.3	21.5	7.2	4.5	366	4.3
697	*Gurr*	SAW5	KE	39.0	31.0	11.3	5.3	618	18.8T
698	Thompson	V169	BS	25.3	21.5	7.2	4.5	366	4.3
699	*Rigel*	WA21	SL	29.6	24.5	9.3	5.0	438	9.2
700	Frazer	CO50	SL	20.5	18.5	6.5	4.5	199	1.4
701	*Moody 66*	M66	KE	66.0	48.0	16.5	8.0	1621	35.5
702	*Bowman 54*	BY	KE	53.6	40.3	14.0	6.0	1066	23.3
703	Wade	V170	BS	25.3	21.5	7.2	4.5	366	4.3
704	Martinez	CO51	SL	20.5	18.5	6.5	4.5	199	1.4
705	*Vertue II (GRP)*	PB	BS	25.7	21.5	7.9	4.4	369	4.1
706	Bumgarner	V171	BS	25.3	21.5	7.2	4.5	366	4.3
707	Holt	M52/	KE	51.8	39.0	14.2	6.8	398	19.1
708	Brown	CO52	SL	20.5	18.5	6.5	4.5	199	1.4
709	No name	GK24	SL	24.0	19.7	9.3	5.0	200	1.8
710	Gilsul	CO53	SL	20.5	18.5	6.5	4.5	199	1.4
711	Nemeth	V172	BS	25.3	21.5	7.2	4.5	366	4.3
712	Underhayes	V173	BS	25.3	21.5	7.2	4.5	366	4.3
713	Emmerton	V174	BS	25.3	21.5	7.2	4.5	366	4.3
714	True	CO54	SL	20.5	18.5	6.5	4.5	199	1.4
715	*Longbow Fisherman*	PB	MB	31.6	Not built	—		—	—
716	*Badley*	CO55	SL	20.5	18.5	6.5	4.5	199	1.4
717	*Atlantis*	OD	LA	45.9	—	—	—	—	—
718	*Vertue II*	PB	SL	25.6	21.5	7.8	4.4	358	4.1
719	Mayhew	V175	BS	25.3	21.5	7.2	4.5	366	4.3
720	Pensoy	B16	KE	52.9	39.8	14.4	7.4	1273	20.1
721	*Westerly 33 MK III*	PB	SL	33.3	27.6	10.9	5.5	473	6.7
722	Quilter	V176	BS	25.6	21.5	7.8	4.4	358	4.1
723	Robinson	CO56	SL	20.5	18.5	6.5	4.5	199	1.4
724	Banum	CO57	SL	20.5	18.5	6.5	4.5	199	1.4
725	Playdon	WA22	SL	29.6	24.5	9.3	5.0	438	9.2
726	Giles 38	G8W1	SL	38.8	30.6	11.0	5.3	754	10.8
727	Ollis	V177	BS	25.3	21.5	7.2	4.5	366	4.3
728	Harps	G8M	CU	38.8	30.6	11.0	5.3	745	10.8
729	Cranfield	V178	BS	25.3	21.5	7.2	4.5	366	4.3
730	Kline	V179	BS	25.3	21.5	7.2	4.5	366	4.3
731	*Starlight*	PB	SL	29.3	24.0	10.0	5.5	479	3.1
732	*Summerscales*	DY2	GC	45.8	38.0	12.3	7.5	1410	24.2
733	*Azimut 42*	PB	SL	41.8	34.3	13.3	7.2	911	26.8T
734	Brown	G8W2	CU	38.8	30.6	11.0	5.3	745	10.8
735	Williams	G8W3	CU	38.8	30.6	11.0	5.3	745	10.8
736	Strut	V	BS	25.6	21.5	7.8	4.4	358	4.1
737	Buxton	WA23	SL	29.6	24.5	9.3	5.0	438	9.2
738	*Giant Killer*	PB	SL	29.3	24.0	10.0	5.5	479	3.1

No.	Name	Class	Rig	LOA (ft)	LWL (ft)	Beam (ft)	Draft (ft)	Sail (Sq ft)	Disp (Tons)
739	*Podmore*	OD	KE	—	80.0	Not Built	—	—	—
740	Clarke	ST1	SL	29.3	24.0	10.0	5.5	479	3.1
741	Fier	ST2	SL	29.3	24.0	10.0	5.5	479	3.1
742	Jack	ST3	SL	29.3	24.0	10.0	5.5	479	3.1
743	Van Meurs	ST4	SL	29.3	24.0	10.0	5.5	479	3.1
744	*Kocak*	OD	KE	65.3	50.0	16.0	8.6	1722	40.0
745	Gjerde	ST5	SL	29.3	24.0	10.0	5.5	479	3.1
746	Garrison	CO58	SL	20.5	18.5	6.5	4.5	199	1.4
747	Badley	MCO	SL	20.5	18.5	6.5	4.5	199	1.4
748	*Bluewater*	PB	SL	29.3	24.0	10.0	5.5	479	3.1
749	*Wulfing*	MWA	CU	33.1	27.0	9.5	5.8	611	8.6
750	Niemiec	CO59	SL	20.5	18.5	6.5	4.5	199	1.4
751	Baldwin	V180	BS	25.6	21.5	7.8	4.4	358	4.1
752	*Sorceress*	DY3	GC	45.8	38.0	12.3	7.5	1410	24.2
753	Whitehouse	CO60	SL	20.5	18.5	6.5	4.5	199	1.4
754	Butler	V181	BS	25.3	21.5	7.2	4.5	366	4.3
755	McFaden	M52/4	KE	51.8	39.0	14.2	6.8	398	19.1
756	Storer	WA24	SL	29.6	24.5	9.3	5.0	438	9.2
757	*Buccaneer*	PB	S/K	39.0	31.0	11.3	5.3	618	4.3
758	Jauncey	OD	CU	44.5	—	—	—	—	—
759	Eddy	OD	KE	57.4	41.7	14.2	7.8	1468	24.0
760	*GK34* (Not built)	PB	SL	34.0	28.5	11.5	4.3	468	6.8
761	*Fastnet 27*	PB	MB	27.0	22.0	9.5	2.6	NA	2.5
762	No information								
763	Bristow	V182	BS	25.3	21.5	7.2	4.5	366	4.3
764	Caprio	V183	BS	25.3	21.5	7.2	4.5	366	4.3
765	Watling	V184	BS	25.3	21.5	7.2	4.5	366	4.3
766	Smith	CO61	SL	20.5	18.5	6.5	4.5	199	1.4
767	Peterson	V185	BS	25.3	21.5	7.2	4.5	366	4.3
768	Raftery	CO62	SL	20.5	18.5	6.5	4.5	199	1.4
769	*Moody 46*	PB	KE	46.5	36.0	12.2	6.0	851	12.5
770	Colebrook	ST6	SL	29.3	24.0	10.0	5.5	479	3.1
771	Courtenay	WA25	SL	29.6	24.5	9.3	5.0	438	9.2
772	Terry	TE	SL	46.3	33.8	12.0	7.0	1087	16.3
773	Marks	WA26	SL	29.6	24.5	9.3	5.0	438	9.2
774	Federighi	ST7	SL	29.3	24.0	10.0	5.5	479	3.1
775	Dogan	ST8	SL	29.3	24.0	10.0	5.5	479	3.1
776	*Martanne*	OD	KE	55.0	41.3	14.4	7.4	1193	21.2
777	Vigor	OD	SL	29.3	22.8	9.9	5.5	215	2.9T
778	Atrer	V186	BS	25.3	21.5	7.2	4.5	366	4.3
779	Ouborg	V187	BS	25.3	21.5	7.2	4.5	366	4.3
780	*Carbineer 46*	PB	KE	46.5	36.0	12.2	6.0	851	12.5
781	Pierson	V188	BS	25.3	21.5	7.2	4.5	366	4.3
782	Luce	OD	KE	36.0	—	—	—	—	—
783	*Benneti 16M*	PB	KE	52.5	45.3	15.6	7.6	1119	28.0
784	Wagemans	MWA	GC	29.6	24.5	9.3	5.0	438	9.2
785	*Westerly 34*	PB	SL	34.0	28.5	11.5	4.3	468	6.9

No.	Name	Class	Rig	LOA (ft)	LWL (ft)	Beam (ft)	Draft (ft)	Sail (Sq ft)	Disp (Tons)
786	Singleton	WA27	SL	29.6	24.5	9.3	5.0	438	9.2
787	*GK34*	PB	SL	34.0	28.5	11.5	4.3	468	6.8
788	Hunter	CO63	SL	20.5	18.5	6.5	4.5	199	1.4
789	No Name	MV	BS	25.3	21.5	7.2	4.5	366	4.3
790	Martin	SAW	KE	39.0	31.0	11.3	5.3	618	18.8T
791	Davies	AQ	KE	39.6	30.5	11.5	5.6	542	11.0
792	*Bennetti 19M*	PB	KE	64.6	54.0	18.5	9.0	1873	46.0
793	Mathews	AQ	KE	39.6	30.5	11.5	5.6	542	11.0
794	*Westerly 28.5*	PB	SL	28.5	25.5	10.8	5.3	430	3.6
795	*Starlight*	GK29	SL	29.3	24.0	10.0	5.5	479	3.1
796	No name	WA42	SL	29.6	24.5	9.3	5.0	438	9.2
797	De Grande	OD	KE	56.7	41.3	14.4	7.4	1348	21.2
798	Kendal	MCO	BS	20.5	18.5	6.5	4.5	199	1.4
799	*Moody 134*	PB	KE	44.0	34.5	13.5	6.3	864	14.5
800	Haig	MBU	S/K	39.0	31.0	11.3	5.3	618	4.3
801	*Southern 40*	PB	KE	39.0	31.0	11.3	5.3	618	10.3
802	Elton	MCO	BS	20.5	18.5	6.5	4.5	199	1.4
803	Boe	MWA	CU	33.1	27.0	9.5	5.8	611	8.6
804	O.Y.C.	OD	KE	58.0	48.0	—	—	—	—
805	No name	GRE	K/S	38.5	29.0	12.5	6.0	631	10.1
806	Deckhams	OD	KE	70.0	52.7	17.1	8.5	1830	82.2T
807	Quelch	WAII	GC	23.9	20.9	7.1	4.9	395	4.5T
808	*Andrillot II*	OD	GC	25.5	21.5	7.2	4.2	366	4.3
809	Engles	CO63	SL	20.5	18.5	6.5	4.5	199	1.4
810	*Moody 52*	PB	KE	51.8	39.0	14.2	6.8	1123	19.1
811	Allred	TE	SL	46.3	33.8	12.0	7.0	1087	16.3
812	Hodge	CO64	SL	20.5	18.5	6.5	4.5	199	1.4
813	*Westerly*	PB	MS	37.7	31.5	11.9	6.0	200	11.0
814	*Westerly 36*	PB	K/S	35.8	30.4	11.2	4.7	732	7.8
815	Standen	SA	KE	39.0	31.0	11.3	5.3	618	10.3
816	*White Gull*	OD	SC	154.0	128.0	30.0	13.0	11500	370.0
817	*Bucklers Hard*	PB	KE	45.7	35.0	13.2	6.0	756	14.4
818	*Dullcibella*	PB	SL	33.0	26.5	10.5	6.5	450	7.0
819	Crowe	CO64	SL	20.5	18.5	6.5	4.5	199	1.4
820	Tradwell	CO65	SL	20.5	18.5	6.5	4.5	199	1.4
821	*Moody 183*	PB	KE	60.0	48.0	16.3	8.0	1490	35.5
822	*Bennetti*	OD	MS	80.8	67.1	20.5	9.9	24413	4.8T
823	*Riding High*	V190	BS	25.6	21.5	7.8	4.4	358	4.3
824	Cavanagh	V191	BS	25.6	21.5	7.8	4.4	358	4.3
825	*Windsong*	CO66	SL	20.5	18.5	6.5	4.5	199	1.4
826	Young	V192	BS	25.6	21.5	7.8	4.4	358	4.3
827	No name	BA	BC	19.7	17.5	5.3	3.7	208	0.4
828	Spratt	CO68	SL	20.5	18.5	6.5	4.5	199	1.4
829	Bates	CO69	SL	20.5	18.5	6.5	4.5	199	1.4
830	Punter	WA28	SL	29.6	24.5	9.3	5.0	438	9.2
831	Johnson	WA29	SL	29.6	24.5	9.3	5.0	438	9.2
832	Baillargen	V193	GC	25.6	21.5	7.8	4.4	358	4.3
833	Gable	V194	BS	25.6	21.5	7.8	4.4	358	4.3
834	Newman	V195	BS	25.6	21.5	7.8	4.4	358	4.3

Index